GLASS LIFE IN A HOUSE

THE MINISTER'S FAMILY AND THE LOCAL CONGREGATION

GLASS
LIFE IN A
HOUSE

THE MINISTER'S FAMILY
AND THE LOCAL CONGREGATION

CAMERON LEE
JACK BALSWICK

FULLER SEMINARY PRESS
PASADENA, CALIFORNIA

FULLER
SEMINARY PRESS

Published in the United States of America
by Fuller Theological Seminary
135 North Oakland Avenue, Pasadena, California 91182

www.fullerseminarybookstore.com

ISBN: 1-881266-23-0

Contents

Preface

Why should anyone want to read a book on the minister's family? Many of you, having been in the ministry, want to get a better grasp on how the ministry affects your family life. You may be asking yourself questions like, What is happening? Why? Is there anything we can do about it? These questions may be reason enough for you to read this book. There is yet another pragmatic reason, however: if you are a minister, understanding the strengths and stresses of clergy families will help you to be more effective in your ministry. As J. C. Wynn has written,

> The minister's interpersonal difficulties affect his entire parish. . . . [W]hen his professional life and his family life are at odds because he has still to come to terms with both, when he suffers from a professional role conflict and is unsure of the expectations of church and community, and when these are compounded by the minister's own immaturity in faith and work, the church membership is certain to feel effects. Paul's salty word to Timothy is apropos: "If a man does not know how to manage his own household, how can he care for God's church?"[1]

The quality of a pastor's ministry cannot be neatly separated from his or her interpersonal or family life. The interaction cuts both ways. On the negative side, family problems can complicate ministry, just as difficulties in the parish can affect the family. But there is a positive side, too: the minister's own family and the congregational family can be mutually reinforcing sources of strength.

Thus, for you who are already in the ministry, this book is written to help you come to grips with some of your experiences as a minister's family. For you who have yet to enter the ministry, this book can serve the purpose of what sociologists call "anticipatory socialization," that is, it can help prepare you for the realities of the ways parish ministry can affect your

7

family. Theological and biblical training, while preparing you to preach and teach with integrity, is not enough to get you ready for the experience of pastoral ministry. Field education is better, but even this is not the same. To use a somewhat loose analogy, dating a person does not always prepare you for the shock of living with that same person on a day-to-day basis. Once you have situated yourself into a particular congregation, new interpersonal dynamics take hold. The more you can understand what is happening to you, the better you will be able to cope.

Our vision for this book is more than just pragmatic: it is directed toward *understanding*, not just *doing*. This is neither a "how-to" nor an encyclopedic reference on ministry and family life. We are not parish ministers ourselves; our expertise is in the social and psychological dynamics of family life. We will not presume to tell you how to minister. Instead, we hope to introduce you to a new way of understanding the context of parish ministry. This takes us beyond the realms of *description* ("What does the clergy family look like?") and *prescription* ("What should I do?") and into the realm of *perspective* —to ask the question, "How should the minister's family be understood?" We hope that this way of looking at the minister's family will be helpful, not only to current pastors and their families, but also to those studying for the ministry as well as to interested laypeople within the church.

The guiding principle behind our approach is that of a *social ecology*. Simply put, this means that everything you do, in your ministry or your family, occurs in a particular social context. In order to truly understand the relation of church ministry to family life, this social environment must be taken into account. One basic assumption is that the local congregation should be considered as a family. This is not just a metaphor, because the psychological and social principles that apply to nuclear families apply to church families as well. You cannot understand the minister's family in isolation from the congregation as a family, nor even from the nuclear families within the congregation. We shall explain this further in subsequent chapters and demonstrate the usefulness of this perspective.

We are currently conducting an ongoing program of research into the families of ministers. Some of the information for this book comes directly from this research. Little has been written on this subject, and we hesitate somewhat to jump into so large a gap. Our research is not finished; it is only beginning. Neither do we consider this book a finished product; it is our way of initiating a dialogue with those who are in the "trenches" of ministry. We seek to bring a sense of coherence to the family experiences of current ministers, their spouses, and their children. We hope also to raise matters of concern for prospective ministers. We invite you, the reader, to take what we have written, reflect upon it, criticize it, and dialogue with it and with us.

The book is divided into three parts. In part 1 we discuss our social ecological perspective of the minister's family, which is the conceptual heart of the book. Chapter 1 introduces this perspective, emphasizing the meaning of "ecological" through an analogy drawn from the natural environment. In chapter 2 we add the "social" by drawing upon the concept of emotional triangles found in family therapy. Chapter 3 takes the general discussion of these first two chapters and focuses specifically on the social ecology of the pastor's family. Chapter 4 rounds out part 1 by showing how a knowledge of different types of families can help us to understand the interaction between the clergy family and the congregation.

Whereas the first part emphasizes the importance of seeing the clergy family in its social context, part 2 focuses on the social expectations placed on a minister and the members of his or her family. Chapter 5 examines expectations of the role of the minister. Chapter 6 in turn considers the minister's spouse. The stresses of ministers' children, known as "preachers' kids," or "P.K.s," are addressed in chapter 7.

In part 3 we turn from an emphasis on individuals to look instead at the clergy marriage and family as units in their own right. Chapter 8 addresses the typical problems faced by clergy families, and chapter 9 focuses on how the parish ministry interacts with the clergy marriage. In chapter 10 we move beyond the local congregation and ask, "How does the denomination fit in? And are there any larger social or cultural trends that have an effect on the life of the pastor's family?" While that chapter takes the ecological model beyond the confines of the local church, chapter 11 adds the dimension of time. Here we introduce the idea of ages and stages in a family's life, and show how the clergy family, too, must change as parents and children grow older. Finally, in chapter 12 we attempt to bring some practical suggestions to light, addressing ministers and their families, prospective ministers, and concerned laity.

Throughout the book we will be using case studies of clergy families and other families to drive home certain ideas. Unless specifically stated otherwise, these cases and the names used in them are fictional. The case examples are composite sketches, using both theoretical and clinical material culled from different sources and specifically tailored for illustrative purposes. Actual quotes from ministers' families have been edited to preserve their anonymity.

A final word on style. We have attempted to keep our language nonsexist. In general, however, throughout the book, we will use male pronouns for ministers and female pronouns for their spouses, who will often be referred to as "ministers'/pastors'/clergy *wives*." This is not meant to reflect any prejudices on our part. We have chosen these terms for two reasons. First, although our research was designed to use nonsexist language, nearly all the ministers who responded were men, whereas the ministers' spouses were women. Second, this usage brings the current work in line with what has already been published elsewhere on ministers' families.

Please bear in mind that the concepts we present are not intrinsically bound by this gender distinction. Comments regarding ministers or their spouses may apply equally well to males or females. We would be remiss as researchers, however, to make such a generalization without further evidence. We enthusiastically support the increasing trend of gifted women being called to pastoral ministry, and we anticipate appropriate and timely research designed to serve their needs. In the meantime, we hope that female readers will be patient with us and see for themselves whether or not our perspective on clergy families helps them to understand their own situations.

We would like to thank the following people for their assistance and encouragement at various stages of our research and writing: Dr. Bill Hogue, Rev. Michael Carlisle, Rev. Donald Piper, and Ms. Leslie Nation. We have also greatly appreciated the enthusiasm and diligence of our editors, Mike Smith and James Ruark. Finally, we are continually grateful for the patient endurance of our spouses, who ministered grace to us in the eleventh-hour madness of manuscript deadlines.

PART ONE

WHAT IS A SOCIAL ECOLOGY?

1

Setting the Stage

Pastor Miller was stumped and frustrated. Two years ago, when he accepted the call to the First Church of Kirkdale, the congregation and the board had seemed unanimously enthusiastic. He and his family had moved thousands of miles, leaving the community where he had planted and nurtured his own church for years, and where the children had been raised. All the family members regretted leaving, but the pastor felt he had done as much as he could at that church. It was time to move on. They were warmly received upon their arrival in Kirkdale and moved into the well-furnished and roomy parsonage.

At first, everything seemed to be all right. Pastor Miller noticed some reserve among board members whenever he proposed changes in the ministry program. Though relationships seemed strained on occasion, they were generally amiable. He dismissed his concerns as matters that would work themselves out in time.

His wife, Arlene, was well-educated and had professional aspirations of her own. She wanted to do some minor remodeling of the parsonage and proposed that if she could find work nearby, the extra income would pay for the modifications. What Arlene had not expected was the murmuring this was to cause in the congregation. "You would think that with all the money the church has spent on furnishing the parsonage, she would be satisfied. And there's nothing wrong with their salary either; she should be serving the church instead of working." Over the months, the murmuring became more frequent and less covert.

Arlene's resentment mounted. She found another woman in the congregation to whom she confided her frustrations, and for a time this helped her to cope.

The Millers' daughter, Nancy, was a senior in high school; their son, Steve, was beginning his sophomore year. In their previous community, both of the children had been popular in school and had good academic standings. It was difficult for them, however, to feel comfortable at Kirkdale High. Their father had been an important person in their smaller hometown, and the status of being his children had been more beneficial than not. At Kirkdale High School they felt like two little fish in a very large pond. They knew they would miss their old friends, and their parents had assured them that in time they would make new ones. But Nancy and Steve felt that it was taking much too long. Occasionally one of them would hear some derogatory remark about "preachers' kids." They tried to ignore it. At any rate, they thought to themselves, Dad has his own worries, and we shouldn't bother him with our problems.

As the pastor sat in his study reflecting over his two years with the church, he became increasingly perplexed. "What happened?" he asked himself. Nobody had anticipated the split that the church was now experiencing. He felt betrayed. His associate in charge of the educational ministry, Frank Collins, had been supportive at first. Frank was now openly critical, claiming that the pastor wielded far too much power in the church. A number of church members rallied around Frank, and thus the church was split. Arlene, too, had felt the sting of betrayal. Her confidante had joined the other side of the split and was now publicly revealing what Arlene had shared in private.

Besides that, somehow school never seemed to get any better for Nancy or her brother. Steve had never seen marijuana before, though he had heard about it. When it was offered to him, he initially resisted. But then he reasoned, "Why not? It's probably the only way I'll be able to shake this P.K. image and make some friends around here. If it gets bad, I'll quit." He tried it a few times, but ultimately decided it wasn't for him. By then it was too late. Word of his experimentation with marijuana had leaked through the adolescent grapevine to the congregation. This, too, now became an object of public debate, but was greatly distorted by false rumors. Stories circulated that Steve had tried everything from pot to cocaine. A number of members suspected that Nancy, too, must be involved in some form of scandalous behavior. She resented their vigilance and felt that the whole world was waiting to see her fall.

Pastor Miller shook his head. "I never would have figured Frank Collins to be that kind of man," he mused. He thought wistfully of the warm reception he and his family had originally received. "What made them change their minds about us?" The pastor felt a surge of anger and bitterness, but gradually suppressed it. He sighed with resignation and asked himself again, "What happened?"

*   *   *

The Millers' story, while fictional, is a composite portrait of the lives of many in the parish ministry. All too often our training fails to prepare us for the interpersonal crises that occur in face-to-face ministry. We are left, like Pastor Miller, feeling bewildered and frustrated.

It is not only the pastor who must live with the day-to-day stresses of ministry. Others in the family are also intricately entwined in the social life of the church. Sometimes the family is affected only indirectly, as when parish demands leave the minister with little time or energy for family life. Yet often the impact is more direct, as when expectations are placed on the minister's spouse and children.

Our goal in writing this book is to help both present and future ministers grapple with the stresses and strengths of living in a clergy family. Although numerous recent works teach how to minister to families,[1] little has been written regarding the minister's own family. A few references deal briefly with the subject, but treat it as if it were of little importance or interest. It is, of course, necessary that pastoral ministry literature focus primarily on ministry and, in particular, ministry to families. But the lack of emphasis on the minister's own family passively promotes a sense of "set-apartness," which discourages ministers from examining their own family life.

This self-reflection does not require that ministers turn inward at the expense of their concentration on ministry. Does an emphasis on family, especially the minister's family, compete with an emphasis on a minister's responsibilities to the congregation? It certainly can. This has led one writer to suggest that the current evangelical emphasis on family has missed the New Testament teaching that family life should flow from the life of the church.[2] The family of biblical times, he asserts, was more extended and community-based, as opposed to the more nuclear modern family. This is a good reminder that saves us from an extreme of privatism and inwardness where the family is concerned. Within the church, concerns regarding families in the congregation must always be balanced with the life of the congregation as a family.

We must also remember that in biblical times no emphasis on family was needed. Devotion to family was so strong that our Lord found it necessary at times to emphasize commitment to God over and against commitment to the family. Mainstream American culture is not the same; we prize individualism and opportunity more than commitment to relationships and a connection between generations. In such a social climate, a renewed emphasis on the family is both legitimate and necessary.

Many articles focusing on the minister's family, however, are simply reminders to busy ministers that they need to find time in their schedules for their families. One writer, for example, advises overzealous pastors, "We need to be quiet sometimes, relax sometimes, and be with our family."[3] The author concludes,

> Each of us can minister effectively and still have time for our family. Someday we will stand before God and hear those words, "Well done, thou good and faithful servant." We will hear those words not only because we have faithfully served the church; we will hear those words because we have also served the ones God has placed closest to us—our family. They are our ministry too.[4]

Here we have the faithful pastor who in the midst of his service finds the time to minister to his family. We agree with the positive emphasis on time spent with the family. In our own studies, though, we have found that pastors are in fact aware of this need and often strive against frustrating obstacles to have family time. It is misleading to place the pastor's family on the same level as every other ministry, especially in a culture such as ours, which tries to keep home and workplace separate. Do members of the clergy family want the pastor to think of them as

one of his many ministries? Besides, he in turn is ministered to
by his family.

Our approach to the minister's family is different. We are not
promoting an inwardness that competes with the outward
responsibilities of ministry. Nor do we intend just to remind
pastors to spend time with their families. Many would simply
respond, "I'd love to. Show me how." And it is simply wrong to
treat the clergy family as one more item on the minister's
agenda. The core of our perspective, which is largely missing in
these other views, lies in understanding both the parish ministry
and the minister's family in terms of *their relationship to each
other*.

Our basic thesis is that parish ministry constitutes a unique
environment and that the clergy family cannot be fully understood apart from its relationship to this environment. The life of
the congregational family is intricately intertwined with that of
the minister's family. In some congregations this intertwining
can seem restrictive to the clergy family; in others the relationships are much less involved. The point is not to make value
judgments as to whether living in a minister's family is
intrinsically good or bad, stressful or not stressful, healthful or
unhealthful. The goal is rather to understand the nature and
sources of the stresses and strengths of clergy families in order
to put that knowledge to constructive use. We will suggest
throughout this book that ministry and clergy family life cannot
be fully understood if considered in isolation from each other.

We hope to provide useful insights into the internal and
external lives of the clergy family. Many questions may come to
mind. What is life in a minister's family like? What kinds of
problems do they face? Is your experience similar to that of
others? What can you do to improve your family life? To
improve your ministry?

But before we can continue to unfold the drama of the
minister's family, the stage must be properly set. As mentioned
in the preface, we will address the concrete issues of description
and prescription—of helping pastors and their families to make
sense of their social environment and to take steps to improve
their ministries and family life. We also have a larger goal,
namely, to teach you a new way of understanding the ministry
environment. The information about ministers' families is like
the script of the play. You can understand the play to some

extent by merely reading the dialogue. But a full appreciation of the drama requires that the script be performed in its proper setting. To set the stage is to provide the backdrop that gives meaning and context to the interaction between the characters.

Part 1 will set the stage, sketching the background perspective that gives coherence to what follows and developing the social ecology of clergy families. When you have finished the book, you may want to reread the first four chapters, reflecting carefully on the rest of the book and on your personal experiences. This will help you to begin to "think ecologically," as we are fond of saying. Learning to see your own social environment in a new way will help you to deal with more situations than we can cover in a book like this.

What does it mean to think ecologically? The word *ecology* should trigger many associations from the news of recent decades: the Environmental Protection Agency, nuclear and chemical waste, pollution of the air and water. What all these have in common is a concern for the physical and biological environment. More specifically, they point to the tendency of humans to ignore the environmental implications of their actions, unanticipated consequences that must be corrected at great expense. One dictionary definition of ecology is "the totality or pattern of relations between organisms and their environment." Human organisms in particular tend to be ignorant of their relation to the environment. The divinely given mandate to exercise dominion over creation can turn into short-sighted exploitation, often with disastrous results. In the following section, we will present an example taken from the realm of nature. This will provide the foundation for the subsequent discussion of a *social* ecology.

The Case of the Dying Lake

Just to the east of Yosemite National Park, nestled into the Sierra Nevada mountains of California, lie the deep blue waters of Mono Lake. The most immediately striking feature of the lake is its tufa towers, oddly shaped columns of a limestone-like substance formed by the peculiar chemical properties of the water. The tufa, originally formed beneath the water's surface, have been exposed by the lake's constantly receding water level. The towers now jut out here and there from the lake surface and the surrounding landscape, giving the scene an eerie, other-worldly appearance.

Though the lake is salty, alkaline, and sulfurous, it supports a closely interwoven network of wildlife. The waters contain algae that feed brine flies and half-inch-long brine shrimp. Visitors to the lake at the turn of the century reported that the shrimp were so numerous that the noise of their swarming sounded like a distant storm. The flies and shrimp in turn fed numerous species of birds, including the California gull. The cycle was completed as the decomposition of dead birds, shrimp, and flies on the lakebottom provided nutrients for the growth of the algae. Mono Lake, in its prime, was a living example of a balanced, thriving ecological system (*ecosystem* for short). At present, however, it is slowly dying. Why?

Over three hundred miles south of Mono Lake lies the city of Los Angeles. In the early part of this century, Los Angeles, too, was thriving. In that often desert-like climate, however, the limited water supply threatened to curtail the city's expansion. Aqueducts were built from the Owens River near Mono Lake to Los Angeles to serve the growing need for water. In 1941, engineers expanded the aqueduct system, diverting into the Owens River water from mountain tributaries that fed Mono Lake. In 1963, they built a second aqueduct to draw upon these mountain streams.

The designers knew of the salinity of Mono Lake, and to them it seemed a shame to "waste" water from clean mountain streams on a salty lake. Mono Lake has no outlet. Water comes into the lake mostly from mountain streams and only minimally from underground and shoreline springs and precipitation. It leaves only by evaporation. Diversion of the stream water cut off the lake's major source of inflow. Water began to evaporate from the lake faster than it could be replaced, and the water level began to drop rapidly.

Probably unaware of the cycle of life that depended on the lake's water level, these designers could not anticipate the impact of the aqueduct system on the lake's natural ecosystem. Since the diversions began, the water level has dropped more than forty feet, cutting the volume of the lake in half. This has had three important consequences. Previously, gulls living on the lake's Negit Island had been isolated from natural predators living beyond the shore. With the water receding at a rapid rate, however, Negit could not remain an island for long. In 1979 a land bridge formed between the island and the shoreline, allowing coyotes to invade and prey on the gulls' chicks and eggs. The second consequence was that the saline concentration of the lake doubled to a point where the brine shrimp could no longer survive. In turn, the gulls that fed on the shrimp dwindled in number.

Third, increasing expanses of exposed, dry lakebed have created an alkali "smog." Windstorms in the Mono basin carry clouds of alkali skyward, to be borne through the air and deposited miles away. The alkali is toxic not only to plants and animals, but to humans as well and has been linked to respiratory problems in neighboring communities.[5]

Our purpose is not to make environmental activists of our readers. The story of Mono Lake, however, graphically illustrates the principles of ecological awareness that undergird the more social perspective that we shall present shortly. What can we learn from the lake?

The Living Earth

The natural world is not an inanimate *thing* to be used or exploited. The earth is neither a thing nor a collection of things. It is a living system, a complex web of relationships between living organisms. Normally these relationships are balanced. For example, California gulls feed on brine shrimp in Mono Lake. As the number of birds multiplies, the supply of shrimp declines. Eventually the decrease in the supply of shrimp will limit the increase in the number of gulls, and the shrimp will once again repopulate the lake. And so it goes, a never-ending cycle of give-and-take, an interdependent balance.

The interdependence of gulls and shrimp, however, is only one simple level of the ecosystem. As we have seen, the survival of the shrimp is dependent on the salinity of the lake water. Here we must broaden our focus to include the lake's dependence on the weather system. The average rainfall and snowfall supply enough water to keep the salinity of the lake within tolerable limits. When water is diverted away from the lake, however, salinity levels increase beyond the shrimp's ability to adapt. This endangers the survival of all forms of life dependent on the food chain that the lake supports. The ecological system includes many levels of interdependent relationships. When the balance is disturbed at one level, other levels may be equally affected.

Nature is tolerant of change, but change within limits. The population of either birds or shrimp is allowed to fluctuate, but not to the extent that the natural balance would be disrupted. As we have seen, however, forces intervening at another level of the ecosystem can disrupt the balance. If the natural balance is continually disrupted, one part of the environment must die or become severely atrophied in order that another may live. A bustling city lives at the expense of a lake. We would not think of deliberately poisoning the lake or heedlessly shooting gulls. But because we fail to appreciate the ecological impact of our actions, a seemingly harmless act such as diverting stream water can have the same net effect. What may seem at first glance to be only a minor or irrelevant disruption to this balance may have remote but grave consequences.

The physical connection between Mono Lake and Los Angeles is a thin one. Think of what it would look like on a map. Considering the hundreds of intervening miles, the aqueduct would appear as no more than a mere thread linking the two. The impact is nonetheless significant for the life of the lake. If we are to learn to think ecologically, we must avoid believing that all important connections will be obvious.

We can summarize the ecological perspective into four basic assumptions. First, organisms must be understood in the larger context of their relationship to the environment. As biological creatures, we are part of the living earth. When we fail to recognize this, we run the risk of disrupting our own relationship to nature as we plunder the environment. There will always be people who care very little that a lake is being turned into a chemical sump. But can they also ignore the resident of Los Angeles who wastes water and thereby contributes to a chain of events that culminates in polluted air and health problems for others?

Second, nature is a vast network of relationships, which can be understood in terms of smaller networks. These networks can be arranged into levels of varying complexity. We saw, for example, that the give-and-take between the gull and shrimp populations was dependent on the salinity of the water. The salt factor, in turn, is kept within limits by a reliable influx of fresh water. This, then, depends on the weather, which is itself a vast system operating in seasonal cycles.

Third, the entire ecological system is in dynamic balance, both within and across its levels. Though the absolute numbers of birds or shrimp, the level of salinity, and the amount of rain and snow may vary from year to year, an overall balance is maintained within certain limits of tolerance.

Fourth, if a disruption occurs at any level of the system, the overall balance will be upset. The effects of this imbalance may become visible at some different level of the system and only after a period of time. This makes it difficult, especially if we think only unidimensionally, to understand the connection between and among the events.

Usually we must be prodded into thinking ecologically. It is not until someone notices the changes in the lake's immediate ecology (or more remotely, the alkali smog and the higher incidence of respiratory problems) that people begin to ask questions. We don't tend to think in ecological terms; it is not a significant part of the philosophical, scientific, or cultural heritage of the Western world. In recent decades, however, an environmental consciousness has been awakened. Planners and engineers are increasingly requiring "environmental impact" studies before they launch new projects. We are learning about our past oversights through trial and error. This is only the first step. As we immerse ourselves in an ecological perspective, we must learn to think correctively about the present and preventively for the future.

The Nature of the Social World

But what does a dying lake have to do with the minister's family? Here we must make a mental shift. We have illustrated the connection between events in nature, in the physical environment. A social ecology is concerned with the social and psychological environment rather than the physical. This may make the chain of events less tangible, but they are no less real. We contend that certain characteristics of the social environment of the minister's family make it unique among the helping professions. In describing the organization of the book, we used the metaphor of the relationship of stage to script in the presentation of a play. The same image is useful here. The

state. In another sense, we have already seen a similar principle
at work in the give-and-take among wildlife of Mono Lake.

How does homeostasis apply to a social ecology? Social
groups are governed by certain implicit or explicit rules
concerning goals of the group, who is a member and who is not,
norms of appropriate behavior, and the like. This is similar to
the "rule" that the brain must have a certain amount of oxygen.
And just as the brain's survival is dependent on keeping this
rule, the preservation of the group is linked to its ability to
maintain the boundaries of meaning defined by its social rules.
Usually some room is permitted for deviation, but only within
tolerable limits. This means that the group can "acclimate," but
only to a certain extent.

Congregations, for example, may have a strong but largely
implicit group consensus about the biblical norm for marriage.
In such a church, the married couple with children may be
viewed as the norm. Though singleness may be accepted as a
tolerable deviation, single adults will feel vaguely uneasy,
especially if they are single by intent. Church members who
divorce may be ousted from the congregation, and those who
have previously divorced will not be allowed to become
members.

It is important to realize in these cases that it is not simply that
a matter of doctrine is at stake. When doctrine is used to define a
group's identity and membership, such doctrine will be defend-
ed as if the life of the group depended on it. And in a way, it
does. Anyone who deviates from the group norm implicitly or
explicitly challenges the way members define themselves. This
causes stress, a sense of imbalance, and the homeostatic need to
do something about it. The "something" may be change and
growth, a parallel to evolution in the biological realm. Often,
though, the group regains its stability by returning to baseline,
lapsing back into more familiar patterns.

The fourth principle follows closely from the third. Whenever
the balance or homeostasis of the group is disturbed, the
disruption can set off a chain reaction as the system seeks to
regain its equilibrium. We have already seen how a city's need
for water can play havoc with the ecology of a lake three
hundred miles away. Similarly, the subtle way that groups are
connected in the social ecosystem may make it difficult to see
the relationship between events. Families in the church are not

isolated. What affects one family in the congregation may affect them all. The minister's own family is no exception. A conflict between a pastor and a parishioner, for example, may seem like a matter of doctrine, or perhaps a clash of individual personalities. Both are one-dimensional ways of looking at the problem. Thinking ecologically, we might find instead that the conflict stems from disturbances in the parishioner's family, the pastor's family, or from a complex interaction of both. We will explore this further in chapter 2.

In summary, a social ecological perspective makes four basic assumptions. First, humans must be understood in relationship to their social environment. Second, the social world is seen as a network of interpersonal relationships that has horizontal, vertical, past, and present aspects. Together these two assumptions teach us that the social world is vast but interconnected. People who may seem remote from us can influence our lives, and we theirs. Third, social groups try to maintain a homeostatic balance. Fourth, when this balance is disrupted, ripples may be felt throughout the system. What may at first appear to be random events in the life of the ministry may actually be connected by a subtle but significant ecological relationship.

We believe that the social ecological perspective is one key to the sometimes confusing world of the clergy family. Throughout this book we will refer to Pastor Miller's family and similar cases in an attempt to unravel the social web surrounding the clergy family. We will approach the family through the experiences of each of its members: the pastor, his wife, and his children. Later chapters will examine the stressors impinging on clergy marriage and family life as well as more general cultural and life-cycle issues. Before we begin our discussion of these more specific matters, the remainder of part 1 will attempt to expand the ideas of this chapter into a broad working model of the ecology of the minister's family.

2

Triangles in the
Pastoral Ministry

If we are to think ecologically, we must see events in terms of their larger social context. Interactions among people do not happen in a vacuum. Most of us are members of several groups, such as the family we grew up in, our present family, or the local congregation. Because of the connectedness of our social settings, we are affected by others in ways that we might not see unless we look carefully. The life of a minister's family is intertwined with the lives of families in the congregation. Stresses that affect one will affect the other. In this chapter we hope to show how members of a social group are connected to one another through what are known as *emotional triangles*. The concept of triangles, together with the related concept of *differentiation,* helps to create a more dynamic view of how we relate to one another. This will form the backdrop for a more detailed discussion of the minister's family in chapter 3.

The social ecological model is meant to help us understand people in their proper social context. We tend to think too much in terms of isolated individuals and separate social groups, and too little in terms of the connections between them. Chapter 1 was an attempt to make this point using a naturalistic example, the story of Mono Lake. But this example is not enough in itself to explain the particularly *human* phenomenon of social interaction.

If we stick solely to naturalistic models, we will be guilty of creating the impression that people are like cogs in a machine. All cogs, gears, and levers work together to form a functioning

29

whole, but no single part operates under its own motivation. This would be a misleading and one-sided view of social interaction. People are active, not passive. We are not cogs in either a biological or social machine. We both act upon and respond to our social environment in ways that help us satisfy our goals and motivations. Thinking ecologically about our social context does not mean seeing ourselves as victims of a process over which we have no control. It means instead that we are connected to a vast network of people who are all goal-directed in their own way. Thus we need to understand both our own motivations and theirs, and how these interact in our social relationships.

In chapter 1 we spoke of homeostasis in human interaction. This means that individuals and groups often behave in ways that preserve a sense of psychological and emotional balance. To understand human motivation in its social context, we must look at how people maintain balance in their relationships. Psychiatrist and family therapist Murray Bowen offers a useful model for understanding this process.[1] At the core of Bowen's model are two important concepts: *differentiation of self* and the *emotional triangle.* The concept of differentiation enables us to understand the emotional connection between our social settings by giving us, if you will, something of the *why* of human interaction.

Beyond this, the notion of triangles describes *how* connections in the social environment are established. Our first goal in this chapter will be to introduce these powerful concepts through our own adaptation and reinterpretation of Bowen's theory. Though the concepts are general and can be applied to any social group, we hope to show how useful they can be in understanding what can happen in a church. We will conclude the chapter by returning to the First Church of Kirkdale to see whether we can help Pastor Miller and his family untangle their confusing circumstances.

Do I Have to Give Up Me to Be Loved by You?

The question "Do I have to give up me to be loved by you?"—taken from the title of a best-selling book—expresses a basic dilemma.[2] How much of myself do I have to change or give up to have the love and acceptance of another person? As individuals who are also members of social groups, we find ourselves in an endless process of give-and-take in our relationships. Other people make demands on us, on our identity, on how we define ourselves. In all our relationships we need to strike a balance between who we are and who others want us to be. It is a matter of the "fit" between individuals or between the individual and the group. Sometimes the fit is natural, but other times it feels as if we are square pegs being pounded into round holes. The question is, What then? Do we round off the peg or square the hole?

Ideally there will be some mutual compromise. All too often, however, one person ends up feeling that he or she has had to give up more than anyone else, to sacrifice himself or herself for the sake of belonging. This is most readily seen and keenly felt in the relationships we hold most dear: in our families and marriages.

Consider, for example, the relationship between a child and her parents. Her identity is formed over the years in a give-and-take relationship with her family. On the one hand, she has numerous inborn characteristics that make her unique as an individual; on the other hand, she is born into a family that already has rules and values. Some of the child's characteristics will be affirmed and valued, while others will be discouraged or rejected. Let's say that she is naturally exuberant and curious so that as a toddler she is constantly getting into things. If her parents give a positive value to her curiosity, they will encourage it and allow her to explore and learn. But if they see her explorations as only messing up their otherwise orderly home, they will punish and discourage her. What the child learns is that if she wishes to have her parents' love and approval, she must curtail her own impulses and behave according to their standards. The child's unspoken feeling is that she must give up herself to be loved by her parents.

In reality, of course, the issue is seldom so black-and-white. There is usually a reasonably fair balance between encouragement and discouragement in a child's life so that she learns both that she is valued as an individual and that she must be willing to compromise in order to belong to the group.

The same tension between individual and group interests is found in adulthood. It is often the case, for example, that a person will marry someone whom he or she has idealized. She may think to herself, "He's everything I've ever wanted in a man," or he may think, "There's no one else in the world who can understand me better than she does." Their vision is clouded by love, and it is not until after the wedding that the mist begins to clear. They may become hurt and disappointed that their spouses are not the persons they thought they were. Then comes the long and arduous process of reforming the spouse. The messages, which are more often felt than spoken, follow this form: "If you loved me, you would (wouldn't) do (be) this." In truth, however, what each partner experiences is the message, "*I* won't love *you*, unless you do this." In more extreme cases, one or both spouses feel that they must give up much of their own self-identity to keep the other's love.

In any social setting, therefore, whether it is our family, our marriage, or even our church, we have to balance who we believe ourselves to be as individuals with who others want us to be. This social fact forms the foundation of Murray Bowen's concept of *differentiation*. The basic idea is that all personal relationships and social groups, including the family, are emotional systems. The tension between the individual and the group, between who I want to be and who you want me to be, is experienced as anxiety and emotional pressure. Differentiation refers to the individual's ability to be objective rather than overwhelmed by the emotional demands of others. The term is used in two ways. First, it is used to describe a *process* of developing a secure and separate sense of identity as an individual. This happens normally as a child develops within the context of the family. Second, the term describes an *end-state*, that is, the relative *level* of security achieved through this process. Thus Bowen speaks of both the process of "differentiating" and of the "level of differentiation" achieved.

All of us fall somewhere on a continuum between low and high levels of differentiation. People who are poorly differentiated tend to be dominated by their feelings. In particular, when faced with the anxiety that comes with social pressure from others, they find it difficult to stand back and be objective. They feel compelled to *do something* to quell their anxiety, and thus their social responses are often automatic, dictated by what they feel rather than carefully reasoned. People with relatively high levels of differentiation, by contrast, are able to keep their emotions from unduly contaminating their thinking. They are aware of their feelings and able to experience them without needing immediately to do something about it. They feel what they feel, they tolerate anxiety, but their feelings don't tell them what to do or how to act. Bowen writes:

> At the low extreme are those whose emotions and intellect are so fused that their lives are dominated by the automatic emotional system. . . . These are the people who are less flexible, less adaptable, and more emotionally dependent on those about them. They are easily stressed into dysfunction, and it is difficult for them to recover from dysfunction. They inherit a high percentage of all human problems. At the other extreme are those who are more differentiated. It is impossible for there to be more than relative separation between emotional and intellectual functioning, but those whose intellectual functioning can retain relative autonomy in periods of stress are more flexible, more adaptable, and more independent of the emotionality about them. They cope better with life stresses, their life courses are more orderly and successful, and they are remarkably free of human problems. In between the two extremes is an infinite number of mixes between emotional and intellectual functioning.[3]

People who possess a high level of differentiation can respond rationally to emotional pressures. Again, this does not mean that they have no feelings, only that their responses are not dominated by their feelings. People who are poorly differentiated respond to such pressures automatically on the basis of their emotions. Placed into a relatively conflict-free and supportive environment, such people may never show any outward signs of emotional trouble. The difference between low and high levels of differentiation, however, will show itself in stressful situations. The well-differentiated person can experience emotions and yet *choose* how to respond; the poorly differentiated person's response will be *dictated* by feelings.

There are two parts to a person's self: what Bowen calls the *solid self* and the *pseudo-self*. The solid self represents the core of who we are as individuals: "The solid self says, 'This is who I am, what I believe, what I stand for, and what I will or will not do,' in a given situation. The solid self is made up of clearly defined beliefs, opinions, convictions, and life principles."[4]

The solid self is secure and doesn't depend on a person's social context. There are, however, parts of our identities that change as we go from group to group. If one group wants us to believe something or to behave in a certain way, we comply when we're with them, but not when we're apart. This is the pseudo-self, namely, parts of the self that are created in response to demands from others and thus may come and go. Bowen writes:

> The pseudo-self is created by emotional pressure, and it can be modified by emotional pressure. Every emotional unit, whether it be the family or the total of society, exerts pressure on group members to conform to the ideals and principles of the group. The pseudo-self is composed of a vast assortment of principles, beliefs, philosophies, and knowledge acquired because it is required or considered right by the group. . . . The pseudo-self is a "pretend" self. It was acquired to conform to the environment.[5]

Differentiation has to do with one's levels of solid self and pseudo-self. The person who has a higher level of solid self is more differentiated, more stable in stressful social situations. The person who has a higher level of pseudo-self, however, is more vulnerable to manipulation and more emotionally reactive.

Through both childhood and adulthood we are building, reinforcing, and modifying our sense of who and what we are. Some of our beliefs become deeply rooted and virtually unshakable. Others are more superficial, grafted on in response to social pressure. What is disquieting, Bowen notes, is that "the level of solid self is lower, and of the pseudo-self is much higher in all of us than most are aware."[6]

During a recent windstorm, a large tree in our neighborhood was completely uprooted. It had been planted in a small rectangle of soil next to the sidewalk. With the asphalt pavement on one side and the cement sidewalk on the other, the tree's roots had been restricted in their growth. The growth that had occurred had gone mostly into the trunk and branches instead of into the roots. Buffeted all night by sixty-five-mile-an-hour winds, the top-heavy tree came crashing down, dislodging a huge slab of the sidewalk as it fell.

This is the dilemma of the poorly differentiated self. What shows on the outside may be in full bloom, but what counts when the storm hits is how deep our roots are, how much solid self we have. Some people who are more pseudo-self than solid self live in perpetual crisis, from one storm to another. Others avoid crisis by stunting their feelings to protect themselves from the possibility of any emotional storm. Both kinds of people live with a deep-seated sense of instability and insecurity.

We are not dealing with a question of either/or: either you have a solid self or you have a pseudo-self. Rather, it is a matter of balance. The person with a higher degree of solid self as opposed to pseudo-self is more secure in social situations. There is the sense of having something, an identity, that no one can take away from you. The one who is well-differentiated is able to *act* rather than simply *react*. In an emotionally demanding situation, this person is aware of his feelings, but his feelings will not determine how he responds. The poorly differentiated person, however, is one who has a higher degree of pseudo-self. Since his identity at this level is dependent on the social environment, he is insecure. Social situations often feel threatening, and he avoids settings that strain his self-esteem. He will tend to react in an automatic fashion, being unable to stand back from his emotions. He does not see himself as having a choice about how to respond, and thus he constantly feels like a victim of circumstances.

Parents who are not secure themselves will often pass this insecurity on to their children, unconsciously interfering with the children's differentiation. This can be readily seen in the way parents respond to two of the most commonly frustrating periods of their lives as a family: when the children are in their "terrible twos," and when they become teenagers. What is at stake in both cases is the child's ability to distinguish himself from his parents.

The two-year-old has already mastered the ability to walk and is in the process of mastering language. Once he starts to walk, he can get into all manner of trouble. All the breakables in the house which were once safe from curious and chubby fingers now become fair game for the exploring toddler. Parents begin to restrict the child and set limits, and they find themselves saying "no" over and over again. Eventually the day comes when the child makes an important discovery: he, too, can use the magic word "no" and seems to take great relish in doing so.

How the parents respond will depend on how they interpret the child's behavior. Their interpretation, in turn, will depend on their own level of differentiation from *their* parents. Parents who have achieved a relatively high level of differentiation can appreciate and value the child's newfound independence. They have the emotional stability needed to find ways to set appropriate limits without crushing the toddler's independence and, with it, his self-esteem. They understand that the child's behavior has meaning *for the child,* and they act accordingly.

Parents who have a relatively low level of differentiation, however, are more apt to focus on what the child's behavior means *for the parents.* Typically, they will take the child's behavior as a personal affront and then will either overtly or covertly punish the child for his willfulness. In an extreme case, the child will be trapped in a no-win situation, having to choose between his need for individual selfhood and his love for his parents.[7]

Similar issues are raised when a child reaches adolescence. The teenager is now trying to establish a sense of identity that does not depend on her role in her family. She may begin to question the parent's rules, even become critical when parents are inconsistent. Yet despite the teenage bluster and bravado, she still needs the guiding support of her parents to make a successful transition into productive adulthood. Again, the question is how the parents will respond. Often the parents' unresolved conflicts from their own teenage years will be reactivated as their children enter adolescence. The differentiated parent will recognize the difference between the parent's issues and the teenager's issues and try to keep them distinct. Such a parent will allow the teenager to struggle through her "identity crisis" but will still be available to offer support when needed.[8] The poorly differentiated parent, however, has a difficult time determining whose feelings are whose. This parent will be overly reactive to the adolescent's emotional struggles, unconsciously trying to work out his or her own past rather than being of any help to the teenager in the present.

Whether speaking of the interaction of parents with toddlers or with adolescents, the effect is the same. A child who is trying to explore and define his separateness provokes anxious feelings in a parent who is poorly differentiated. If the parent and child are not able to let go of each other, the parent's anxiety about separateness, about being a well-defined individual, will be passed on to the child. And so it may go down through the generations.

How do children respond to a lack of differentiation in their parents? As we mentioned, a child may feel that he must choose (again, unconsciously) between the right to be a separate self and his love for and need to be loved by his parents. Ideally he should never have to choose one over the other. No one should have to feel that he has to give up himself in order to win his parents' love and approval. This is, however, precisely the experience of the child reared in a poorly differentiated family. How the child responds when he comes to adulthood will then usually take one of two forms, depending on which of the two choices is made. There is the child who even as an adult will not dare to risk physical nor emotional separateness from his parents: he stays close, shuns disagreements, and generally toes the line. At the other extreme is the child who "unplugs" from his family or, in Bowen's terms, "cuts-off" emotionally. He may move to another state and either refuse or conveniently forget to contact his family.

Neither choice resolves the basic problem of the lack of differentiation. Those who cut themselves off from their families often have the illusion of independence. As long as they keep out of contact, the illusion holds; but when contact is reestablished, the façade quickly melts. For example, many first-time pastors must relocate hundreds or thousands of miles away from their childhood family. As they pursue their ministry, they begin the long process of building a professional identity as people who are skilled and competent. But what happens when one of these pastors visits his parents? When away from his family and in a different social context, he may feel like an able and professional adult. But he may experience this self-concept being stripped from him as he walks through his parents' doorway and may almost automatically slip back into the role of the undifferentiated child. The professional veneer gives way to feelings left from childhood, and the pastor may become angry, petulant, depressed, or withdrawn.

The congregation, too, is an emotional system that can test the differentiation of the pastor. An example of a differentiated minister is given by David and Helen Seamands, who recalled their own initiation into a new pastorate and their sense of being "owned" by the congregation. The couple had determined beforehand that once they moved to the new church, they would uphold their prayerfully considered convictions despite whatever pressures they might experience from parishioners. In his very first sermon in the new church, David used quotes from

Bonhoeffer and Niebuhr. After the service, the pastor was approached by the wife of a seminary professor, who said sweetly, "You're very new, and we understand; but there are certain people we do not quote in this church."

How would you have responded in such a situation? A poorly differentiated person would probably respond with either mortified submission or angry defensiveness. The pastor's clearly differentiated response, however, was, "Well, I'm sorry, but I believe that all truth is God's truth, so you'll have to get used to hearing some strange people quoted from the pulpit."[9] This is the kind of response that many would have thought of when it was too late. It is to Seamands's credit that he was differentiated enough to respond as he did when the situation required it. As we shall see throughout this book, the pastor and his family must balance social expectations stemming from numerous sources. Those who are more highly differentiated will be better equipped to handle the stress.

Differentiation is an issue that affects all social systems. The level of differentiation we have achieved within our families will be tested in our other groups. If we have cut ourselves off from our childhood families, we will probably try to reactivate old family issues somewhere else:

> People who cut-off with their own parental families are the most vigorous in the effort to create "substitute" families from social relationships. There is a growing trend toward cutting-off from "bad" parental families and finding "good" substitute families. . . .
> If social relationships become significant, the relationships are duplicates of their relationships to parental families. When they encounter stress, and anxiety increases, they cut-off from the social relationship and seek another, better relationship.[10]

As we shall see in the next chapter, this phenomenon is particularly important when discussing the church as "family," for the church is a likely place for unresolved family issues to arise. In a more general sense, how we deal with differentiation from our own families can have a profound impact on how we approach other relationships.

Bowen's concept of differentiation, therefore, can be used to understand the dynamic, emotional connection between our various social settings. In summary, the term can be used to describe both the process of becoming an individual in our childhood families and the end result of this process. The differentiated self, in Bowen's own words, is a person who is able to "maintain emotional objectivity while in the midst of an emotional system in turmoil" without abandoning or cutting off from the system itself.[11] The poorly differentiated person, however, is one who is emotionally reactive; he sees himself as a victim and acts accordingly. Whatever level of differentiation we have reached in relation to our families, we bring it with us to our marriages, to our parenting, to our churches, and to our ministries.

The point of discussing differentiation is not to divide humanity into two camps, those who are healthy and differentiated and those who are not. In the first place, each of us will find it easier to remain emotionally objective in some circumstances or relationships and more difficult in others. We have our own panic buttons and pet peeves, and when these are pushed or provoked, we are more likely to react automatically than to act objectively. In the second place, to divide humanity thus would put people in too passive a light. As we have said, human beings are not machines; they are active in sculpting their social settings.

But how do people shape their social environment, and how are the connections in a social ecology forged? To understand this, we must turn to the second central concept in Bowen's theory, that of the *emotional triangle*.

Three Is Company, But Two Is a Crowd

Pastor George MacMurray and his wife Gracie have been married ten years and have three children. Over the past few years, they have both become increasingly dissatisfied with their marriage, though neither one is exactly sure why. Gracie has tried to tell George that she wishes he wouldn't put in such long hours at the church, but she usually backs off and says that she understands and it's okay. For his part, George finds little in his home life to bolster his sagging self-esteem and prefers to stay at work because he gets fulfillment out of his ministry.

Both George and Gracie are somewhat surprised and confused about the strength of their growing discontent. They have seen other marriages dissolve after long years of bitter fighting. However, they never really seem to fight in earnest, at least not about each other; their disagreements are usually about the children, the church, and occasionally, the in-laws. Their disagreements never come to any kind of resolution and seem to be more trouble than they are worth. What could you say to George and Gracie that would help them see their relationship more clearly?

From what you know already, you might have guessed that both of the MacMurrays are poorly differentiated. Their expectations for the marriage have not been realized because they were built on the hope that the other spouse would solve the differentiation problems for them. Their lack of solid self-esteem also shows itself in their interaction. Though dissatisfied with their relationship, neither is able consistently or directly to express this to the other. The result is that they have created a safe emotional distance between them. He cuts off by escaping to church; she, by bottling her emotions inside.

The MacMurrays illustrate the process of emotional triangling through which they escape direct conflict with one another. People who are well differentiated are able to take social risks and are willing to be vulnerable because they are less afraid of being victims of their own or someone else's emotions. Those who are less differentiated are more insecure and are highly motivated to find ways to keep things on an even keel. This is done through the process of triangling. Here is Bowen's definition:

> A two-person emotional system is unstable in that it forms itself into a three-person system or triangle under stress. . . . As tension mounts in a two-person system, it is usual for one to be more uncomfortable than the other, and for the uncomfortable one to "triangle in" a third person by telling the second person a story about the triangle[d] one. This relieves the tension between the first two, and shifts the tension between the second and the third.[12]

A triangle begins with two people in a poorly differentiated relationship. When there is tension between them, one of them will try to deflect it by involving a third person or thing. It can be as simple as changing the subject whenever a sensitive issue is raised. The key is to understand the purpose of the triangle, or why people resort to such means. Whatever form a triangle takes, its purpose is always the same: to help one or both people in a relationship to avoid facing their conflicts with each other. Thomas Fogarty has expressed this as follows:

> If two people can get interested in a third person, object, issue, fantasy, etc., they can avoid facing the real, threatening, scary issues between them. Thus, a husband and wife may stay together "for the sake of the children." They may get into an argument over his girlfriend—does he have one or not? They can argue over the right way to do anything. The right time for the children to go to bed. The right amount of TV to watch. Which child causes what trouble. As if there were answers to these questions. The process can cross generations. Be like my father and mother. Be different than my father and mother. In the long run, no matter what the emotional problem, the purpose of the triangle remains the same. Only the details vary. It is the avoidance of real, hard emotional issues inside of and between the members of the twosome. It is to avoid my changing myself, my part in the problem.[13]

Gracie and Pastor George have tried to work out their differences. But somehow it never seems to happen. Every time they begin to discuss their relationship with each other, they end up fighting about the kids or church or something else— anything but their relationship, how they feel about being with each other. This is hardly accidental; it is a way of avoiding a highly charged emotional issue. Something or someone else is drawn into the conflict to defuse the tension. George has already become overinvolved with his ministry to compensate for the lack of closeness in the marriage. Rather than face his dissatisfaction, George has become "married to the church" instead of to his wife. This is only one example of how spouses distance themselves from each other emotionally, only to fuse with another person or thing. In George's case, the third "thing" is his ministry. Other spouses use their careers, whatever they may be, in the same way. In more serious cases, the triangle could be completed by an extramarital affair or perhaps alcohol.

When Gracie complains to her husband about his long hours at the church, George will usually counter with some remark about needing to be about the Lord's work. All well and good except that this is not Gracie's point. Pragmatically George's response simply serves to deflect the tension between him and Gracie. For her part, Gracie, too, is anxious and accepts George's move, letting the matter drop rather than pursue it. The problem is that neither of them has faced the real issue: their relationship. Instead of talking to George directly about their marriage, Gracie also "triangles in" the church by talking about how much time he spends there. This is a much safer subject. For his part, George may at some level recognize that his work is not the issue, but he avoids addressing the marital relationship as well. Instead, he responds by triangling in still another safe topic, their dedication to ministry. Here both spouses are on sure ground. After all, isn't this what being in the ministry is all about, to serve others regardless of how much personal sacrifice is involved? But having reached such an obvious conclusion, the conversation has nowhere to go. The interaction is stymied, the discussion fizzles out, and confrontation with their dissatisfaction with the marriage has been neatly avoided once again.

Triangling is not something that simply happens to people. It is something people do to avoid taking a stand, to avoid defining themselves in relationship to someone else. There are many ways to do this.

First, I can triangle a person, issue, or thing by drawing your attention *to* it and *away* from the real conflict between us. It doesn't matter if the person or thing is present or past, living or dead. All that matters is that it is sufficient to distract you from talking about us. George and Gracie did this by talking about church or the children instead of themselves. In the same way, as suggested in Bowen's definition, I can triangle in a third person by telling you a story about him or her. If you and I have a conflict, I can distract you by asking, "Do you know what Joe said about you?" Then I become the one with the inside information, letting you in on a secret. Instead of risking our openly being at odds with each other, I have manipulated it so that you and I are now on the same side, and Joe is the odd man out.

Second, I can actively drag someone else into a conflict, essentially to help do my fighting for me. This is different from the first instance, where I detour the tension between us by distracting you with something else. Here a third person is actually brought into the fray. Parents often involve one or more children in their marital squabbles, each parent trying to win the child over to his or her side. Siblings, rather than work things out between them, also drag parents into their fights, by shouting, "Mom! Billy hit me!" And young people seem to have a knack for marrying someone their family will dislike. What

they don't realize is that they have chosen someone who will fight with their family *for* them, someone who will supposedly help them accomplish the differentiation from their families that they couldn't accomplish for themselves. In all these examples, the effect is the same: "If I can't fight with you, maybe I can find someone who will." Eric Berne has phrased it neatly: "Let's you and him fight."[14]

Third, we must recognize that triangling is a two-way street. For a triangle to exist among three people, someone has to initiate it and the other two must accept it. Triangling begins with the lack of differentiation between two people in a relationship. Let's say that Mr. Black and Mrs. Blue, both members of the same church, have a running disagreement with each other. Neither one can bear the thought of actually confronting the other person directly, so the conflict goes on and on. If Black were the more uncomfortable of the two, he would involve a third person, and who better to fill the position than the pastor! But the triangle is not complete unless Blue is willing to be distracted in this way and the pastor is willing to be involved. This means that the one who is triangled is not a passive victim. He allows himself to be drawn into others' conflicts because of his own lack of differentiation. When he sees other people in tension with each other, his own stress level rises and he feels that he has to fix the situation. Thus a triangle can also be created by a third person who jumps into a relationship between two others in order to reduce his own anxiety.[15]

There are more ways to construct an emotional triangle than we can show. Furthermore, in real life there is usually a combination of the kinds of triangling used so that the third person may be simultaneously talked about, actively drawn in, and made a willing participant. George and Gracie, for example, may avoid facing their marital relationship either by fighting *about* the kids or by fighting *with* the kids. As the children sense tension between their parents, they may "draw fire" by behaving in such a way that their parents will fight with them instead of each other. Or their anxiety may provoke them to jump into their parents' squabbles to try to calm them down before the parents have had a chance to get to the real issues. As you may already know from your own experience, all these triangling maneuvers can occur at the same time.

Triangles offer the security of predictability. The problem with being yourself in a relationship and facing up to interpersonal tensions is that you can never be quite sure how others will respond. Being straightforward means being vulnerable, taking the risk that people won't like what they see in you. Triangles function as a safety hatch, an emergency escape to be used when the stress in a relationship becomes unbearable. Eventually, however, their use becomes habitual, like an addiction to painkillers. Some drugs help to stimulate the body's natural ability to deal with pain, but when we overuse them, we deaden their effect. We become dependent, taking the drug at the first hint of discomfort, no longer capable of bearing even minor pain without chemical assistance.

So it is with triangles. We can become so used to drawing in a particular person or sidetracking to a particular issue, that even minor stress in a relationship activates an automatic triangling response. In this way triangles become institutionalized. The various favorite triangles become imprinted on the group as part of its habitual, unconscious way of life. It is our way of inoculating ourselves against the threat of unmanageable anxiety in our important relationships.

When all is at peace, triangles remain dormant. At the slightest sign of trouble, however, they are automatically reactivated. The MacMurrays had a solid repertoire of possible maneuvers to avoid facing each other. As soon as the stress level rose in their marriage, they automatically brought into play one or the other form of triangling. In a sense, this is a stable relationship, not because it is good but because it is predictable. George and Gracie are both dimly aware that they will never have to face what they fear most: their feelings about each other and the belief that sharing those feelings will result in the destruction of their relationship. They can rely on their arsenal of triangling maneuvers to avoid that threat. Meanwhile, they continue to drift further and further apart.

Triangling in some form happens in any social group where a problem with differentiation exists. The church is no exception. As we have suggested, many church members are adept at drawing the well-meaning pastor into their disagreements. This is especially true of the poorly differentiated pastor who has a personal need to maintain harmony in the congregation at all costs. If he consistently either allows himself to be triangled between two church members or triangles himself into their relationship, two things will happen. First, he will quickly become burned out emotionally from having to carry tensions that really don't belong to him. Second, he will ensure that there will be no change despite his fondest hopes. The purpose of triangling is to avoid facing the relational issues that frighten us. As long as the pastor continues to allow himself to be triangled by the congregation, he helps them to keep avoiding each other.

We do not, however, want to create the impression that triangling is simply something that a congregation does to a pastor. Sometimes it works the other way around. Tensions in the clergy family may be deflected, only to surface somewhere else in the church. As one author has written, "An emotional triangle is an integral part of American middle-class society, marriage, and business. The institutional church is not unique— its triangle incorporates priest, parish, and wife."[16]

Let's suppose that Peter, a senior pastor, wants his wife to be more involved with the ministry. She has other aspirations, however, and prefers to pursue a career outside the church. He is angry and disillusioned with her, but doesn't want to make an issue of it. He may have any number of reasons for not facing his discontent: he is afraid of her anger; he knows she is right, but he is too proud to admit it; he doesn't want to risk making a scene in front of a watchful congregation. So what does he do? Enter his unfortunate female associate pastor, Paula. He is highly critical of everything she does, and he becomes resentful when she takes any action without clearing it with him first. He regards her as unreliable and too independent; she regards him as unreasonable and too controlling.

This pastor is maintaining a superficial closeness with his wife at the expense of his relationship to his associate. And everybody loses. The marriage loses because the closeness between the pastor and his wife is a sham. The pastoral staff lose because the chronic friction among them results in an inability to work together. And the church loses because its leadership is fragmented.

In summary, then, triangling is one way we try to circumvent our anxiety about relationships. Because we are insecure and poorly differentiated in some personal issues, we cannot confront problems in our relationships directly and confidently. Instead, we avoid each other, avoid focusing on the tension between us. We deflect issues, steer around conflict, and preserve the peace to keep from rocking the boat. The immediate payoff is obvious; after all, getting down to the real, hard issues between us is risky and delicate business. We are more comfortable kidding ourselves into thinking that everything will work out by itself, so let's just deal with it later. The long-range effect, however, is that we stay mired knee-deep in an emotional swamp of our own making while waiting in vain for someone to rescue us.

The way out of the morass is to admit that we continue to triangle others and allow ourselves to be triangled because we are afraid to take a stand. When we take a stand, when we define what we believe and who we are, we risk having others reject us, get angry with us, or just plain prove us wrong. That is the cost of differentiation, and it is not to be taken lightly. The alternative, however, is to sacrifice depth of honest, truly personal relationships.

But where do we go from here? How do we apply the notion of triangles to our social ecological vision? Triangles are but the starting point in understanding social networks. To Bowen, the triangle is "the basic building block of any emotional system, whether it is the family or any other group."[17] This means that any group of more than three people can be viewed as a web of interlocking triangles. Connections between events in the social environment, therefore, can be traced through a chain of triangling maneuvers.

Let's return to the example of Peter and Paula. In their church is an important elder and his wife, Mr. and Mrs. Stern. What is the connection between the senior pastor's marriage and that of the Sterns? Can one affect the other? Imagine the following scenario:

One morning Pastor Peter has an argument with his wife because she has applied for a job outside the church without consulting him first. Much as it was with George and Gracie MacMurray, this argument never quite gets around to focusing on their relationship—what they expect of each other and whether or not their expectations are fair. Instead, they resort to the time-tested triangle of arguing about devotion to the ministry. Even that argument doesn't go far, however, because they are too caught up in pursuing the image of the perfect pastoral couple. So Peter predictably brings his unresolved marital stress with him to work and takes it out on the associate pastor.

Paula, unfortunately, has recently made some executive decisions regarding the life of the congregation. The senior pastor is incensed. Why wasn't he consulted? What gives her the right to make such decisions? In her defense, she claims that the situation demanded that someone in authority make *some* decision and that the decisions she made were appropriate and well-considered. What she has not recognized in herself, though, is her reaction to panicky church members ("Do something quick") and her desire to carve out a niche for herself in the congregation ("Now's my chance").

Neither Peter nor Paula has faced the relationship directly. When they do argue, they talk not about themselves, but about the right way to do ministry. The senior pastor's conflict with Paula is a little too close to home (literally) to be comfortable. For her part, Paula feels overwhelmed and abused when Peter treats her this way; it reminds her of the years of painful struggle she has spent trying to define her rightful place as a woman in the pastoral ministry.

[margin note: Substitution of ministry for real topic of conflict in the relationship]

Occasionally, to detour the conflict, Paula will triangle in one of the elders, Mr. Stern. Peter is willing to accept this move, and so is the elder who always has a bone to pick with the pastor. Mr. Stern argues with the pastor about how ministry *should* be done in this church or about how the previous pastor did things. Peter, tired of hearing about the exploits of his predecessor, usually ignores the elder's long-winded diatribes. This leaves Mr. Stern feeling belittled; rather than pursue the issue with the powerful pastor, he takes out his bitterness on Mrs. Stern. We could go on and on. The point is that there is, in fact, a direct connection between the pastor's marriage and that of the Sterns. It is a chain of linked triangles, held together by everyone's willingness to be distracted from truly resolving his or her own interpersonal conflicts.

Does this sound implausible? Then take the time to examine your own church and marriage and family. Write your own example, the story of *your* social context. Connections like this are a part of the everyday life of families, and the church family is no different. If it sounds too far-fetched, it may be because you're not used to thinking in terms of triangles and interconnected relationships. We will try to show in chapter 3 how the

[margin note: Δ's interconnected relationships]

life of the clergy family is intertwined, sometimes inseparably, with the lives of the families in the congregation. Triangles can help us to understand this.

Tangled Webs

"Oh, what a tangled web we weave," Sir Walter Scott reminds us, "When first we practice to deceive!" Lies have a way of reproducing themselves. Even a small lie, which seems innocent enough, can snowball into a mountain of deception as more and more untruths are required to cover the original one. Triangles are a form of deceit. They are ways to steer around the truth about a relationship. And like lies, triangles are capable of producing tangled webs of relationships, a network of interlocking triangles, held together by a common desire to avoid facing the truth. Mr. A and Mr. B begin by triangling in Mr. C, creating a pseudo-conflict between B and C. Mr. B and Mr. C then triangle in Mrs. D. And so on: C and D triangle E, D and E triangle F, ad nauseum. An entire social group may be kept together by crisscrossed emotional triangles. Mr. A and Mr. B need to keep Mr. C triangled to avoid facing their relationship with each other. The same is true all the way down the line. Everyone in the web has a personal investment in keeping things the way they are in a peculiar kind of balance that is precarious yet stable. It is stable in that group members have the false security of avoiding their most anxiety-provoking emotional issues. But it is precarious because their stability is shallow as unresolved tensions constantly threaten to shake the system from within.

To some extent, the behavior of a poorly differentiated group is predictable. This is because people who are not well differentiated generally live according to certain rules of relationship:

1. If you are a friend of my friend, then you are my friend, too.
2. If you are an enemy of my friend, then you are my enemy.
3. If you are a friend of my enemy, then you are my enemy, too.
4. If you are an enemy of my enemy, then you are my friend.[18]

We are using the terms "friend" and "enemy" loosely here. It would be more accurate, but also more ponderous, to substitute "someone with whom I have a positive relationship at this moment" for the word "friend." True friendships have their ups and downs and are able to weather them without destroying the relationship. The point is that if I am poorly differentiated, then I will feel compelled to respond to you, not on your own merit, but on the basis of my relationships to others. If you like someone whom I like, then all else being equal, I will feel compelled to like you. If, by contrast, you like someone whom I dislike, it makes it difficult for me to like you. A more differentiated relationship would mean that those whom I like and whom you like should have little to say about whether or not we like each other.

Think for a moment what it would mean if you were to violate one of these rules in a relationship. For example, consider the second rule, "an enemy of my friend must be my enemy." Let us say that Smith is a good friend of yours or at least someone with whom you would like to keep a positive relationship. Jones then comes to you with a criticism of Smith. From our discussion of triangles, you know that Jones is implicitly asking you to take sides. What would you do? The immediate temptation would be to follow Rule 2, that is, to consider Jones your enemy by rejecting the criticism and defending your friend Smith. To do otherwise would require a well-differentiated person indeed.

The dilemma faced by ministers and their family members, however, is more complicated than this. If Smith and Jones are both members of the congregation and you are the pastor or a member of his family, you cannot resolve the situation so easily by rejecting Jones. The problem is that *you* want to keep a positive relationship with both, but *they* will each want you to side with one against the other. Again, it takes a secure sense of your own differentiation to be able to stay out of such a triangle and let Smith and Jones work it out between themselves.

Let's assume that we are members of a certain church who follow the four rules listed above, lacking the differentiation to do otherwise. We keep the rules in order to maintain a feeling of psychological balance; it causes too much anxiety to break one of them. If we are consistent, then our group will fall into one of three "balanced" patterns.

The first pattern is the most obvious one: we must all be friends, pushing Rule 1 to its limits. There are no enemies. As we have said, any realistic friendship will have its ups and downs. In a poorly differentiated relationship, however, the

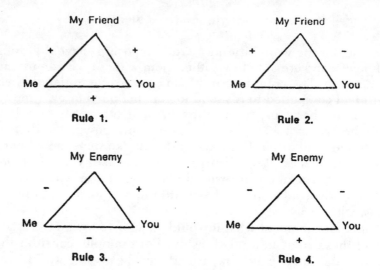

Figure 2.1. "Balanced" triangles: the four relationship rules

downs cannot be tolerated. This means that the church can maintain a sense of balance and follow the rules by always *pretending* to be friends and turning a blind eye to interpersonal difficulties.[19] If there are any underlying negative emotions, they are covered over by a false display of togetherness. The unconscious motto of our group is "Let's put a good face on it" or "Smile even if it kills you."

The second and third patterns are harder to see. If you are the kind of person who likes to be convinced by personal experience, try the following exercise. Draw three dots on a piece of paper and connect them with lines. The dots represent people, and the lines represent the relationships among them. Each of the four rules can be illustrated by placing plus signs (+) or minus signs (-) next to the lines. The plus signs represent friendly relationships; the minus signs, enemies. Figure 2.1 illustrates this.

Note the two basic patterns in this illustration. Either all the signs are positive, as in the first rule, or one is positive and the other two are negative, as in the last three rules. Pragmatically this means that a relationship among three people can follow the rules in only one of two ways: either everyone is friends or two are friends while the third plays odd man out.

What happens if we expand the network? Adding a fourth person means adding three more relationships for a total of six. Draw four dots now with six lines connecting them. We already

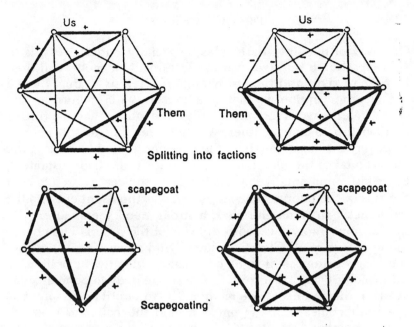

Figure 2.2. Balancing a group, with splits and scapegoats

know that we could balance the foursome by making all the relationships positive. Instead, throw in one negative relationship somewhere, and then add in plus or minus signs for the other relationships. Remember, each triangle must have either three plus signs or one plus and two minus signs.

There are two basic patterns of solutions to the puzzle, two patterns of relationship for the group. Can you begin to see them? With only four dots, of course, it's hard to generalize. If you really want to see the patterns clearly, you will need to extend the network even further. Add a fifth or even a sixth dot. Again, draw all the connecting lines, label one line negative, and then follow the rules to label the rest of the lines as well. If you were to do this several times, you would find many different solutions. All of the solutions, however, would fit into two overall patterns, which are illustrated in figure 2.2.

The first pattern splits the group into two smaller groups. Within each of the smaller groups all the relationships are positive. But between the two groups all the relationships are negative. If you are a member of my group, then you are my friend. If you are a member of the other group, then you are my enemy. Sound familiar? This is the stuff of which church splits are made. A general lack of differentiated relationships in our congregation means that we will be bound by the four rules.

One way of obeying these rules, especially under stress, is to split the church into two warring factions. Our motto will then be "We're right and they're wrong" or "It's us against them."

The other option is that one person will emerge as the common enemy. Everyone else in the group has a positive relationship to one another. All lines leading to the enemy, however, are negative. He is the outsider, the odd man out, the one who takes the blame, the scapegoat. In the Old Testament, the priest ceremonially laid his hands on the goat chosen to bear the sins of the people. The scapegoat was then sent out into the wilderness. In some churches, a strong need seems to exist to saddle some individual with the sins of the group. The church motto is "we're all Christians here," and anyone who tarnishes the congregation's self-righteous image is dealt with swiftly. An entire congregation can rise up as a single body to denounce the sexual indiscretions of one member. It isn't until much later that the truth comes out: the one who led the battle to have the errant member kicked out was guilty of the same sin.

Scapegoating is a way of ridding the congregation of its sin by dumping it all in another's lap. A poorly differentiated family, church, or other group "chooses" someone to be the scapegoat so that the rest of the group can say, "We're all friends here." In the church setting, of course, that person is often the pastor or a member of his family. When we as church members experience tension among ourselves, we can deflect it by carping about the pastor, his wife, or his children. Our motto then will be "If it weren't for him" or "It's all his fault."

We are *not* trying to say that every church must fit one of these patterns of false togetherness, a split into opposing sides, or scapegoating. The assumption behind each of these is that the members of the group are poorly differentiated and therefore feel compelled to follow the four rules of relationship. It is possible, of course, for the members of a church or any other group to be differentiated enough to avoid falling into one of these unsatisfactory patterns.

But let the wise be forewarned. As Bowen suggests, we are all probably less differentiated than we would like to think. And if we are honest with ourselves, we may have to admit that as Christians we have more invested in denying negative emotions than most people. That makes us prone to slip into a superficial togetherness. And in some cases it may be important enough for us to maintain this false closeness that we search for a cause, a flag to rally around. We do this by finding an enemy to fight—perhaps a person (scapegoat), perhaps a group (factions).[20]

The church of which we are members may not fit one of these patterns exclusively. But the seeds of these patterns will exist in every church since, realistically, in no church will all the members be completely differentiated in every way. If we take the easy way out, to continue to triangle one another, to allow ourselves to be triangled—in essence to avoid facing the conflicts among us—then we will be drawn toward one of the three patterns. If in our congregation triangling is more prevalent than differentiation, we might as well hang a banner over the church door bearing one of the three slogans: "Smile even if it kills you," "It's us against them," or "It's all his fault."

If we return now to Pastor Miller and the First Church of Kirkdale, we can begin to see how triangling and a lack of differentiation have contributed to their situation. Again, let us suggest a learning exercise. Go back to the beginning of chapter 1 and reread the story of the Miller family. As you read, reflect upon where and how the people involved were avoiding the interpersonal issues among them. What triangles do you see? When you have done this, read the concluding section of this chapter and match your insights against ours.

*   *   *

Kirkdale Revisited

First, we must ask ourselves what it is that led the pastor to feel that his ministry at his previous church had ended. What made it "time to move on"? Pastor Miller had planted his church, nourished and tended it, and watched it grow over the years. When the church stopped growing, when it seemed to stagnate, he became restless. True, it was still one big happy family. But is that all there was to it? Some churches can grow only to a point and then a change is required to keep it growing. Pastor Miller came to the conclusion that the change that was needed, both for him and the congregation, was for him to leave.

A family analogy is helpful here. There comes a time in the lives of most families when both parents and children begin to feel that the children should be on their own. The converse of this, of course, is that the parents should also begin to redefine themselves as something other than adults with dependent children. This is a difficult transition for many on both sides of the generational line. Some parents and children have a very difficult time letting go of each other. Yet they must let go for the healthy differentiation of all concerned.

What we don't know is whether or not Pastor Miller's separation from his previous church was accomplished in an appropriately differentiated fashion. Was the congregation party to the decision? Did they fight it? Or did they just look the other way with a hasty good-bye? What we do know is that the pastor and his family have just experienced an important transition in their lives. If the separation from the previous church was clean, they would be able to make a relatively fresh start in their new church home. If not, they would be more likely simply to try to recreate the church family they left behind, using the Kirkdale church as the raw material.

The congregation in Kirkdale, too, had just been through a transition. The question for them is whether their previous pastor made a clean separation. Did they let go willingly and lovingly? If not, then they too will want to mold the Miller family into the image of the previous pastor and his family, to finish old business and unresolved feelings. Any pastor who moves to a new congregation should want to know why the previous pastor left.

If you think that you've been called to a congregation solely on the basis of your theology and your preaching ability, think again. These are important criteria, but they are often less important than the emotional issues left behind by your predecessor. Indeed, discussions about theology may be used as a socially acceptable way of avoiding more personal issues.

If the Millers had known, they might have recognized the clear signs of a lack of differentiation, both in their own family's behavior and in that of the congregation. When the pastor tried to take leadership in the new church, it created tension. But rather than face the personal differences that prompted their anxiety, both pastor and church were content to believe that everything would work out on its own. Transitions take time, of course. But there is a difference between recognizing this fact and fooling ourselves that time itself will resolve the tensions. There was almost an implicit agreement among everyone in the

Kirkdale church to cover their anxieties with a display of cordiality. This is not to say that their feelings of friendship were completely artificial; it is rather that positive feelings of togetherness were used by all to deny any separateness.

Arlene's aspirations also fanned the flames of anxiety in the church. Her wish to remodel the parsonage was bad enough. As if to add insult to injury, however, she proposed to do this by working outside the church. Heresy! The previous pastor's wife had devoted all her time to the church. How could the new pastor's wife be so selfish?

Naturally there are two sides to every story. It is clear that some church members were incensed by what appeared to be Arlene's declaration of independence. They were not prepared for a minister's wife who wanted to be separate. But have they completely misread the situation? Why didn't Arlene ask the church for the money? Whether or not they would have agreed is beside the point. Her proposal to work outside the congregation may be just as much an attempt to cut off as it is to differentiate. And since neither Arlene nor those who complain about her are able to face each other directly, a lack of differentiation is probably the better guess.

These are the rumblings that everyone tried to ignore, until the rumble grew into a quake and sundered the congregation. Up to that point the congregation had been playing "Smile even if it kills you." The stress in the ecosystem, however, had built to the point that the game had to change to a deadly earnest combination of "It's all his fault" and "It's us against them." What forced the change?

If a group is not well differentiated, it takes only one person to cause enough anxiety to set off a chain reaction. Frank Collins was the random element. What Pastor Miller had not realized or taken the time to find out was that Frank had also been at odds with the previous pastor, claiming that he, too, wielded too much power. Nor did Frank himself understand why this made him so angry. He had grown up as a P.K. under a dynamic but overly controlling father. Frank had sworn to himself that he would never go into the ministry, even up to the day he submitted his application to seminary. Even now, he prided himself on having no ambitions to be a senior pastor.

But Frank had never differentiated from his father. The emotional baggage left from his childhood was always waiting to be dumped on the unsuspecting senior minister who didn't affirm Frank in the way that he so badly needed. The force of his anger and resentment caused an anxiety wave in the congregation, which carried the poorly differentiated congregation into an us-against-them split.

And the Millers' children? It was difficult enough for them to make their own adjustment to a new town, a new school, and a new set of potential friends. But when they sensed the tension in the congregation, they decided to keep their problems to themselves and go along with the game of putting on a good face, no matter what. Now they were caught. Steve's indiscretion would probably have made little difference to anyone in the church had he not been the minister's son. With the congregation spiraling toward a split, however, his fling with marijuana became a hot topic and made him a prime candidate for many a triangle. Eager to keep the triangling process going, numbers of church members now watched and waited for Nancy to provide them with another convenient excuse.

Again, we must emphasize that no one in First Church, Kirkdale, should be considered purely a victim of the system. Everyone has a role in keeping the game alive. But if it takes only one person in the right place to set the game in motion, it also takes only one person to be resolute enough to stop it. One person in a key position who refuses to be triangled will force others to face up to the real issues. Differentiation is not an accident. We become differentiated either because our parents have intended it, or because we intend it for ourselves. It is a human irony that we can come together authentically only if we are secure in our separateness. We cannot truly be the body of Christ unless we recognize our gifts and functions as different organs with individual identities, yet at the same time one body. When we cannot allow for this diversity but let our anxiety get the best of us, the health and growth of the body suffers.

The concepts of differentiation and triangling point to some of the essence of what it means to be human. As such, they are applicable to all social groups, family and church included. They give us a dynamic foundation for building a social ecology, for understanding the nature of our connectedness with each other. In chapter 3 our task will be to focus more specifically on the uniqueness of the ecology of the clergy family.

3

A Family Within a Family

So far we have discussed our assumptions only broadly and have made general applications to the minister's family. In chapter 1 we outlined the foundations of our social ecological perspective. In chapter 2 we gave more content to this framework by showing how triangles function as the basic building blocks of social systems. But these general comments may be applied to any family; indeed, to any social system. In this chapter we intend to speak more directly to the clergy family itself, since nothing we have said to this point clearly distinguishes the clergy family from any other social system.

Let us first point out, however, that there is nothing unique about the clergy family when considered as a family. Furthermore, if we focused our discussion solely on the clergy family itself, we would be going back on our commitment to an ecological perspective. We have purposely emphasized the ecology of the minister's family for one reason: it is not the clergy family as a family, but their *social environment* that is unique.

We must make a careful distinction here between the structural characteristics of professional ministry, or ministry as a *job*, and the broader ecological issues that we seek to address. The families of other professionals must deal with some of the same causes of stress that face clergy families, such as extended hours, a high degree of responsibility for others, and the unpredictability that comes from being on call twenty-four hours a day. These external structural factors are related to the vocation and as such

are not singular to ministry. Rather, our ecological thesis is that
the uniqueness of the clergy family's experience is rooted in its
relationship to a local congregation. The minister's family is a
social subsystem, or system-within-a-system, seated squarely
within the larger context of the local church. It is the relationship between these systems that is our primary focus in this
book.

One of the metaphors that the apostle Paul uses to describe
the church is the family. Christians are to see themselves as
members of a divine family of which God is the Father. Thus
Paul, quoting from the Old Testament, writes, "I will be a
Father to you, and you will be my sons and daughters, says the
Lord Almighty."[1] We are also told, "Because you are sons, God
has sent the Spirit of his Son into our hearts, the Spirit who calls
out, 'Abba, Father.'"[2] And as Paul describes our bonds to each
other, he writes, "Consequently, you are no longer foreigners
and aliens, but fellow citizens with God's people and members
of God's household, built on the foundation of the apostles and
prophets, with Christ Jesus himself as the chief cornerstone."[3]
We believe that the language of family is not just applied to the
church as one applies a metaphor; Paul is describing the reality
of our relationship to one another, founded in God's relationship
of grace to us.

This reality is more than a theological reality—it is a social
one as well. Edwin Friedman has written that of all work
systems, "the one that functions most like a family is the church
or synagogue."[4] Here, too, family is more than just a metaphor.
Friedman suggests that no other work environment functions
more like a family than the ministry. The church is not just the
place where the minister labors; it is not just another work
system to which we may apply some dispassionate organiza-
tional theory. The church, the local congregation, is a family,
subject to the same emotional processes, the same joys and
sorrows that all families must face. One minister's son speaks of
his home church as "an extended family of one thousand." We
must keep in mind that the clergy family lives and breathes in
the midst of a larger, extended family: the congregation.

Moreover, Friedman continues, the clergy family and the
congregation "are plugged into one another and their respective
states of homeostasis join in a new overall balance."[5] This is
essentially an ecological view. It is not merely that the church

has an "impact" on the clergy family or vice versa. To cite Friedman again:

> The concept of "impact" suggests two different, discrete entities that influence one another from outside each other's space, as might occur in a crash between two boulders, two trains, or two billiard balls. . . . The model being developed here is more analogous to electricity. The deepest effects that work systems and family systems have on one another come from the fact that they both run on the same current, if not the identical energy source.[6]

It would be shortsighted to focus on the external impact of ministry on the life of the clergy family, just as the one-dimensional thinking that led to the crisis of Mono Lake was shortsighted (see chapter 1). The minister's family and the congregational family are but two subsystems of a larger social ecosystem that includes them both. As we shall see, a full description of all the relevant social systems would go beyond the local congregation to include, for example, the community and the denomination (chap. 10). The absolute minimum context, however, for understanding the minister's family is its relationship to the congregation.

How might we understand this relationship? Our own research and a review of the literature suggest two broadly overlapping themes. The first theme is that intense and often emotionally charged *role expectations* are placed on members of the clergy family. These expectations can stem from several different sources. The diversity of the expectations that a minister's family members must juggle can lead to a great deal of personal stress. We shall discuss these role expectations in general terms in part 2.

The second theme concerns the ways in which problems of expectations are experienced at the different *boundaries* in the ecology of the clergy family. This is a somewhat more structural approach to understanding the social environment. In particular, we outline three stressful "boundary problems" that face the minister's family. The first is called *idealization,* in which superhuman expectations of members of the clergy family effectively prevent them from forming differentiated peer relationships with church members. The second, which we call *impoverishment,* reflects the additional difficulty of forming supportive relationships outside the congregation. Finally, the problem of *intrusion* deals with what is commonly called "the fishbowl syndrome." We shall discuss each of these difficulties separately and show how they interact in the lives of clergy families.

The Price of Exampleship

Our first general theme is the role expectations placed on the members of the minister's family. Many clergy and their families have experienced a lack of freedom to be just another family in the congregation. Their roles are invested symbolically with particular personal, religious, and emotional significance. William Douglas addresses this issue with his metaphor of the "royal family complex":

> The minister still tends to be regarded as the father of an extended family, of which his wife is the mother. Furthermore, like the British royal family, which symbolizes the Empire and Commonwealth to a world community, the minister and his family symbolize the congregation to a local community. In their representative function the "royal family" is given love and respect, without earning or necessarily deserving this response. But the price of respect and love is exampleship.[7]

Members of the minister's family are expected to be spiritual and moral examples to the congregation. The minister and his spouse must have a model marriage. Other couples within the congregation may confess their marital difficulties and perhaps even be praised for their openness and honesty in doing so. For the minister to acknowledge marital problems, however, may provoke disillusionment, anxiety, and doubts about the minister's spirituality. In some churches the minister's wife is expected to be the ideal wife and mother; the children must be upright and moral, often with the implicit expectation that they are to be groomed for positions of church or civic leadership. The failure of the clergy family members to meet the expected standards may bring social condemnation.

A congregation's spiritual expectations can leave members of the minister's family with the sense that they dare not show themselves, beyond certain narrow limits, to be fallible human beings. The matter of spiritual standards, however, is only one dimension of the issue. Debates within the congregation regarding the spirituality of the clergy family may be an indication of an underlying process of emotional triangling. Remember that no other organization functions more like a family than the church and that the clergy family functions as the symbolic head of this complex family. The practical effect of this situation, as Friedman notes, is that "the intensity with which some lay people become invested in their religious institutions makes the church or synagogue a prime arena for the displacement of important, unresolved family issues."[8]

People on both sides of the ministry, clergy and congregation alike, bring with them a personal history. This includes a reservoir of thoughts and emotions from previous relationships, particularly from one's family. The familial nature of the church makes it all the more likely that unresolved family issues will surface in that setting. Therefore debates regarding the spirituality of the clergy family can be merely the occasion or even the excuse for church members and clergy to hash out unresolved emotional issues within their families.

Consider the church member who always criticizes the minister's children for their behavior. To some extent, concern over whether or not the children live up to some standard of behavior can be legitimate. But is that all there is to it? The more important factor will usually have to do with that member's frustrations regarding his or her own children or childhood. The same may be said of how the minister and his spouse will react to such criticism. Ministers or parishioners who are overly strict with the P.K. may on a conscious level appear to be standard-bearers, perhaps even advocating a particular prescription for righteous behavior. Unconsciously, though, they may also be trying to resolve old feelings about their own religious upbringing.

When role expectations are so emotionally laden, the person in the role feels greater pressure to conform. As we shall see more clearly in the next chapter, this is complicated by the fact that many expectations from different quarters may simultaneously hang in the balance. There are specific and explicit demands that may be made by various church members, the more vague sense of expectations stemming from the congregation as a whole, denominational expectations, and the clergy family members' own perceptions of their roles. What happens, moreover, when some of the expectations conflict with one another? When members cannot agree with each other? When the congregation's expectations are at odds with the clergy family's own vision of ministry?

Thus the multiplicity of role expectations, together with their highly charged nature, can create a precarious juggling act for the clergy family. And while it may be necessary for sanity's sake to sort out conflicting expectations, this may be difficult work indeed, especially where covert triangling is involved. If, for example, the pastor receives contradictory messages from members Smith and Jones, it may be because Smith and Jones are at odds with each other and triangling the pastor. Confronting the discrepant expectations will meet the resistance of the two members who are avoiding facing their own conflict. This makes it doubly important that the clergy family be able to distinguish between legitimate differences of opinion regarding roles, and pseudo-conflicts that mask emotional triangles. Where bona fide differences of expectations exist, open communication and negotiation will be necessary. If the apparent difference is only a pseudo-difference, however, as in the case of Smith and Jones, then even the most well-meaning negotiation process will be fruitless as it fails to confront the real issue.

In summary, then, the clergy family lives in a social environment characterized by a variety of role expectations stemming from diverse sources. Where these expectations are realistic and in harmony with one another, the life of the clergy family will usually be relatively conflict- free and fulfilling. But where there are conflicting expectations members of the minister's family will experience what sociologists call "role strain," the stress of being unable to enact one's roles successfully. This is complicated by the fact that the image of the minister's family as the "royal family" means that it is more likely that unresolved family issues from the congregation will be played out on the clergy family.

The theme of role expectations will be carried through in subsequent chapters.

Our second theme, regarding boundaries, goes hand in hand with the first. The uniqueness of the ecology of the minister's family can be expressed in terms of the relationship among the clergy family, the congregational family, and the community— at the boundaries where these systems meet. In particular, the minister's family is confronted by the triple threat of three interrelated *boundary* problems: idealization, impoverishment, and intrusion.

The Importance of Clear Boundaries

The boundary of any social system is an actual or socially agreed upon "skin" that distinguishes the system from its environment and from other groups. Boundaries can be both physical and social, and families vary greatly from one another in the extent to which they guard their boundaries. The family is bounded physically by the walls of its home. In some instances this physical boundary between the family and the outside world may be characterized by fences, security systems, and locked doors. In other families, doors are left unlocked, and family and friends come and go at will.

More importantly, however, a family's physical boundary is a concrete indication of a social boundary, an underlying social posture toward the outside world. Where the physical boundaries are more closed and locked, the social posture is one of defensiveness. Such a family will carefully regulate the incoming and outgoing traffic of family members, visitors, and friends. Where the physical boundary is more open, the posture is also more open, with allowances made for influence from the social environment. At the extremes of openness, it may appear that there are no social boundaries whatsoever; indeed, there may be little distinction between what is family and what is outside the family.[9]

Whatever its style or preference, the way in which a family maintains its boundaries is a function of its family identity. The family that emphasizes its collective identity as a family and a devotion to the group over against individual differences, is likely to have a more closely kept boundary. Families that by contrast stress the importance of individual identity are likely to have more loosely defined family boundaries as the individual members seek their primary source of identity outside the family's walls. Beyond these structural differences, however, lies an important point: the boundary of the family is the keeper of the family identity. A family's behavior toward the outside world, in terms of how boundaries are maintained, is a reflection of its own sense of identity.

Within a family's larger social environment, certain patterns of boundaries are typical for our culture. Take the simplified case of a nuclear family with two employed parents and one school-age child. These three share a family identity, separated from the outside world by a boundary as described above. The father's workplace, the mother's workplace, and the child's school are additional social environments in which the individual family members participate. In general, however, these environments do not involve the other family members in any consistent, face-to-face way. Although father and mother are involved with the child's schooling, parent-teacher conferences, and the like, they are not a part of the child's daily school activities and peer groups. If you have had children in school, you know how important these boundaries can be to them. When they have identified enough with their school and peer group, they may be embarrassed if you show up at school. Similarly, some adults feel varying degrees of awkwardness when spouses or children visit their place of work.

What these people are experiencing is a form of _role confusion._ To a great extent, our behavior and attitudes depend on our social context. How we behave at school or at work when among peers is not necessarily the same way we behave at home. This does not make us split personalities; every person plays a number of roles, and certain role behaviors are cued by our social environment.

Each of our social settings has a relatively consistent cast of characters, and for the most part our roles in these settings are predictable. But occasionally family members are present in extra-familial settings, and some confusion can result. A man or woman who has a dominant role at work and yet is more passive at home may be uncomfortable when the spouse makes a surprise visit to the office. A child who is a leader among his or her peers may feel awkward and embarrassed when Mom or Dad shows up to take the child home. The more divergent our roles in different settings, the more awkward such a situation can be. This does not mean that crossovers from one setting to another are necessarily disruptive. The important point is that our roles—and thus to some extent our behavior and sense of self—are partially defined by the social context. Variations in the predictability and continuity of these contexts may create tension.

The consistency and stability of our social environments, in turn, are protected by clear and adequate boundaries. Typically there is a clear boundary between a family and the other social settings in which the individual family members participate. In addition, each family has what Kantor and Lehr call a *social intraspace*.[10] This is the gap between the family boundary and the interpersonal relationships therein. An outsider to the family may be allowed into the family's "space," but extra effort is required if the outsider wishes to negotiate his or her way into a more personal relationship with a family member. For example, a door-to-door salesperson may be able to get in the door fairly easily. Family members will continue to relate to this person in a formal way until he or she can win their confidence. The sales pitch occurs in the family's social intraspace. This intraspace helps to safeguard a family's integrity by serving as a buffer to the outside world. Boundaries, then, can be physical and concrete or pragmatically established by a group's social behavior. Moreover, physical boundaries are often symbolic of a family's perception of its relationship to the outside world. Whether physical or social, a family needs clear and adequate boundaries to maintain its identity and stability.

Renowned family therapist Salvador Minuchin focuses specifically on the relationship of boundaries to healthy family functioning.[11] Minuchin has a multi-leveled view of the family system. Families, considered as a unit, are interactional systems in their own right. This means that a family is more than just a collection of individuals. To understand a family, one must go beyond the personalities of the individual members and consider the implicit rules that govern how family members relate to each other and to the outside world. Pragmatically, for Minuchin these rules constitute the boundaries of the family.

As we have seen, families differ in their rules regarding how members come and go and what is required of strangers before they are admitted into the family's social space. Minuchin, however, emphasizes more than just the boundary between the family and the outside world. He also sees boundaries between family members and between subsystems within the family. For example, the husband-wife relationship as spouses is one family subsystem, the relationship of the adults as parents to their children is another, and the relationship among the children is still another.

A healthy family must have rules of relationship that clearly demarcate the boundaries of these subsystems. For example, if the marital relationship is weak and the spouses are emotionally distant from each other, this is not yet a boundary problem. If, however, one spouse substitutes an intimate relationship with one of the children for what is missing in the marriage, this is a violation of boundaries. Children should not fulfill roles appropriate to spouses. This is just one common example of a type of boundary problem found in families that seek out therapy.

There are, therefore, rules and boundaries that distinguish subsystems from each other at all different levels of a family's ecology. These boundaries must be clear and must allow for interaction. In problematic families, boundaries can be either too rigid, resulting in what Minuchin calls *disengagement,* or too diffuse, resulting in *enmeshment.*[12] Disengagement is characterized by emotional distance and aloofness; the boundaries are too closed to permit free give-and-take personal interaction. People who are disengaged show a lack of concern or interest in each other's activities or welfare. Enmeshment, on the other hand, is a more fused pattern of relationship where those involved often have difficulty telling where one person stops and the other begins. In enmeshed relationships, personal boundaries are blurred so that in some cases persons react with hair-trigger sensitivity to each other's feelings. One person's depression triggers the other's depression; one person's anxiety triggers the other's anxiety.

It is possible to find both enmeshed and disengaged relationships in the same family. A common pattern, for example, is for the mother to become emotionally overinvolved or enmeshed with one or more children, becoming overconcerned with every difficulty the child faces. Meanwhile the father/husband remains disengaged and detached from the family, perhaps compensating by becoming overinvolved with his career. Such a family needs to reestablish clear and appropriate boundaries between the various sets of relationships. The boundary *between* mother and child is too fuzzy, while the the boundary *surrounding* the mother-child relationship is too rigid and excludes the husband/father.

A positive change would entail strengthening the boundary around the husband-wife relationship, making the personal boundary between mother and child more appropriate and reestablishing contact between father and child. Unfortunately, the individuals involved may find it easier unconsciously to maintain such a pattern than consciously to change it. The spouses, anxious about their own relationship, remain disengaged from each other to avoid confrontation. Meanwhile, the child may feel that the mother's overconcern is better than no concern at all and will thus encourage her overinvolvement. The point, however, is that clear boundaries are needed both within and around the family. Every healthy relationship must have a balance of separateness and togetherness. Where boundaries are too rigid, togetherness is sacrificed; where boundaries are fuzzy or diffuse, separateness is lost.

The foregoing examples illustrate the fact that within any family, clear boundaries go hand in hand with balanced and appropriate role expectations. What is true for families in general is also true for the clergy family in particular: clarity of boundaries is needed both within the family and without. We can think of this in either of two ways.

If we consider the congregation as the immediate social context of the clergy family, then the emphasis falls on the need for clear boundaries between the clergy family and the congregation as "the outside world." Remember also, however, that the clergy family is a family within a family or, perhaps, a subsystem within a larger congregational family system. In this way the emphasis falls on two boundaries: the one between the clergy family and the congregation as subsystems within one larger family, and the boundary between the congregation and the community where the community now takes the role of the external environment.

One or the other way of thinking will be more appropriate for a particular congregation. Either way, however, we can state our thesis for the general case: many ministers' families face social boundaries that are either inappropriately rigid or diffuse. This results in the particular relational difficulties or boundary problems that we shall now discuss.

What we call the problems of idealization and intrusion refer to the boundary problem between the clergy family and the congregation. The phenomenon of impoverishment refers to the boundary problem between the clergy family and the community beyond the congregation.

It's Lonely at the Top

To understand the phenomenon of *idealization,* think about this: Have you ever had a conversation with a person who somehow didn't seem to be speaking directly to you, but instead to his or her inaccurate *image of you?* I remember many such interchanges with my grandmother. As a boy I was short and slightly overweight. Adolescence changed all that; in one year I grew over five inches and in subsequent years lost twenty to thirty pounds. My grandmother, however, could not keep up with the changes in my appearance. Each time she saw me, she expressed surprise that I had grown taller and lost more weight since the last time we met, whereas in reality I had long since stopped mutating. I received the same reaction when later I decided to sport a mustache. The first time Grandma saw it, she made some confused comment about my having "whiskers." And each time thereafter she again registered her surprise as if she were unsure that I was really her grandson.[13]

The point of the story has nothing to do with advancing senility. It is rather that all of us, in our ongoing relationships, relate to others partially on the basis of the images we have of them. My grandmother's image of me was of a prepubescent and chubby twelve-year-old. Each time she saw me, she was jarred by the disjunction between her mental image and my actual appearance. Even then, this did not prompt her to revise her picture of me in her mind.

Our mental images can be extremely resistant to change because our perceptions of others are inextricably intertwined with our perceptions of ourselves. This also is a matter of differentiation. It is difficult for some parents to let go of their images of their children as young and dependent because to do so would change the nature of the parent-child relationship and hence the parent's self-image in relation to the child. If, say, a mother has a strong need to be needed, it will be difficult for her to acknowledge her children's growing independence and competence. To give up the image of her children as needing her help would entail modifying her image of herself. In general, our self-concept is greatly dependent on the roles we play vis-à-vis others. This in turn requires that others play roles that complement our perception of ourselves, and our images of these others will be based on these complementary roles. When we have a heavy emotional investment in a particular role, the associated images of ourselves and others will be highly resistant to change. When we are not appropriately differentiated, your role and my role are too closely enmeshed; I cannot play my part in the script unless you are also playing your part.

Relating to others on the basis of our images of them is a fact of everyday interaction. It is neither good nor bad, healthy nor unhealthy in and of itself. It becomes problematic only when our images are no longer realistic, when they keep us from acknowledging and adapting to the reality that is before us. "Adapting to reality" means modifying internal images; for the poorly differentiated person, this is tantamount to giving up a piece of one's identity.

The severity of this problem will depend on the context. My grandmother's inflexible image of me had a relatively innocuous effect on our relationship. I saw her only on infrequent visits and viewed my interchanges with her as both curious and amusing. If I had lived in her home, however, the effect would have been dramatically different. People who live or work together eventually establish a pattern of expectations of each other, or what is usually called "a working relationship." But what happens when such expectations are based on an inaccurate image of a person's identity, capabilities, feelings, or desires? In that case, what would normally be experienced as reasonable expectations will instead be experienced as unfair, restrictive, and unreasonable role demands. It is important to recognize that the intensity of our role expectations is not necessarily problematic in itself. It is rather a question of "fit"; whether or not an expectation seems reasonable depends on how well it fits with our own self-perception and personality.

Each member of a church congregation has some image of the roles of the minister, the minister's spouse, and the minister's child. The images derive partly from theological and ideological beliefs and partly from experiences with other ministers in particular and the church and one's own family in general. The less differentiated the person, the more likely images from the past will determine relationships in the present. Since, as Friedman asserts, no other work setting functions more like a family than ministry in a congregation, church members are unlikely to be emotionally neutral about their images of these roles. Again, the intensity of these images is not problematic in itself; the more important question is whether or not they are compatible with the images that members of the clergy family have of themselves.

As Douglas's metaphor of the royal family suggests, however, the images that we hold of our clergy tend to be idealized or larger than life. They must be more than human but less than God. The bottom line is that the special nature of the clergy family's roles too often requires some form of moral, spiritual, or emotional "differentness." The net result is inflexible images, fixed relationships, and a perpetual sense of a personal chasm between members of the minister's family and members of the congregation. This is the pragmatic result of idealization: members of the clergy family experience a fixed, rigid social boundary that makes it impossible to engage in true peer relationships within the congregation.

This social isolation raises a crucial question: where does the pastor or a member of his family turn during times of spiritual or emotional crisis? Margaretta Bowers has poignantly described the importance of this question for the mental health of the clergy:

> The nature of the ministry with the awesome demands it places on the self-image of the individual minister constitutes the most formidable obstacle in the path of clerical psychotherapy. It is an integral part of the priestly self-image that if the minister is sick in his religious life, he should be able to cure himself. And when he finds that the Sacraments do not heal him, and that all of the beneficent services of the Church do not heal him, when he finds himself unable to pray, he feels that this means only one thing— he is bad.[14]

Whereas the members of a congregation are exhorted to bear one another's burdens, the members of the minister's family may be effectively excluded from this process. In such a situation the clergy family is cut off from the healing potential of a community of peer relationships. Members of the clergy family find themselves ministering grace to the congregation and having no one to minister to them in return.

Yet it is important to recognize that idealization and the resulting isolation are not simply forced by the congregation upon a clergy family. The minister and his family may themselves affirm a sense of calling in which they are to be set apart.

In so doing they may support an image of specialness and a differentness of role. Ruth Rehmann, a minister's daughter, describes the loneliness that attends this two-sided separation:

> ... this particular kind of loneliness, which doesn't look like loneliness at all because it is surrounded by well-meaning people; it's only that the one who is lonely has no way of approaching them except from above by bending down as St. Martin from his lofty steed to the poor beggar. This can be given a variety of names: to do good, to help, to give, to counsel, to comfort, to instruct, even to serve; this does not change the fact that above remains above and below below and that the one who is above cannot have others do good to him, counsel, comfort, or instruct him no matter how much he may be in need of this, for in this fixed constellation no reciprocity is possible—no matter how much love there is, there is not a spark of what we call solidarity. No misery is enough to make such a person come down from the lofty steed of his humble conceit.[15]

Two important lessons are to be learned from this passage. On the one hand, Rehmann gives us a vividly emotive description of the unbridgeable moral chasm that confronts many clergy. Ministry is often a one-way street, a fixed role relationship in which the one who ministers gives but does not tangibly receive. On the other hand, Rehmann reminds us that the congregation does not simply force this station upon an unwitting or unwilling pastor. The minister's "humble conceit" is that he may reap private, even unconscious, satisfaction from his morally superior position. This creates the situation in which the congregation and the minister implicitly cooperate with each other to maintain the idealized image of the minister and his family. We shall address this issue again in the next chapter, in the discussion of "collusion."

The point is that this double standard for the clergy family often results in the loneliness of not having the kind of peer relationships where one can truly be oneself.

You're All I Need to Get By

The interaction between a clergy family and its congregational family is further complicated by the factor we call *impoverishment*. Whereas idealization addresses the rigidity of the psychological boundary between the clergy family and the congregation, impoverishment refers to the restrictive nature of the boundary between the clergy family and the world beyond the congregation. Either for superficially pragmatic or more deeply emotional reasons, a clergy family may have few or no significant social ties outside the congregation.

One researcher asked ministers' wives this question in a survey: "What social ties do you and your husband have together outside the usual church functions?" Of the 119 responses received, 69 of the women answered simply, "None." In longer responses, many wives indicated that lack of time was the culprit; so much of the family's time was consumed by church involvements that further outside contacts would have to compete with the family's time for itself. Only a few of the respondents listed any social ties external to the church.[16] Limiting the social network of the clergy family in this way both reduces the available sources of personal support and increases the importance of its relationship to the congregation.

As we have suggested, the cause of such boundedness and impoverishment may be that there are simply too few hours in a week for socializing, given the minister's often stringent schedule. A deeper reason, however, may be that either the minister or the congregation or both may believe that the pastor-parish relationship *should* be the only social network that the clergy family either needs or desires. In some instances, particularly with a caring congregation, this can be a strength and not a weakness. Often, however, the minister's family experiences a sense of separation from much-needed emotional resources.

Picture a married couple in chronic conflict who come to you for counseling. At home Don and Lisa Fredericks spend most of their time avoiding any form of intimacy or closeness with each other. The time they do spend together is taken up with useless bickering and petty arguments. Neither spouse, it seems, is able to meet the other's needs; at least, they seem unwilling to give until they have received their due.

When they first married, the Frederickses were an inseparable twosome. To their friends and family they seemed like one person living through two bodies. They did everything together, even thinking the same way. But eventually the inevitable disagreements arose. At first Don and Lisa refused to let such insignificant disagreements puncture their near-perfect bubble. But as time passed, those unresolved disagreements piled up, and the couple began a downward spiral of heated argument and depressed withdrawal.

In the course of interviewing them, you realize that this couple is removed from virtually all social contact outside their relationship to each other. What began as a charming young-couple-in-love togetherness has degenerated into a desperate seeking of each spouse to have all emotional needs met by one person.

Don and Lisa are at an impasse. While they are beginning to realize that their marriage cannot possibly carry all their emotional expectations and hopes, they are still unwilling to let go of their fantasy of the perfect couple who never disagree and need only each other. Their ideal fantasy relationship worked for a time. But when genuine differences arose, they were stuck. Their ideals prevented them from acknowledging the differences that held them apart. As a result, Don and Lisa cut themselves off from the only source of emotional sustenance they allowed themselves: each other.

Suppose now that instead of looking at the relationship of a husband and wife, we consider the relationship of a clergy family to its congregation. When a pastor is called to a new congregation, there is often a honeymoon period when both pastor and congregation may avoid conflictual issues. Members of the clergy family are seen at every church function; there is a tangible togetherness between the minister's family and the congregational family. But what happens when the honeymoon is over? Some clergy-church family marriages will go the way of the Frederickses; when differences arise, the unhappy couple will try to solve their disputes by denying their separateness and trying to buttress their cherished togetherness.

The problem is that sometimes only a solid relationship with a more objective third party can give one the perspective needed to approach conflict constructively. If Pastor Miller (chap. 1) had had the opportunity to discuss his dilemma with a friend—perhaps even another pastor—outside the church, he might have gotten a better handle on his situation. He would have needed to be careful not to let it become a way for him to triangle out of his relationship to the congregation. Whatever objectivity he gained in his conversations with a friend must be put to use in his ministry.

From school-age onward, we all need peer relationships

outside our families. Such relationships help us to firm up our sense of identity, gain a different point of view, broaden our horizons, and provide ample resources for personal support, especially during family crises. This is true whether or not the family is relatively well-functioning. In healthy families, members are capable of relating to each other on a peer basis inasmuch as they respect each other's individuality; demands for family togetherness are appropriate and do not violate family members' own sense of self. When such peer relationships are not possible within the family, as with the problem of idealization, then peer relationships outside the family take on added importance. The problem with impoverishment is that the clergy family, for either pragmatic or personal reasons, is effectively prevented from making social contacts outside the congregation. The result is an impoverished social network and the experience of being isolated from additional sources of emotional support.

Of Glass Houses and Fishbowls

Today the buzzword in discussions of the clergy family is *fishbowl*. A recent cartoon showed a ponytailed young girl running up to a befuddled clergyman and announcing, "Reverend Browning! Come quick! Your son is exploiting his inherent yearning for independent selfhood in reaction to the ministerial family fishbowl syndrome again. Come enhance his individualism."[17] In this little girl's trendily sophisticated plea, the cartoonist has captured the sense of intrusiveness often experienced by members of the minister's family. Like goldfish in a bowl, clergy family members feel hemmed in by watchful eyes. The metaphor conveys the sense shared by pastors and their families of constantly being on display. There is not only a lack of privacy, but also an everpresent sense that each family member must live up to some vague set of social expectations held by the congregation.

The fishbowl metaphor, however, is too one-sided; we prefer the more humane metaphor of a glass house.[18] A fishbowl is like a cage in a zoo; the animal is held captive against its will and put on public display for the entertainment of others. A glass house is not a cage, and the clergy family is not held against its will. Far from being passive or unwitting pets, the pastor's family moves into the glass house willingly as part of the expected role. Unlike a fishbowl, the house has doors, and the family may enter and exit as they wish. But even when the doors are closed, family members can still share the vague discomfort of feeling as if the walls are transparent, that there is no firm sense of the boundary between inside and outside. Thus even in their private lives, clergy family members continue to live in the shadow of the expectations of members of the congregation.

This sense of intrusion is a consistent theme in the literature on ministers' families and results from unclear or fuzzy boundaries between the clergy family and the congregation. This contrasts with other families, where the boundary between the family and the parents' workplace is usually well-defined. In many instances the clergy family is not clearly separated from the pastor's workplace, the church. All family members either participate directly in the church or must fulfill some role expectation of the congregation. To the minister's wife, for example, the church is not simply where her husband works; there are usually strong expectations of her behavior. If she chooses to have some vocation other than that of a pastor's wife, she must often either produce some guilt-allaying rationalizations or even rebel openly. Wallace Denton has written:

> To marry the minister of a church is a decision to marry more than a man. It is a decision to become part of a role with a long tradition. . . . [The minister's wife] can extricate herself from this role only at a risk to herself and her husband's ministry.[19]

The boundaries between the congregation and the clergy family are often too diffuse. People in other professions would be aghast if their employers began to make direct demands on their families. But this is precisely what happens in the clergy family. And this creates an ambiguity of boundaries that is often characteristic of the clergy family-congregational family relationship.

In a different context, researcher Pauline Boss has studied the phenomenon of boundary ambiguity in the families of POWs and MIAs.[20] These families suffer from a painfully unique kind of ambiguity—that of not knowing whether a family member is alive or dead, returning or gone forever. If they knew this person to be dead, they could grieve. Their uncertainty, however, prevents them from bringing closure to their pain.

This kind of boundary ambiguity, of not knowing who is in and who is out of the family, is an important variable in understanding the stressors faced by these special families.

The boundary difficulty faced by the clergy family is somewhat different. The issue is not that there is a gaping hole in the family membership, but rather that the boundary between the clergy family and the congregation is unclear. Yet whatever the reason for this lack of clarity, be it fate or design, the net effect is similar in both cases: clear boundaries protect a family's ability to define and regulate itself, while fuzzy boundaries allow intrusion that interferes with this self-definition and thus creates stress.

A concrete illustration of the problem of intrusion is given to us in one of the most prevalent themes in the literature relating to ministers' families: the stress of living in the church parsonage. Keith Madsen, writing on clergy divorce, relates the following example:

> One Methodist minister now serving a special appointment referred to the stress of living in a parsonage, noting that it was hard on his former wife living "in the literal shadow of the church." This was especially true since she wanted some improvements made, which were denied, and she wanted to convert to a housing allowance, which was also denied. Living in a parsonage can bring stress to a marriage because many church people see the house as theirs and hence feel they should be able to use it in any way they see fit. Some people come into the parsonage unannounced. Others feel the pastor is obligated to use the parsonage for all kinds of functions, from holding Sunday school classes to babysitting during church meetings. . . . The result is that the parsonage does not really feel like home to the pastor's family, and the family members do not feel they have the privacy any family needs.[21]

For this couple, living in the shadow of the church involved two types of intrusion. The first and most obvious is physical intrusion. As in Madsen's example, this can be carried to the extreme, with church members feeling they have the right to come and go as they please. Second, however, even when parishioners are not intruding bodily, the clergy family can feel a sense of psychological intrusion—an ever-present watchfulness whereby family members are monitored by the congregation. This fuzziness of psychological boundaries is less tangible, especially to the outside observer; it is nevertheless quite real to the family under scrutiny.

There is more than just a question of privacy at stake here. In a deeper sense, the parsonage is symbolic of the relationship between the minister's family and the congregation. One writer has said that "the parsonage stands as a symbol of the pastor-people relationship and the problem of striking a balance between material and spiritual aspects of church life."[22] This is true on one level: the tension between the spiritual and the material can be a legitimate issue. Recall the case of the Miller family. Some of the members of First Church began to grumble when Arlene Miller decided to take a job outside the church. The membership felt that they were being more than generous with salary and accommodations, so they interpreted Arlene's behavior as unnecessarily materialistic. Objectively speaking, they may be right to some extent.

As we noted in the previous chapter, however, issues such as this may camouflage more important matters of relationship. The matter truly goes deeper than the spiritual-material debate. Conflicts regarding the parsonage reflect a question of differentiation and personal boundaries: who has the right to define the roles that the clergy family will play in relationship to the congregation? The question, therefore, is not simply who owns the parsonage, but to put it bluntly, who owns the minister and his family? The expectations placed on the members of a clergy family can leave them feeling that they have no right to be seen, heard, and experienced for who they really are. Gerald Jud has recorded the response of one former pastor who bitterly remonstrates with the congregation that crushed him with their expectations:

> If you feel it just and fair to hire a man and his wife—who have together put in approximately 12 to 15 years of study and training for required degrees—to work for you, to be religious for you on a full-time basis for the part-time salary of one unskilled, untrained, and uneducated individual; if you feel that it is a Christian virtue—preparing one for sainthood—to allow one's self and family to be exploited physically, emotionally, spiritually, and financially; then you are probably a typical and average American congregation calling yourself the body of Christ.
>
> My recommendation is that you give up the phoney church image, put away your pious platitudes, your saccharin sentimental-

ism of the nineteenth century, blow out the candles of your churches, lock the doors of your neo-Gothic buildings, and go home and forget the whole thing and become *real people*.[23]

If the balance between the material and the spiritual were the only issue here, one might think this pastor left the church because he was not getting enough money. This would be a one-sided and unfair conclusion. The larger issue is what the salary symbolizes for the minister: appreciation and recognition of his worth. Furthermore, as one can infer from this pastor's experience, such tangible symbols are especially missing for the pastor's wife, who is expected to fulfill an important role even though her position is not salaried.

All of us should be able to recall some experience in which our hard work and diligence were simply taken for granted. Wives often complain about their husbands who have the remarkable ability to sit through an entire painstakingly prepared gourmet meal without noticing the food or the effort that went into it. When our best efforts go unappreciated, it makes us feel depersonalized: we feel that there is nothing we can do to make another acknowledge our value. Even when we merely do what is expected of us, we still wish to be appreciated, affirmed, respected. When our children do something we have asked them to do, we should thank them; in so doing, we communicate to them that we value their cooperation, and we earn their respect in return. But when we are taken for granted, we feel that we are not being treated as human beings, with our own thoughts and feelings, but rather more like pieces of property.

When the pastor admonishes the congregation to become "real people," there is a simultaneous but unspoken plea: let *us* be real people, treat us like real people. The clergy family is not an appendage of the church, nor a piece of church property. No self-respecting congregation, of course, would ever consciously take such an attitude. Yet the truth is that because of unrealistic expectations, many church members may leave the clergy family feeling precisely that way.

In summary, the problem of intrusion has both physical and psychological importance. Some clergy families, especially those living in parsonages or on church property, experience the physical intrusion of church members into their private lives. This interferes with the family's ability to define and regulate itself, and thus causes stress. More important, perhaps, is the more profound sense of psychological intrusion, which can exist whether or not physical intrusion is present. This is the sense of not being appreciated as a separate person, with the same rights to privacy and appreciation that are usually accorded to all others.

The Triple Threat in Ministry

You may feel that we have painted the clergy family in overly stark and dismal colors. Or perhaps you are beginning to think that you must be worse off than you thought you were! If you find that the typical problems we describe are not true for your situation, then you have cause to rejoice and be thankful. We do not intend to be gloomy any more than we intend to be Pollyannaish. Life in a clergy family in and of itself is neither wonderful nor terrible. Rather, it is life in a family within a family and must be understood in that larger context. What we want you to focus on are *patterns* not judgments.

In our reading and research we have discerned certain patterns of relationship to be true of many ministers' families, which we have expressed in terms of difficulties experienced at the boundaries of the social ecosystem. To what extent these boundary problems either are or will be true for you depends on many factors that we cannot anticipate. We only hope that once you have read this book, you will have some general tools to understand your particular social context so that you can be active on behalf of your own family as well as your congregational family.

To conclude our discussion of the boundary problems, let us pose a thought-question: How do idealization, impoverishment, and intrusion interact with each other? These three processes in tandem create a triple threat that is common to clergy families. Again, our emphasis is on pattern and interaction. While each of the three boundary problems can be considered separately for the sake of exposition, in real life they are not so independent of one another. Problems in one area can exacerbate problems in another; a strength in one area can help to compensate for a weakness in another. How is this so?

First, let us reemphasize how we understand the nature of these boundary problems. It is easy to forget that the term

"boundary" is largely metaphoric. Whenever we give a phenomenon a name, there is the temptation to view it as a "thing" in its
own right. What we are talking about, however, is patterns of
relationships, not things. The term "boundary" is meant as
shorthand for interactions that occur where two social systems
meet.

At the boundary where the clergy family and the congregation
meet, the relationship can be characterized by either idealization, intrusion, neither, or both. Where boundaries are clear and
mutually respected, neither of these difficulties will arise. In
some cases there may be a degree of idealization, but little
intrusion; at other times there may be more of the latter and less
of the former; in still other instances there may be both.

Remember that idealization has to do with our perceptions
and images of others to the extent that these images fit their
perceptions of themselves. Intrusion points to the experience of
being taken for granted physically and psychologically. These
are related but distinct qualities that can be applied to the same
relationship. Think of the relationship between a parent and
child. There are parents who are overly intrusive, who need and
want to know about every facet of a child's everyday life. There
are also parents whose preset images of what their children are
like or will be are highly resistant to change. Though there is
probably good precedent for believing that these go hand in
hand, it is not necessarily so.

An intrusive parent may be able to perceive the child in a
relatively undistorted way. Likewise, a parent who has a rigid
and distorted image of a child may not do so in an intrusive
manner. There are parallels for the clergy family. Some congregations may be intrusive, but without making exaggerated
claims for the clergy family's differentness. Other congregations
may largely leave the clergy family to itself but still carry larger-
than-life expectations of them. To put it in another way: it is
possible both to put others on a pedestal and to act as if you own
them. But it is also possible to do one and not the other. The
most difficult situation occurs when a congregation both in-
trudes into and unrealistically idealizes the clergy family.

The interaction between idealization and intrusion occurs
within the congregational setting. The third factor, impoverishment, involves the relationship between the congregation and
the outside world, but particularly between the clergy family

and that world. The degree of impoverishment affects the relationship between the congregation and the minister's family for better or worse.

If the relationship between clergy family and congregational family is positive and supportive, then even a nearly total lack of outside contact need not be experienced as impoverishing. We all probably know families or married couples who focus all their emotional energies on each other, who care for and identify with one another, and who have little to do with outsiders. Clergy family-congregational family relationships can be like that. They do not experience their togetherness as a problem and do not wish for outside relationships. The disadvantage here is that togetherness is usually purchased at the cost of growth. Though the minister's family and the congregation may feel as comfortable with each other as one does with an old pair of shoes, too much boundedness can result in a stagnant and ingrown church.

What shall we say when interaction between the minister's family and the congregation is experienced more negatively? Any sources of personal support outside the congregation will help the clergy family to have a more balanced perspective. Pastoral support groups can be particularly effective in this regard, provided they are not allowed to degenerate into weekly gripe sessions. If, however, the boundary around the congregation prohibits outside support, then interaction within the boundary can take on a desperate quality, such as that which we saw earlier between the Frederickses. There we have persons who are unable to relate to each other supportively, unable to meet each other's needs, yet confined to that one relationship as the only source of nurture. This is truly a no-win situation and the worst case of triple-threat.

Let us repeat that we do not support the view that ministers' families are passive victims of their congregations. Those who enter ministry do so with their own expectations of themselves, which may be just as demanding and unrealistic, if not more so, than any external expectation stemming from the parish. The point is not to assign fault, but to locate what may need to be changed in the way the clergy family and the congregation relate to one another. Clergy and congregation alike must assess their relationship by asking themselves questions such as, Who has the right to determine the clergy family's physical and emotional boundaries? Are they allowed, or do they allow themselves, to be real human beings within the context of the congregation? What personal resources do they have? Do they have any external social ties beyond the congregation? In chapter 12 we will give practical suggestions for current and prospective clergy.

Summary

The major focus so far has been to create an ecological model in an attempt to stimulate a new way of thinking about the minister's family. Chapter 1 introduced the ecological metaphor, emphasizing the importance of seeing social events in context. The dynamic interconnectedness within our social ecology was stressed in chapter 2, using the concepts of differentiation and emotional triangles. In this chapter the structure of the social setting of ministry has been described as a family within a family, where the relative health of the family as a whole can be assessed by looking at its internal and external boundaries.

Not every church and not every clergy family will experience the boundary problems we have described. Our central emphasis is that the nature of ministry makes the life of the clergy family closely intertwined with the congregation. Because of this, the phenomena described in this chapter, while not universal, are in fact common.

But what accounts for the difference between one setting and another? Why do some pastors' families experience problems while others do not? And why might the *same* pastor's family have difficulties in one church but not in another? Differentiation is one possible answer, but is that the *only* answer? These are the kinds of imponderable questions that give family theorists insomnia. While we are not foolish enough to claim to have the answers, we can suggest a productive line of thought. Families differ from one another in terms of their guiding values for family life. What happens between a minister's family and a congregation will to some extent reflect how well their respective values match. That proposition is the subject of chapter 4.

4

Family Types or Stereotypes?

Families, families everywhere. The life of the minister's family does not occur in a social vacuum. We have described the clergy family as a family within a family, namely, the local congregation. The local congregation in turn includes both the clergy family and other nuclear families. So at its most basic level, the social ecology of the minister's family comprises the interaction between three "families": the clergy family, the congregational family, and the various families in the congregation. This interaction, as Edwin Friedman suggests, is one of the "pervasive triangles for all clergy."[1]

Being human, we tend to understand those who are like us better than those who are different. Families have their own unique styles: their own rules, goals, and ways of doing things. Sometimes we encounter another family who is so unlike us that we believe they must be either crazy, immoral, or both! If we were sufficiently differentiated, we would be able to accept the difference without feeling compelled either to make them more like us or to make us more like them. Instead, we often create an image of what a family should be, especially a *Christian* family, and then expect others to live up to the code.

Whether there is such a thing as a Christian family ideal, or an ideal Christian family, is an open question. The point is that the very *notion* of such an ideal often leads us toward division rather than unity. If truth be told, we Christians have a remarkable talent for using our moral and supposedly biblical ideals in the service of emotional triangling. How is this so?

When we are confronted with others who are different from us and have different values, we become somewhat uneasy. Their differentness seems to challenge what we believe and who we are. And the more undifferentiated we are, the more nervous we get. All too often, our knee-jerk response is to quote Scripture rather than to deal with the tension of differentness. The point is not whether there is a proper time and place for quoting Scripture. Rather, we need to recognize that we can pervert the purpose of God's Word by using it to escape our responsibilities in relationship to others.

We can triangle the Bible or even God himself. If others make us uneasy, we can avoid dealing with them directly by confronting them with Bible verses. Indeed, we may need to arm ourselves with an entire arsenal of memorized verses just in case! The Bible becomes a shield, not against the arrows of Satan, not against temptation, but against other people and the anxiety they trigger in us.

When the Bible speaks of unity, it does not exclude diversity. Being one body does not mean being all the same. The apostle Paul wrote to the Corinthian church:

> The body is a unit, though it is made up of many parts; and though all its parts are many, they form one body. . . . God has arranged the parts in the body, every one of them, just as he wanted them to be. If they were all one part, where would the body be? As it is, there are many parts, but one body.[2].

It appears that the matter of spiritual gifts was becoming, or had become, a divisive issue in the Corinthian congregation. Here Paul judiciously answers the church's query by emphasizing the importance of unity. This unity, rather than being the opposite of diversity, thrives on the richness of a variety of talents and gifts. All gifts are of the same Spirit and from the same God for the sake of edifying the church. The focus is not on individuals, but on the common good. Paul removes all cause for division by placing the matter in its proper context: our unity is in Christ, in being members of the same body. Our unity is not the bland oneness of uniformity, but the colorful and variegated unity that lies in diversity and interdependence.

Paul has given us a central metaphor for understanding the nature of the church. The body is made of diverse parts, each with its own gifts and all contributing to the unity of the whole.

In any congregation, however, a single facet of this diversity can give rise to division—that is, when anxiety causes us to lose sight of our unity. This is especially true when there is diversity in matters that are close to the heart of a church's life and work. One of these matters is the family.

Every church is made up of many families. These families differ from each other in several ways in regard to structure and values. At one level there are the demographic differences. We can no longer afford to harbor the illusion that the "typical" family in the church has a father, a mother, and two children, more or less. There are now many alternative family forms that force us to rethink our stereotypes about a typical family. For example, in many quarters the church has only recently begun to deal realistically with ministry to the divorced and remarried. Moreover, our American culture shows changing trends:

1. An increase in those who have never been married and intend to remain single[3]
2. An increase in those who choose not to have children[4]
3. The social and economic confusion of growing numbers of dual-career families[5]
4. Dramatic increases in the number of single-parent households, the fastest-growing lifestyle in America[6]

Our ability, individually as Christians or collectively as churches, to reevaluate our own family values and assumptions, is lagging far behind the pace of these social currents. If we ourselves do not fit one of these categories, we nevertheless rub shoulders with someone in the congregation who does. If our ministry is to have any impact on real people in their real family situations, we need to reassess our goals and presuppositions in light of these changes. A ministry based on unchecked assumptions about the families to whom we minister will be naïve at best and harmful at worst. Ministry cannot be founded on stereotypes.

Demographic diversity is only one obvious level of the differences between families. They also differ in the way they perceive themselves, the way their members relate to one another, and the way they relate to outsiders. This is a diversity of identity, purpose, and values that cuts across structural differences such as whether or not a family has any children or two parents in residence. To understand this type of variety, we need something more than a table of demographic statistics. We need a working *typology,* a descriptive model that brings these differences to life.

One such model is the "Cambridge typology" of *closed-,* *open-,* and *random-*type families, created by David Kantor and William Lehr in the now-classic work *Inside the Family.*[7] After we present the typology we will show how it is to be used to think ecologically about the interaction of families in the church, particularly as it applies to the minister's family. We believe that a dynamic understanding of *family types* is a far better foundation for church life than stereotypes.

Inside the Family

How do we develop a typology of families? Researchers have wrestled with this question for years. In the early sixties, therapist Jay Haley called for "the development of a descriptive system which will rigorously classify families and differentiate one type from another. The basis for classifying families into groups is only now beginning to be explored."[8] Much has happened since he issued this appeal. Researchers of all stripes have worked diligently to construct valid models to help us understand the ins and outs of family interaction.

Of the models created, Kantor and Lehr's is one of the most complex. Their family typology is only one part of a more comprehensive model. What sets their model apart is the way in which it was derived. Kantor and Lehr selected nineteen families for their study, many of whom were considered "normal" by clinical standards. This immediately set their study apart, for most studies used only individuals and families who were undergoing some form of psychological treatment. Instead of bringing the families to the researchers (into an artificial laboratory environment) the reseachers went to the families (to their homes). One student research assistant was assigned to each family—to live with them, to eat with them, to observe them. The student gathered information through interviews, reports, tests, and tape recordings. Kantor and Lehr's intent was to create a model that would study the family from the inside and take its cue from the actual, daily interactions of existing families rather than from an abstract theory.

Why was this distinction important? If we begin by emphasizing theory, then what we see will be shaped more by what we expect rather than by what a family actually does. Part of the theory will include some standard by which we judge whether or not a family is "normal." But when the theory is developed from inside the family, such judgments become presumptuous. It is only from inside the family that we can learn to appreciate families *on their own terms*, rather than by the standards we set for them. This means that a family's behavior must be understood in light of their particular goals.

As we have said, we often have trouble understanding people who are different from us. Their behavior may seem nonsensical. If we are poorly differentiated and thereby given to making moral judgments, we see the different or nonsensical as *bad*. Instead of trying to understand them, we try to change them and to convert them to our way of thinking. What we fail to realize is that families differ from one another, not only in their behavior, but in their goals. How others behave, which may make no sense with respect to *our* goals, may make a great deal of sense with respect to theirs.

This is part of the genius of the Cambridge typology and the reason why we use it here. Each of the three family types is understood to have its own *core purpose*, which is valued in its own right. Each type also has a characteristic way of developing problems when distressed. Together these two notions mean that every family has something of value and that no family is immune to problems. This steers us away from absolutes of either "healthy" or "sick" family types. To Kantor and Lehr, each of the three family types, whether closed, open, or random, tries to put into practice "a core purpose consistent with the values of Western civilization."[9] Every different social group, however, including the religious denominations and church communities, will decide for itself which family design it likes best. This means that the judgments we make regarding families are based largely on our own values and goals as individuals, families, and groups. We cannot simply label other family types as good or bad until we have at least tried to understand and appreciate how their goals differ from ours.

Does this mean that all family behavior is morally relative? That what works is therefore right? Not at all. We do not intend to be morally simplistic. Family life today is beset with complex moral questions regarding such diverse issues as abortion, a teenager's right to privacy in sexual matters, test-tube babies, embryo freezing, surrogate motherhood, gay parenting, and a parent's right to decide whether a newborn with severe birth defects lives or dies.

There are no simple answers to such questions. Our point is more general: Coming to grips with the diversity of families in the church does not mean deciding who's right and who's wrong. It means that we attempt from within their frame of reference to understand those who are different from us. Conversely, we must challenge our narrow stereotypes, taking a hard look at how our own family values reflect personal preference and not timeless truth. In this way we can begin to transcend prejudices and biases that divide us and move toward a true unity in diversity.

The Three Family Types

A family faces two challenges as it interacts in a larger social environment: (1) to adapt to the demands of life in its particular community, and (2) to maintain a coherent sense of identity that helps to link the present with its experience and future goals. Adapting successfully requires a balancing act between change and continuity (a theme that will emerge again in chapter 11). To some degree, families will change their structure and their patterns of relationship as they progress through life. Kantor and Lehr write:

> As a family grows and matures, its structures are frequently challenged, torn down, and built up again. Thus, since structural change is an inherent function of the family's organic develop- ment, the three terms *closed, open*, and *random* are relative. We are not offering descriptions of the fixed structural characteristics of different kinds of systems. Rather we are designating three stereotypically different ways in which the . . . family can maintain itself and achieve its purposes, ways that may often be mixed in family practice.[10]

The Cambridge typology developed by Kantor and Lehr recognizes growth and change. Families will differ according to how closely they stick to one type rather than to another. This depends upon their particular context, history, and so on. Our aim is not to categorize any family once and for all time, but to see that families organize themselves around goals and purposes. Kantor and Lehr suggest that there are generally three main goals that families pursue and a typical family style accompanies each goal. These styles are called closed-, open-, and random-type families. Let's take a look at three families: the Clovers, the Oppenheimers, and the Randalls. As you read, think about which families in your church remind you of each of these three.

The Closed Clovers

The Clovers are what Kantor and Lehr call a closed-type family. The parents, Carl and Claire, pride themselves on running the family like a "tight ship." They are clearly at the top of the chain of command, and every member of the crew has carefully prescribed roles and duties. Order is maintained through an extensive system of rules. There is a proper time and place for everything, and any deviation from the rules is discouraged or punished. Yet when the family works well together, they are like a well-oiled machine or an efficient ship's crew. Dad and Mom do not lord it over the kids; rather, everyone recognizes to some degree that rules serve the common good of the family. The identity of each person is closely intertwined with the identity of the family as a group. The rules are believed in and followed willingly. In general, the interests of the individuals are secondary to those of the family.

The Clovers watch their boundaries carefully. The family limits its interaction with the community at large because it lives in a high-crime neighborhood and the environment poses a continual threat to family stability. Doors to the outside are always locked or in some cases double-locked. There is a chain link fence in the front yard; a wood fence in the back protects the family's privacy. Mr. and Mrs. Clover have set careful rules for who is allowed in or out and under what circumstances. If the children break rules, they will be grounded. Usually enforcement is unnecessary, however; the children share their parents' values and monitor their own behavior without complaining. This is because for all family members the rules create a feeling of meaningful security, a feeling of "apprenticeship to something bigger than the self."[11]

The family runs on a joint schedule, or "family clock." Members are expected to adjust their own schedules to the family clock, with no exceptions. Carl comes home from work at 5:15 in the evening, and Claire has dinner on the table at 5:30, no sooner, no later. The one time their daughter Cindy came home at 6:00, she found the dinner table had been cleared and the food put away. No dinner for her that night! She was never late again. Both Cindy and her brother, Carl, Jr., have strictly observed bedtimes on school nights, and nothing is allowed to interfere with this rule. The kids don't fight to stay up late. When bedtime comes, they put away their schoolbooks, brush their teeth, put on their pajamas, and bid their parents good-night. Overall, the predictability of their schedule helps all the Clovers to feel that they are in control of the events of their lives rather than being controlled by them.

The Clovers have a warmly composed and stable emotional life. For example, when Carl, Jr., received all A's on his report card, he didn't jump up and down, nor did he expect his parents to do so. With an expectant smile, he handed the report card to his father, whose face melted into a warm grin as he read. He handed the card to his wife, took his namesake by the shoulders, and said in deep earnest, "I'm proud of you, son." The same kind of composure extends to feelings in all aspects of family life. The parents have genuine affection for each other, but refrain from hugging and kissing in front of the children. When discipline or punishment is necessary, it is accomplished without screaming, sometimes even without the parents raising their voices. The feelings that family members share for one another are rooted in their sense of belonging, in pride at being part of the group.

The core purpose of the closed family is *stability through tradition*. The Clovers work together to preserve a strong sense of family identity, of who *we* are as opposed to who *I* am. "Tradition" is a word that captures the kind of continuity they thirst for. Carl likes to tell tales of his childhood, his parents, and his grandparents. And rather than dismiss their father's stories as just so much boring nonsense, the children enjoy them as a time of closeness. Even now, Carl, Jr., dreams about what it would be like to follow in his father's footsteps. Everyone in the family feels some connection to generations past, and they take great pride in the Clover family name.

The key to closed families like the Clovers lies in their emphasis on order, control, and certainty. From these the family can derive a sense of security and stability. These are positive core values that characterize many families. But there are other values around which families can organize themselves. The Oppenheimer family is one example.

The Open Oppenheimers

A few blocks down from the Clovers lives the Oppenheimer family: Oscar and Olivia and their three children, Oliver, Marcy, and Max. They are Kantor and Lehr's open-type family.

The Oppenheimers' motto is "Let's talk." In contrast to the Clovers' rather one-directional chain of command, Oscar and Olivia prefer a style that emphasizes negotiation and gives every family member equal say. This does not mean that the children have equal authority with the parents. It does mean, however, that at the earliest opportunity in each child's life, the parents sought ways to include him or her in family decision making.

The Oppenheimers arrive at their goals by consensus, sometimes by actual vote. Once the vote is in, family members are expected to respect the democratic process and adhere to the group decision. Every year, for example, the group sits down to discuss where they will spend their family vacation. For the last few years it seemed as if everyone wanted to go somewhere different. Their solution? If they couldn't reach consensus on where to go, they drew lots to see who would decide. No griping is allowed after the decision is made. This year Max, only seven years old, won the right to choose and he chose Disney World.

This family has more individual freedom than the Clovers. The cardinal rule is that no one may violate another family member's rights or trample on any group agreements. Yet, given these simple limits, there is a great deal of latitude. For example, the kids are free to listen to whatever kind of music they wish, but they may not play it so loudly that the parents can't hear themselves think. The rules on coming and going are also lenient. Oscar and Olivia are willing to make exceptions on bedtime and curfew depending on circumstances. One Saturday, Oliver convinced his parents to let him stay out with his friends until midnight—an hour later than usual. He tiptoed in at 1:00 A.M. Oscar and Olivia confronted him in the morning. The issue was not that Oliver had broken an inviolable rule, but that he had broken their agreement. The boy contritely agreed and was allowed to suggest an appropriate punishment. Overall, the traffic crossing the Oppenheimer family's boundary is less carefully regulated than the Clovers'.

As with the closed family, the Oppenheimers have a common schedule, a family clock. As an open family, however, members are allowed to deviate from the schedule—within limits. One afternoon, teenaged Marcy came late to dinner. The family waited for a little while, then began without her. They were still eating when she arrived. She apologized for being late and explained that she lost track of time chatting with a friend whom she had not seen in a long while. Oscar and Olivia saw no reason to make a fuss and invited their daughter to sit, have dinner, and tell them about her reunion with her friend. If Marcy starts being chronically late, however, the family will have to decide what action to take. In general, each of the Oppenheimers has some sense of what the limits of comfort are for stretching the family schedule. They will observe the family clock as a guideline rather than an unbendable rule, keeping one eye on the clock and the other on what they are doing.

Authenticity is the Oppenheimers' emotional ideal. They are much more open to acceptance of overt expressions of feeling than the Clovers, who care for each other deeply but who stay composed at all times. The only rule about feelings among the Oppenheimers is that the emotions expressed must be genuine. Family members are encouraged to share their true feelings and not keep them to themselves.

The Oppenheimers are less rule-oriented than the Clovers. Their faith is not in the system of rules, but in the basic wisdom of the group. They believe that if everyone will participate fully and honestly in cooperative negotiation, they will eventually reach the best or "right" decision. While the Clovers want to keep ideological unity, the Oppenheimers emphasize dialogue. The latter are much better at tolerating different points of view because to them it is more important to be relevant than to keep a firm anchor in tradition.

Kantor and Lehr describe the core purpose of the open-type family as *adaptation through consensus*. Whereas the closed family is controlled through a hierarchical power structure, the open family places a high premium on cooperation. Whereas the closed family is characterized by set structures, rules, and traditions, the open family is characterized by growth and change. The Oppenheimers' family structure and process can always be modified by consensus. In pursuing their core purpose of adaptation, they emphasize relevance over certainty and authenticity of feeling over composure.

Both the closed- and the open-type families clearly reflect positive values inherent to the American culture. Kantor and Lehr have observed:

> In the American culture as a whole, it has been our experience that major institutions, such as schools, hospitals, agencies, and clinics, generally announce a preference for the open-type family, perhaps because the process style of the open system more closely approximates the democratic ideals of our nation. . . . In their day-to-day dealings with families, however, such institutions seem to exhibit an operational preference for the closed-type family, perhaps because it seems to offer the most successful form of organization for maintaining the larger social order.[12]

The open family's focus on consensus and equality and the closed family's emphasis on order and stability are core values that most of us can easily appreciate. There is a third type in Kantor and Lehr's model, however, called the random-type family. Their rather anarchic style can be perceived by some as threatening to social institutions. We believe, however, that the random family also portrays a cultural value: the emphasis on individual rights.

The Random Randalls

Ask any of the kids in the neighborhood, "Whose house do you like to go to the most?" It's not the Oppenheimers'. And it's certainly not the Clovers'; children's parties are rare at their home. Neighborhood children will invariably tell you that they love to visit the Randalls. To borrow an advertising slogan, the Randalls' house is a place "where a kid can be a kid."

Ray and Liz Randall have five children. Their names? They can't always remember their names. Before each child was born, Ray and Liz chose names that struck them as delightful and meaningful. The problem is that when one of the kids is standing in front of them, it takes them a few seconds to figure out what his or her name is. Liz has adopted the strategy of calling out the entire list until she gets to the name she wants.

In a manner quite opposite to the closed Clovers, the random Randalls consider the rights and interests of the individual members to be more important than the group. Their mottos are "Do your own thing" and "Make your own choices." But sometimes this individual emphasis is carried to such an extent that it becomes difficult to say in what sense a random family is a family at all!

At times the boundary around the Randall family can be hard to determine. Family members, visitors, and guests may come and go at will. Any of the five children may bring home one or more friends without warning. Ray and Liz may not even know who all the kids are, except that they are all friends of their children. The Clovers would consider this an intrusion, and the Oppenheimers would prefer that other family members be notified before guests are brought home. For the Randalls, however, this is a common state of affairs, and no one thinks anything of it. Similarly, a student of ours recalls a family who lived in the more rural neighborhood where he grew up. Not only did people come and go, so did the chickens and other animals! This is why families of other types think of the random family as a "zoo."

And what of the family clock? The Clovers strictly observe their family schedule. The Oppenheimers leave a bit more leeway. The Randalls, however, have no group schedule, no family clock. In fact, if you were to look at the walls of their home, you literally will not find a clock at all. Of course, each person has his or her own watch. But some of the watches may be fast, some may be slow, and some may not work at all. And it doesn't matter much where the family is concerned because there is no need or expectation that they will keep a joint schedule. There is always food in the house, but the Randalls seldom sit down to supper as a family. More typically, each person will rummage through the refrigerator when he or she gets home. One child decides to eat in the kitchen. Another eats in front of the television set. Still another takes her food to her room. And, of course, any of the Randalls is free to decide on a moment's notice to have dinner out with friends.

The Randalls' stress on individual rights means that there is no clear authority structure. The Clovers resolve disputes through the chain of command, often referring to "the way it's always been done." The Oppenheimers are more democratic. In the Randall family, however, such differences may not—indeed, need not—be resolved at all. While the Oppenheimers found a democratic way to deal with different views on the family vacation, this problem never rises in the Randall family. Why? Because there is no family vacation! Each child usually vacations with a friend's family. On those rare occasions when the Randalls do all go on vacation together, they spend their days pursuing their individual interests—one goes to the museum, one goes shopping, one sightseeing, and so on. They eventually regroup in the hotel room, straggling in one by one.

Thus the ideals of the random family emphasize individual freedom. As opposed to the closed family, the random family values spontaneous and passionate expressions of feeling. Rapture and whimsy and a broad sense of humor are characteristic. Faith in rules or cooperation is replaced by faith in the creative process of anarchy, and attempts by one family member to coerce another are expressly forbidden. Meanings are generated by personal intuition and inspired originality. The Randalls view the rules of the Clover family as just so many dry legalisms. Moreover, they do not dialogue as the Oppenheimers do, since individually created meanings are valued as ends in themselves.

One minister, hearing the description of the random-type family, was concerned that the apparent chaos and lack of authority would be harmful to the children, leading eventually to ill-manners, delinquency, or worse. This may be true in some cases. Any family that knows only one way of functioning will be poorly equipped to adapt to the demands of the real world. In particular, the random family, which prizes individuality and is unable to restrain personal desires when appropriate, may produce children who have not learned to respect the rights of others. But we are speaking of an excess and not an inherent flaw. Each of the three family types has its own problematic form, which we shall discuss in the next section. This fact should not be allowed to obscure the positive core purpose of the random family.

What is the core purpose? Kantor and Lehr express it as *exploration through intuition*. The catchwords here are creativity, discovery, and spontaneity. Neither tradition nor a need for mutual agreement is allowed to get in the way of the free exploration of ideas, feelings, and personal potential. The random family sets aside universal laws in favor of free intuition. Family members are thereby encouraged to discover what is right or wrong for themselves.

For some of us, the random style seems too undisciplined, too chaotic, too threatening to our ideals of family life. But this says just as much about our own biases as it does about the random family itself. Our focus in this section is on the positive, on what there is to appreciate about each of the three family types. The random family can stimulate individual potential in a way that neither the closed nor the open family can. The Randall children, for example, are not destined to be social misfits or radical political activists. They may willingly join other groups that are ideologically or structurally closed or open in type. It is not that random family members cannot submit to authority, appreciate tradition, or negotiate with others. It is rather that the family itself does not define who the individual will be or what values the individual will adopt as one's own. Values that are discovered are just as meaningful as, or more deeply held than, those that are passed on. The random family member who is or becomes a Christian can have a deep personal faith and may be the one who is best able to appreciate and encourage a diversity of gifts in the church.

We have deliberately accentuated the positive goals of each of the three family types. This is because the first step in learning to appreciate and value the diversity of families is to recognize the positive ideals that each family seeks to attain. Words such as "stability," "sincerity," "consensus," "authenticity," "exploration," and "spontaneity" all express worthwhile goals. The second step, however, is to remember that despite its goals no family is perfect. Each family type has its own problems when it twists its goals into a one-track way of dealing with stress. Something may begin as a legitimate core purpose and solution to a minor problem and become a narrow restriction on how the family *must* behave. Thus solutions themselves may become part of the problem.

When the Solution Is Part of the Problem

Just as no family type has a monopoly on positive values, none has a corner on family problems. Each family has its own goals, worthy in themselves, and a characteristic way of dealing with day-to-day difficulties. Sometimes, though, a problem arises that requires a family to do something different. The closed family's reliance on established rules doesn't always work, especially when the children are reaching adolescence. The open family's emphasis on negotiation is valuable, but some situations require one person to take immediate responsibility and action without waiting for a group decision. And the random family, which is perfectly willing to let differences of opinion go unresolved, offers its members no protection from each other, nor any basis for family unity when differences escalate into all-out war. If any type is unable to change the way the family normally does things, even temporarily, their lack of flexibility will eventually get them into trouble.

This is what family therapists call "more of the same": a family's dogged repetition of the same coping strategies, even when they fail.[13] The family has faith that its usual solutions will work. When the solution fails, the family becomes more anxious. But instead of looking for new or better solutions, the members become even more zealous in applying the old ones. Unable to question their faith in their time-honored patterns, family members lock themselves into a downward spiral of failure that Kantor and Lehr call a "crisis chain," where the positive goals and purposes of each of the types can be carried to negative, destructive extremes.[14] When we know a family's type and thus its core purposes and ideals, we can anticipate the direction this chain of failure will take.

The Autocratic Clovers

When the Clovers are in harmony, their emphasis on family identity, tradition, and authority is felt positively by all. When these goals are carried to extremes, however, the Clover family degenerates into an autocracy. Individual wants and needs are sacrificed on the altar of family rules.

As a high school senior, Cindy decided to try out for the lead in the school play. Carl and Claire were relatively neutral on the subject at first because neither of them had experience in drama, and thus it was an idea for which they had no predetermined values. Cindy auditioned and to her delight won the lead role.

What she had neglected to tell her parents, because she knew they would not approve, was the schedule for the performers. Rehearsals were to be held weekly for months, and as the opening date approached they would become more frequent. There would be less time for school work, less time for family, and many late nights out. She had hoped that if she got the role, her parents would make an exception.

She was wrong. Privately Carl and Claire were incensed that Cindy would keep information from them in what seemed to them a deliberate deception. To her face, they kept their anger under careful control and stated quite clearly that the rehearsal schedule was unacceptable and she would have to turn down the role. Cindy was not surprised, but she was hurt. Reluctantly, out of respect for her parents' authority, she did as she was told.

This was, however, only the beginning. Teenagers should be expected to begin separating from the family to some extent, and Cindy was no exception. Little by little she tried her independence, and each time she was confronted by her parents' unwillingness to bend the rules. The family's rules and traditions, which once were a source of meaning and security, began to feel like shackles. Her respect for her parents began to dissolve into contempt, for they now seemed arbitrary and narrow-minded. For their part, Carl and Claire were at a loss to know what to do with their daughter. They could not understand why Cindy suddenly needed to question the rules that she had lived by for years. All they knew how to do was what they had always done: whenever there was family conflict, enforce the rules and, if necessary, tighten them. This led them into a downward spiral that no one knew how to stop.

Cindy eventually left home. Out of the remnants of her devotion to her family's values, she went to college. But it was not the college her parents wanted for her, and she knew it. She cut off from them and moved to a little-known campus thousands of miles away. She didn't write, and she didn't come home for holidays. Carl and Claire, still hurt and confused, gave her up for lost. Meanwhile, they began to watch Carl, Jr., more carefully, making sure that he broke no rules, in the hope that he would not repeat his sister's story.

The Split Oppenheimers

The flawed version of the open-type family reflects the failure of a democratic approach. The family splits because the members cannot reach the consensus that they demand of themselves. Discussion becomes endless and negotiation futile.

The Oppenheimer family, like the Clovers, began to have problems when the first-born reached adolescence. Oliver, you will recall, had negotiated a one-hour extension to his regular curfew. He had violated the agreement by staying out even later. He was embarrassed enough to have to tell his friends that he had to be home by midnight. Rather than risk more ridicule from his peers, he hoped his staying out past midnight would satisfy his friends, yet still be within his parents' limits of tolerance.

In other circumstances, it might have been all right. Oscar and Olivia would have understood Oliver's plight as well as they could and tried to reach a better compromise. The problem, however, was that Oscar and Olivia did not approve of the friends with whom Oliver had taken up lately. To them, these boys were an unruly gang; to Oliver, they were independent-minded guys who liked to have fun. Oliver and his parents talked and talked about it, but the conversations always ended up in a stalemate. The parents tried to convince Oliver that his friends were no good for him, but Oliver would not accept this. He countered by trying to persuade his parents that his friends were okay. But they couldn't get past their prejudices.

In a closed family the parents would have taken charge for better or worse. In a random family the difference in opinion would not have been an issue. The Oppenheimers, however, were an open family. It was important to have consensus. In this case, their need for agreement led nowhere because neither Oliver nor his parents were willing to compromise.

The matter lay on the family like an open wound. Family members found it increasingly difficult to negotiate meaningfully on anything. Discussions began to seem pointless and trivial. When compromises were made, they no longer felt like resolutions to problems but grudging personal sacrifices. Gradually the members began to withdraw from each other emotionally, becoming separate factions.

The Chaotic Randalls

And what of the random family? When the random family is working well, the individuality of its members does not compete with a sense of mutual identification as a family. But under stress the emphasis on individual freedom can be pushed to extremes, leading to utter chaos. Whatever sense of family identity the individual members possess dissolves into irrelevance and anarchy.

The Randalls' oldest daughter, Amelia, began dating steadily. Ray immediately disliked the boy the first time they met and did not hesitate to say this to his daughter. It wasn't that her boyfriend didn't meet up to some traditional or mutually agreed family ideal; Ray just didn't like him. He couldn't articulate a concrete reason, but felt it was his prerogative to dislike someone if he chose to do so. Amelia, of course, also upheld this value of the random family. It was her right to like the boy and date him merely because she wanted to. Her reasons for liking him were no more coherent than Ray's reasons for disliking him.

In most cases the Randalls are able simply to agree to disagree. Every member of the family can have a different opinion about an issue and it does not jeopardize their sense of mutuality as a family. The dating issue, however, is different. Ray and Amelia have always had a genuine affection for each other; family members often tease Amelia about being a "daddy's girl." Ray feels that he has lost his daughter's affection and that sense of specialness they have shared for so many years. He is not completely aware of this, nor is he able to face this directly in relationship to her. So he triangles the boyfriend. Both Ray and Amelia—even the whole family—sense how important the conflict between father and daughter has become. Because of their overzealous random family ideals, however, they have no protocol to resolve the issue.

Unable or unwilling to face their relationship to each other, Ray and Amelia keep the triangle alive through their bickering. The ideal of spontaneity becomes twisted into a license for taking cheap shots at each other. The other children jump in, often teasing or mocking Amelia and making her feel more and more alienated. Occasionally, in a flash of uncontrollable frustration, Ray attempts to conquer the system by making arbitrary declarations, forbidding her to see the boyfriend again. Amelia, of course, responds in kind with a bitter tongue-lashing of her father.

The positive intent of the random family, of encouraging diverse points of view and free expression of emotion, has deteriorated into a system where none of the individual members is offered any protection against each other's hostility. In the embattled Randall family, it is everyone for himself. Unless they can escape the narrow confines of their ultra-individualism, flawed random families like the Randalls will be torn apart by self-made chaos.

*　　*　　*

We see that each of the three family types can be understood in either positive or negative terms. Positively, each type pursues a core purpose or goal that is valuable in its own right. Negatively, each type has a characteristic way of running into difficulties as the family's positive purpose itself becomes part of the problem.

In reality, most families cannot be easily classified in one category or another. "Pure" types are the exception rather than the rule. Moreover, pigeonholing families is seldom useful and often unfair. Classification is not an end, but a means to understanding. Even if we found that there were more than three types of families, this would not detract from the essence of the model.[15] The heart of the typology lies, in our estimation, in the notions of core purpose and flawed types. Taken together, these two concepts say that (1) we can find something of positive worth in every family, no matter how difficult this may seem at first, and (2) no family is immune to problems regardless of how closely it may match our ideals.

Human life is enormously complex. There are many ways to be "healthy" and just as many ways to be "unhealthy." There are far too many positive values in life to make it possible for any family to major in them all. Conversely, there are so many ways to distort what is positive that there can be no invincible rules regarding the making of an ideal family. As Christians we live under two commandments: to love God and to love our neighbor as ourselves. But while these may be foundational to the Christian life, they do not define how families should interact day by day. If we, as family and church, are to make Paul's model of unity in diversity a living reality, we must keep one question in mind: Does a family's type really prevent its members from fulfilling their commitment to God or neighbor?

This is not a simple question, and it may require serious reflection. We are convinced that any of the family types is capable of a vital faith and just as capable of rejecting God. If this is true, then we must learn to distinguish questions of faith and devotion from matters of family style. This will help us to resist the temptation to play God in the lives of families and to try instead to appreciate the many ways that families live and love.

Unity in Diversity

What, then, does the Cambridge typology have to do with the social ecology of the minister's family? As we have suggested throughout part 1, the pastor's family cannot be fully understood apart from its social context, namely, the congregation. We have attempted to flesh this out by discussing differentiation, triangling, and boundary problems. (In part 2 we will see how role expectations play an important part as well.) We can also use the Kantor and Lehr typology to understand how biases regarding family types play themselves out in the ecological arena.

In particular, recall the quote from Edwin Friedman at the beginning of this chapter. The local church environment includes the interaction among three interlocking groups: the minister's family, the congregational family, and the various families in the congregation. The need to recognize and appreciate the diversity of families applies at each of these three levels. Obviously, families within the church may differ from each other according to type. But we may also apply the typology to the pastor's family and to the congregational family as a whole. Again, we have no interest in mere pigeonholing. But if we can begin to understand the *ideals* and the *core purposes* of each of these families, we will have a much better grasp of the issues and goals they bring with them when they interact.

It is especially in the midst of conflict that we forget or fail to see the positive values that motivate the parties involved. It takes differentiation to appreciate our "antagonists" on their own terms. What begins as a family preference becomes a bias under pressure. Biases in turn become prejudice under conflict. In other words, left to ourselves, our family lives indicate our preferences for some goals or purposes over others. If we are asked about it, this preference becomes a bias: what we believe a family *should* be. When confronted with someone who has different ideas, we can become defensive and adversarial. In the anxiety of a conflict, the bias *for* a certain type becomes a prejudice *against* other types.

This is important when assessing the "fit" between a clergy family and a congregation. Unity in diversity means that growth occurs where diversity is allowed to serve a positive function; there is true complementarity, mutual support, and mutual challenge. In churches where such diversity is absent or is not allowed, growth will be limited. There is a tension here. On the one hand, the clergy family may match the congregational family so well that the fit is virtually seamless. This may mean less friction all around. Or it may mean that neither the congregation nor the minister's family will experience much growth. This is uniformity rather than unity. On the other hand, if the clergy family differs sufficiently from the congregational family, this may give the needed catalyst for either growth or conflict. The pastor's family and the congregation can learn and grow from their differences, or they can each embark on a program to convert the other, a task they may approach with missionary zeal!

The point is that we bring our preferences regarding family into the ministry arena, either as clergy or as church members. The families in any church are so diverse that there is ample opportunity for our preferences to become biases. If sufficiently pressed, our biases will then become prejudices that keep us apart. The first step in transcending our biases and prejudices is to know what they are while at the same time striving to understand and appreciate the preferences of others.

Typology can be applied in many ways. We will not try to be comprehensive, but suggestive. It is neither possible nor desirable for us to anticipate all possible applications of the model. Instead, we want to give enough examples and raise enough questions to stimulate you to think about your particular situation. Let us return, then, to a consideration of the three levels of families in the church: the families in the congregation, the congregational family, and the pastor's family. We can apply the typology to all three. More to the point, however, we can use our understanding of the types to look at the interaction of these families. We will begin by looking at how the diversity of family types in the congregation relates to the congregation's own typal bias. Since the clergy family is also one of the families in the congregation, these preliminary and more general comments apply to them as well. We will then apply the typology to the particular concerns of the minister's family.

Families of different types are in any congregation. We can view this diversity as either a weakness or a source of strength. Despite the potential for conflict that comes with diversity, we believe strongly in the latter view. All three types have something to teach us, not only about family life but about the life of the church and our assumptions regarding ministry. Each type captures something essential to a vibrant and vital faith. And as we have seen, while each type models a core purpose that can contribute positively to our faith and ministry, an excessive and exclusive emphasis on any one of them can be detrimental.

Generally speaking, we can look at the congregation from three vantage points: the individuals and families that constitute the group, the group itself, and interactions among them. These three entities are interdependent; one cannot exist without the others in a vital and growing church. Though any particular congregation may place a greater emphasis on one entity, this emphasis cannot be exclusive if the church is to thrive. We can put this in more theological terms. There are (1) the people on whom God bestows his gifts, (2) the community for which the gifts are given, and (3) the mutual process of edification between the individual or family and the larger community. Each clearly builds on the others.

In the same way, each of the three family types, applied to the core purposes and values of a congregation, will emphasize one of these three entities. Yet every congregation should reflect the values and skills of all three types to some degree.

From the closed-type family we learn the importance of the group and tradition. These help to create the sense of being rooted in the ongoing history of God's dealings with his people. In the Old Testament, family heads were commanded to teach this history to their children so that even generations and centuries later, the sense of being chosen of God remained strong. The closed-type church has a positive emphasis on tradition and history, in the larger sense of biblical history and in the more limited sense of the history of a particular congregation. We can speculate that such a church would value the use of catechetical methods in its ministry to families. The closed-type ideals remind us of the need for a sense of faith that transcends the individual. We are part of more than just a local congregation. We are part of a community of faith, of a universal church that stretches beyond our present social boundaries into our historical origins and into our future.

Such guiding ideals are not enough in themselves, however. Excesses of this type can lead to inflexibility and an inability to minister in timely and relevant ways. Recall our earlier comments about demographic or structural diversity. Many families in the church do not fit the stereotypical image of an intact family with two parents and two children. The imbalanced closed-type church may not know how to deal constructively with families who fall outside the stereotype. There may be a view of moral and biblical standards that results in a recently divorced church member's being disciplined, perhaps even asked to leave. This is not to say that there are no biblical standards or that church discipline is unnecessary. Our concern is pastoral. Is enforcement of the rules a sufficient ministry to the divorced church member? As the Clover family illustrates, closed-family ideals do not in themselves show us the way to healing and reconciliation when someone breaks the rules.

From the open family we learn the lesson of equality under God. We share equally in human frailty and fallibility, and we are all equally in need of grace. Though congregations and denominations have their hierarchies, we all still have equal access to God, the one Lord who is above us all. This equality, like that of the open family, is not just an abstract assumption, but is lived out in a life of mutual cooperation. No single part of the body can say to any other, "I don't need you."[16] There is a give-and-take balance between the individual's responsibility to the community and the community's responsibility to hear what may be prophetic words from its individuals.

This openness cannot, however, be separated from rootedness in the historic Christian faith. If, like the open family, we are to have any trust in the wisdom of the group, it is because this wisdom has been bestowed by a God who works in human history. A lopsided emphasis on open family ideals makes cooperative negotiation an end in itself. For the church, this removes the value of consensus from its proper context. Striving for consensus is not done for its own sake; rather, the church must seek a consensus of vision regarding its mission. All matters of negotiation serve this overarching goal. And this cannot be achieved without a sense of how the church of the present is related to its past and future.

It is the random family, more than the other two types, that teaches us the value of the individual. An emphasis on the body, on corporate life, should not be allowed to overshadow the importance of the individuals who make up the whole. When our physical bodies are functioning properly, we tend to take the parts for granted. It is not until we are sick that we realize how serious it can be to neglect any part of the body. So it is with the church. The fact that God is concerned with his people as a whole does not mean that he neglects individual persons.

But again, we can make too much of a good thing. We must be just as concerned about excesses of this type as we are with the other two. Though we must remember the importance of pesons, individuality is not an end in itself. To speak of a personal relationship with God is valid, but we must keep that in the context of the historic community. There should be no room for narcissism in the church. Gifts are not for the glory of individuals, but for the edification of the group. Individual meanings cannot be prophetic if kept to oneself. There must always be a balance between an individual's experience of God, that person's responsibility to the community, and the community's responsibility to the person.

The unity that grows out of the diversity of gifts in the church means that to complement and enrich each other we need all three family types. God has given his gifts through *individuals* for the edification of the *body of Christ.* Furthermore, the body is a *historic* church, rooted in redemptive history and moving in the present toward a final redemptive future. The nature of the Christian community will be distorted if any of these three emphases is allowed to become an exclusive ideal.

The Ecology of the Clergy Family: Type Meets Type

Every family in the church, including the minister's, can be understood according to its core purposes on the one hand, and its particular way of developing flaws on the other. We have used the Cambridge typology in two ways. First, applying the typology to nuclear families within the church, we argued that a diversity of family types is a strength and not a weakness for the local congregation. Each of the types embodies values essential to a balance of unity and diversity. Second, we applied the typology to the congregation as a whole. Congregational families may show a preference for one family type over another, and this is not inherently a problem. But just as nuclear families can become flawed by becoming too narrow in the pursuit of their core values, so too does a congregational family become flawed by suppressing diversity within its boundaries.

We can apply the typology in one other way. We have shown that it is useful for understanding families at three levels: nuclear families in the church, the minister's family, and the congregational family as a whole. What has only been implied is that the typology is useful for looking at interactions among these levels. What does it mean for families at these three levels to be of the same or different types? We will address this question by focusing once again on our theme for part 1: the interaction between the minister's family and the congregational family.

In chapter 3 we discussed the boundary problems of idealization (where high expectations of the clergy family make peer relationships impossible), impoverishment (where it is difficult to form relationships outside the congregation), and intrusion (the glass house syndrome). If you live in a clergy family, you have probably identified with one or more of these problems. But what makes the difference between one clergy family's experience and that of another? Why is one minister's family, for example, plagued by intrusion while another is not? This is essentially a question of how the social environment differs from one church to the next. We suggest that the notion of family types helps us to understand some of these differences.

First, a congregation's typal preference will influence the kind of treatment given the clergy family. Let's use the closed-type congregation as an example. A closed family emphasizes tradition and history. At the level of a congregation, this may show itself in set structures, policies, and power hierarchies. The new pastor may find himself continually on the outside looking in. Despite his best efforts at negotiation (an open-family trait), he finds himself always at the mercy of tradition. This is what happens when the powers that be in a local congregation smile at the new pastor and say, "This is how *we* do things here." (Recall the example of David Seamands in chapter 2.) The church that embodies more open-type ideals might be more willing to compromise, and the more random-type church might be perfectly happy to let the new pastor do things his own way.

In the closed church, moreover, tradition may embody more than just church structure or policy. The pastor himself may be expected, perhaps without his knowing it, to match up to a favorite pastor who left the church years before. We might speculate, then, that a closed-type congregation may be more prone to idealization than other types.

One characteristic of closed-type families is that they respect privacy. Just as the doors to the outside world are locked to protect the space within their walls, it is common for members of a closed family to have their private spaces, protected against intrusion from other family members. The parents' bedroom, for example, is often off-limits to the children. When the children begin to mature, their privacy is also respected; if a child's bedroom door is closed, the parents will not enter without knocking first. By contrast, the more extreme random-type families have no private space at all.

Might not this distinction also apply to the intrusion that clergy families experience from their congregations? It may be that closed-type congregations will respect the privacy of the clergy family more than a random one would. Or perhaps it is the random nuclear families within the congregation who are more likely to intrude. At present we have no definite answers here. And even if we could show that these relationships between type and intrusion do in fact exist, it would be foolish to assume that this is the entire explanation! Nevertheless, we do believe that typal preference, for both the nuclear family and the congregational family, is relevant to what kinds of boundary problems exist between the clergy family and the congregation.

From the other side of the interaction, we must also suppose that the ideals of the clergy family will determine their reaction to boundary problems to some extent. What if, for example, we were to change the Clover family to *Pastor* Clover and his family? As a closed-type clergy family, the Clovers would desire to keep a well-defined boundary between their family and the congregation. This means that the problem of congregational intrusion would probably be felt quite keenly. When Pastor Clover and his family sit down to dinner, they do not wish to be interrupted. That would be a particularly poor time for a church member to call, either by phone or in person. The Clovers would probably accept the intrusion graciously (especially if they believe this their duty), but the intrusion would still cause stress. Too many intrusions into the closed clergy family would place a strain on their sense of order and security.

Now, if the clergy family were more random, like the Randalls, intrusion would be less of a problem, if a problem at all. A clergy family that opens its doors willingly to outside influence will be more apt to welcome the comings and goings of church members. What would it matter that the phone rings at the dinner hour, if the family were not all eating together anyway? We may speculate that the nature of ministry demands a certain amount of randomness of schedule on the part of clergy. The question then becomes a matter of fit: How easily does randomness fit into the clergy family's preferred lifestyle?

In a more general sense we might ask, How does the clergy family's type preference interact, not just with a particular congregation, but with the demands of the ministry? For example, will a closed minister's family experience more problems with its P.K.s than the open or random styles? This, of course, is too simplistic, for it begs the question of what distinguishes well-functioning family types from their flawed counterparts. But the question does suggest some avenues for thought. What happens in a tradition-oriented family, with several generations of ministers, when a P.K. decides not to go into the ministry? Whether or not this becomes a problem will depend on the family's ability to keep the momentum of generations of tradition from overpowering any individual member. Here the ability to value the random-family emphasis on individuality or the open-family emphasis on negotiation would allow them to accept the P.K.'s decision with grace and encouragement. Other questions could be asked, but we encourage you to create and reflect upon your own.

The Cambridge typology is a tool to help us understand the strengths and weaknesses of families, whether we are talking about nuclear families, clergy families, or whole congregations. The model teaches us that (1) each type has its own core purpose, which is valuable in itself, and (2) a family's positive goals can, under emotional stress, become part of a downward spiral of problems. This twin recognition has enormous pastoral implications. What do we do when confronted with a troubled family? Rather than blaming their typal preference and seeking to change them at that level, we must seek first to understand them on their own terms. Only then can we help them out of their rut by teaching them the skills they lack. It is ill-advised to force-fit a family into an ideal type that may not suit them. Instead, we approach an ailing family by seeking and encouraging their strengths while shoring them up where they are weak.

The sword cuts two ways. We have to steer clear of viewing any kind of ministry as what we do to someone else. Understanding others entails understanding ourselves. Appreciating the strengths and weaknesses of others requires that we are honest with our own. In the ecology of the minister's family, this means that both the clergy family and the congregation must learn to value their differences. Any move by one to change the other before such understanding is reached will be premature at best and destructive at worst.

Summary

Part 1 has been devoted to developing an ecological model of the life of the minister's family. All of us, as individuals and as family members, interact with a variety of social contexts that influence how we live, work, and see ourselves and the world. We can look at these contexts through the conceptual lenses of differentiation, triangles, boundary problems, or family types. We must be careful, however, not to overindulge any of these constructs. To some extent we will find triangles, boundary problems, and the like simply because we are looking for them. If we were to look for something else, we might find that too.

What we have tried to emphasize in these four chapters is the importance of seeing our own life and behavior in its social context. *How* we do this—what lenses we look through—is secondary to learning to see in this way.

In addition, we can focus on the role expectations of clergy family members, both in terms of what is expected of them and what they expect of themselves. As we have suggested, members of the minister's family must learn to juggle roles and expectations that come from many quarters. In part 2 we will look at this sometimes confusing world of competing roles.

PART TWO

FAMILY MEMBERS AND THEIR ROLES

5

The Roles Ministers Play

Members of a clergy family are surrounded by expectations of all kinds: Who has the right to do what to the parsonage? What should the social boundaries between the clergy family and the congregation look like? Which family type is the most ideal? And so on. Parishioners often expect members of their "royal family" to be models of virtue in both church and family life. But the matter is hardly one-sided. Members of the pastor's family also have ideas about how to fulfill their roles as leaders in the congregation as well as how to live together as a family. Thus, in the ecology of the clergy family, the congregation and family members interact with each other, attempting to define appropriate expectations and roles.

Sorting out all the different expectations placed on a clergy family would be extremely complex. First of all, there are potentially several members in the family: the minister, his spouse, and each of the children. Second, there are many roles to be distinguished: the minister as minister, father, and husband; the minister's wife as church leader, wife, mother, and possibly a professional in some other field; and the children as children to their parents, leaders in the youth group, and leaders at school. Third, expectations of the clergy family come from several sources: individuals and families in the church, the congregation as a whole, and the denomination. And of course, the members of the minister's family have their own expectations for their life as a family. Multiply the number of sources of expectations by the number of roles, and there are literally

113

hundreds of possible combinations. And every combination can be a source of either satisfaction and fulfillment or frustration and conflict.

It should come as no surprise, then, that some clergy families feel they are trying to juggle too many balls at once. How much anxiety this provokes depends on how clergy family members perceive their roles. Some clergy treat their various roles as if they were rubber balls. They try their best to keep all the balls in the air, and if by chance they miss one, they trust that the ball will simply bounce harmlessly and can be scooped up later. Other ministers, however, treat their role-juggling as if they were tossing either eggs or flaming torches! They feel that if they are not careful, either something will break or someone will get burned.

What accounts for the difference? Why might one minister view his roles as resilient and flexible while another attaches almost life-and-death significance to them? Our guess is that it is a matter of differentiation. The well-differentiated pastor's sense of identity is more stable and does not depend on how well he fulfills expectations, whether they are his own or the congregation's. As David Seamands's experience shows (chap. 2), the differentiated pastor is able to stand calmly in the strength of his convictions despite emotional pressures from members of the congregation. The situation is not the same for the poorly differentiated pastor. He becomes enmeshed in the ministry. His sense of identity becomes so closely entwined with the fulfillment of role expectations that instead of experiencing failure as temporarily dropping the ball, he experiences a failure of self. Such a pastor responds to emotional pressure defensively, either by cutting-off ("I don't care what you think, so there!") or by becoming oversubmissive and apologetic ("I'm so sorry—just tell me what you want me to do, and I'll do it").

The focus in this part of the book will be role expectations. Our goal is to show the complexity of the variety of expectations that a clergy family faces. In chapters 5 through 7 we will consider in turn the roles of the pastor, the pastor's wife, and the pastor's children.

Once again, however, satisfaction in the ministry or in family life is not just a matter of how a congregation treats a clergy family. That view is too passive. We can talk about how the members of the clergy family must deal with several roles, coming from several sources, and how some of those roles may conflict. But this would still not explain why some people will handle the situation better than others. We must remember that each member of the clergy family also brings to that environment a personal history, a certain level of differentiation that is either developing or already formed. This is the ecological perspective: the environment does not *cause* the organism to behave in a certain way, and the congregation does not *cause* the clergy family to be happy or unhappy. It is a matter of fit, of interaction, of how the clergy family and a congregation work with and adapt to each other. In this chapter, then, we will use our discussion of the minister's roles to show how the expectations of both the congregation and the minister contribute to their ongoing interaction.

Types of Role Conflict

Our discussion of the pastor's roles must begin with our defining a few basic terms.[1]

What is a *role?* It is "a set of social norms and expectations of behavior that is relatively distinct from other sets or roles."[2] Roles are made up of expectations of how a person should behave. These expectations are bundled together in a set, which is given a name such as "doctor" or "pastor." The names are then used as a kind of shorthand for what the person does. If I want to tell you about a friend of mine, I could describe everything he does in a day at home and at work, or I could say he is an attorney who is married and has two children. The latter description will trigger a storehouse of role expectations, and you will conjure up some kind of image related to the roles of "attorney," "husband," and "father." All of us have preconceived notions of what is appropriate to many different roles, including ministerial ones.

The minister's numerous functions can be grouped together under roles of various names. "Pastor" is not just a synonym for "minister"; it is also used as shorthand for such functions as counseling and visitation. "Evangelist" describes a different set of expectations. The role of evangelist is not expected to include pastoral counseling. Thus "pastor" and "evangelist" describe two relatively distinct roles that can be played by the same minister, albeit usually at different times.

The minister, in his position as minister, is expected to play a number of different roles such as pastor, preacher, and administrator. Clergy are expected to be dynamic preachers, warm and empathetic counselors, biblical scholars, and shrewd administrators. This may be true even if the minister has actually had little or no training or experience in some of these areas. There is yet another set of roles related to the home and family, that of devoted spouse and caring but firm parent. Perhaps more than in any other profession, the minister is expected to be "all things to all people."

Expectations must come from somewhere and are received by someone. Thus a person who either verbally or nonverbally communicates expectations can be called a *role sender,* while the person who is the focus of these expectations can be called a *role receiver.*[3] This chapter will focus particularly on the minister as the role receiver; later chapters will look at the minister's wife and children as role receivers in their own right.

Role strain can be defined as "the stress generated within a person when he or she either cannot comply or has difficulty complying with the expectations of a role or set of roles."[4] The variety of roles in the ministry can place an enormous burden on the pastor. Stress can occur when the minister simply has more roles than he has energy to fulfill. But the sheer volume of roles is not necessarily a problem in itself. The problem is, the more role expectations there are, the greater the chance that two or more sets of expectations will conflict. Add to this the complicating factor that expectations of clergy commonly have a great deal of emotional significance attached to them. This means that role conflict is not simply experienced as an intellectual difference of opinion. There is a certain emotional urgency on the part of both role sender and role receiver to resolve the conflict.

Edgar Mills has created a helpful typology of role conflicts that we will use to organize the rest of this chapter: (1) conflicts that are primarily external, (2) those that are primarily internal, and (3) those that arise between internal and external demands.[5] Simply put, external role conflicts arise when the congregation sends incompatible expectations to the minister. Internal role conflicts have to do with confusion in the minister's own expectations. And the third type describes the interplay of these expectations.

Thus clergy (and members of their families) are often confronted by numerous roles. These roles may be interpreted in different ways by the minister, the church, the denomination, and the individual church members. This is further complicated by a general lack of clarity regarding which roles should be played when and in what circumstances. Sometimes the confusion comes largely from discrepancies in a congregation's expectations. At times the confusion arises from within the minister. Often it is a mixture of the two.

External Role Conflicts: You Want Me to Do What?

Sometimes the role conflicts for pastors come from the incompatible expectations of others. Every role is by definition a set of expectations; since the minister must fulfill so many roles, there is bound to be role conflict at some point. It is, if you will, a hazard of the profession. Consider the following example:

Mr. Robbins had been going to Pastor Ogden for counseling for several weeks. The pastor, while not a mental health professional, skillfully helped Mr. Robbins feel secure and understood. Mr. Robbins was not a member of the church and attended only infrequently.

The pastor suggested that Mr. Robbins take a closer look at his faith. He encouraged Mr. Robbins to participate in a Bible study that was to begin that week. At first Mr. Robbins was reluctant. He objected that he really didn't know anyone in the church and didn't know the Bible well enough to contribute anything to the group. The pastor smiled and gently persuaded him that joining the group would itself help solve both problems. Mr. Robbins eventually agreed.

The first meeting was relatively uneventful. It was mostly a time for people to meet one another and learn names. Mr. Robbins seemed slow to warm and said little about himself. By the end of the evening, however, he left with a private feeling that he could actually find a place in the group.

But in the weeks to come, as the group entered into study and discussion in earnest, Mr. Robbins felt more and more left out. Most of the group members were more experienced. Although the group as a whole tried to keep Mr. Robbins involved, the more experienced members would usually end up sweeping the discussion away. Pastor Ogden, who viewed himself as a biblical scholar, also relished the chance to have some in-depth discussion, and as a result he lost track of Mr. Robbins.

Back in their counseling sessions, the pastor felt that there was an emotional distance between them. Mr. Robbins began missing appointments and rarely offered more than a superficial explanation. Soon the confused pastor received a note from him that said simply, "You've been a lot of help. Thanks." Pastor Ogden never heard from Mr. Robbins again.

What happened? For the present, let us forego psychological speculation and focus on the issue of roles. In our example, Pastor Ogden had to wear two hats. In one social context he would put on his pastoral counseling hat and be a warm and understanding listener. This is apparently just what Mr. Robbins needed at the time. In another setting, however, the pastor would don his teacher-scholar hat. When Pastor Ogden was functioning in the role of teacher, he tended to focus less on feelings and more on content and ideas. This does not mean he was an insensitive teacher. The point is that counseling and teaching are different roles; they involve different expectations and different behaviors. Apparently Pastor Ogden recognized this and has little trouble switching hats as needed.

The problem came largely from Mr. Robbins' side. He was able to relate to the pastor in only one way: as client to counselor. The change in setting from counseling office to study group required that both the pastor and Mr. Robbins change hats and thereby change the nature of their relationship. For Pastor Ogden, this was no problem. For Mr. Robbins, however, it was not so easy. He had agreed to join the group only reluctantly, and even then mostly because it was the pastor who suggested it. Had someone else invited him, he probably would have said no. It never occurred to him that he could not expect the same level of patient, listening attention from the pastor in his role as teacher. Mr. Robbins was disillusioned and hurt.

When one person must play many different roles, there is always a possibility of confusion: which role is appropriate when? Pastor Ogden was clear, at least in his own mind, about what behavior was appropriate in what setting; he had little difficulty moving from one role to the other. But Mr. Robbins expected the pastor to continue to play the counselor role regardless of the setting.

This is an example of a source of role conflict that is external to the minister. Why, then, didn't the pastor seem to experience any role stress? Because Mr. Robbins tended to keep his expectations to himself. To be sure, he communicated them indirectly by his emotional and eventually physical withdrawal from the relationship. But by and large, Mr. Robbins was not the type to press the issue. Suppose instead that Mr. Robbins were a loud and belligerent man. Can you imagine the kind of role stress this would have put on the pastor?

To avoid confusion in themselves, their families, and in the people they serve, many professionals have a need to keep their roles clearly delineated from one another. For example, academic professors who are also psychotherapists will often have a rule that they will not counsel their own students. Let's say a professor were to counsel a student whose problems were low self-esteem and a difficulty with authority figures. What would happen if the student began to flunk the class? How should the professor respond—as a professor, a counselor, or a combination of both?

Most professionals would prefer, for both personal and ethical reasons, to avoid thorny situations like this one and not allow their roles to cross. Many physicians will not actively treat members of their own family, especially in cases where they believe a high degree of clinical objectivity is needed. And psychotherapists are familiar with what happens when they slip into their professional role at home; the therapist, in the middle of an argument with a spouse, suddenly "goes clinical" and begins to offer brilliant psychological observations. This is when the spouse usually retorts, "Don't YOU try to psychoanalyze ME!"

The problem for ministers is that while they may be comfortable with their many roles, it is not always clear which role is appropriate at a given time. For most people the immediate social context provides clear cues. When you go to the doctor, for example, you may be ushered into a room with an examining table and a hospital gown. Although the nurse tells you what to do, the setting itself already defines your role, and you already know what to do. The doctor, dressed in clean white linen, has a position of authority over you while you are under medical care. When the doctor says cough, you cough! But if you should run into your doctor at the grocery store, the roles are different. There is no examining table, no hospital gown, no white coat.

You are, for the most part, equals: two people from the same neighborhood shopping for food. The social setting, with all of its accompanying cues, helps define the appropriate role relationship.

It is not so simple for clergy. The difference between a physician and a minister is that the former has a fairly well-defined role that is fulfilled in a well-defined setting. When the physician leaves the office and white coat behind, he or she is no longer expected to behave as a doctor except in an emergency. The minister, however, plays many roles that cross many settings. At any time, in any place, people always expect a minister to *be* a minister. And what it means to "be a minister" will vary according to both the setting and the usual relationship between the minister and the other person. Mr. Robbins expected Pastor Ogden to be an empathic counselor no matter what the setting. Had the two met by chance in the grocery store, Mr. Robbins might have felt perfectly comfortable reciting a litany of the day's woes while the pastor's ice cream melted in his cart.

External role conflicts, therefore, have to do with incompatible expectations that come from outside the pastor. In the case of Pastor Ogden, the conflict was between the role Mr. Robbins wanted him to play and the role demanded by the context of the Bible study. Because of the pastor's numerous roles, some external role conflicts are practically inevitable.[6] Yet such conflicts may not be easy to pinpoint, because role expectations are often fuzzy or poorly defined.[7] This is illustrated by what we call the "double-bind theory of pastoral ministry."

Family therapists use the term *double-bind* to describe a particular pattern of family communication that is thought to be related to the development of psychological problems in children.[8] The essence of the double-bind is that a no-win situation is created for the child. One or both parents send incompatible messages to the child. One message is verbal, the other is nonverbal.[9] The child is expected to respond, but is not allowed to comment on the discrepancy in the messages. Here is an excerpt from a classic example of the double-bind:

A young man who had fairly well recovered from an acute schizophrenic episode was visited in the hospital by his mother. He was glad to see her and impulsively put his arm around her shoulders, whereupon she stiffened. He withdrew his arm and she asked, "Don't you love me anymore?" He then blushed, and she said, "Dear, you must not be so easily embarrassed and afraid of your feelings." The patient was able to stay with her only a few minutes more and following her departure he assaulted an aide.[10]

In this episode the son is confused by the conflicting messages he is receiving. Verbally his mother seems to want him to express his affection for her. More than that, she implies that there is something wrong with him if he doesn't. Nonverbally, however, when she stiffens she communicates to her son that she really doesn't want his affection or can't accept it. He is stuck in a no-win situation. If he is affectionate, he will be rejected. If he is not affectionate, he will also be rejected. And if he tries to get out of the bind, he will still be rejected.

What is it that is so destructive about this interaction? Simply this: the mother's problem is fobbed off on the son. The real problem is that *she* cannot accept a spontaneous display of affection from her son. But this becomes distorted into *his* lack of affection or *his* fear of feelings. And as long as the focus remains on the son and his symptoms, the true nature of the problem will never be discovered.

If interactions like this happen consistently, they can be truly "crazy-making." Of course, the son's psychotic response could be circumvented if he could simply say to his mother, "Mom, I noticed that you're giving me two messages here. On the one hand, you say you want me to express my feelings. On the other hand, when you stiffen up like that, you tell me you *don't* want me to express my feelings. You can't have it both ways. What's going on here?"

Anyone who comes from emotionally undifferentiated families, however, knows that it is far from simple to make such a statement to a parent. The response would probably not be, "You know, you're right. Let's talk about that." What do you think would happen? The parent will probably respond by (1) resorting to more double-binding communication, (2) changing the subject, (3) accusing the child of being an ungrateful wretch, or even (4) disowning the child emotionally. The fear of such a reaction is usually enough to keep the child from trying to clear up the ambiguities.

How might this apply to the ministry? The minister's role

conflicts can be double-binding when, for example, two things happen at the same time: (1) the congregation sends conflicting expectations, but (2) conflict within the congregation itself is denied. Remember our earlier discussion of scapegoating? Members of a poorly differentiated group avoid facing their struggles with each other by singling out a person who then becomes the target of blame and excuse-making. If the group is a church and the scapegoat is the pastor, he will make little headway in trying to sort out conflicting expectations. He will feel frustrated and confused, with a burning question in his mind: "But what do you *want* from me?"

This frustration is all the more acute for the pastor who derives a large part of his identity from being a minister. What the pastor may fail to realize is that the church members may not want to make their expectations clearer. The lack of clarity serves the purpose of masking areas of disagreement. The pastor who tries to clear up these expectations in such a situation will meet with resistance. To a poorly differentiated congregation, clarity of expectations would entail having to face up to their inconsistency and internal conflicts.

External role conflicts can also be complicated by misperceptions of how the minister spends his time. Two researchers who studied twelve Lutheran congregations found that parishioners believed their ministers spent most of their week preparing sermons. Studies show that this definitely is not the case.[11] There is a lack of communication here! This misperception of the true nature of the minister's work can lead to unrealistic expectations and increased role strain.[12]

So clergy role conflicts can come from different external sources:

1. Interacting with parishioners through more than one role can create confusion over what role is appropriate in a given situation.
2. Conflicts within the parish may give rise to incompatible messages being sent by parishioners. These messages can be double-binding in poorly differentiated congregations.
3. Misperceptions of the minister's duties may add to the force of unrealistic role demands.

Again, let us emphasize that looking at what the congregation contributes is only one side of the story. Role conflicts are not necessarily external. There is much that the minister brings to the interaction. Church members are not the only ones who have expectations of the pastor; the minister is heir to a multitude of role expectations learned from his family history and training. These can be the source of internal role conflicts.

Internal Role Conflicts: Just Who Do I Think I Am?

Internal role conflict arises when the minister's various expectations of his role are incompatible or unintegrated. Pastor Carver had grown up as a P.K. His father had consistently preached a strong message of servant-leadership. The way he preached and the way he acted, however, were two different stories. Pastor Carver remembers the power that his father held over the church board and how he relished wielding that authority. Now, in his own ministry, Pastor Carver finds himself feeling disjointed. On the one hand, he truly believes in servant-leadership; on the other, his tendency is to want to rule the board with an iron fist. He feels the conflict, but is unsure of its source. Unless the internal nature of his role conflict is pointed out to him, he is unlikely to resolve it.

The minister's personality, expectations, and perceptions are every bit as important as the congregation's expectations. To some extent the minister's expectations are shaped by larger social trends such as changes in the general image of what a minister *is*. For example, today's ministers tend to view themselves as "professionals." This is in contrast to earlier, more constricting models. One writer describes the earlier ideal this way:

> Our clergy are frequently perceived by their parishioners in non-human terms. . . . By perceiving themselves as some non-human Christ figure, many clergymen are locked in a double bind. To themselves and to others they are not allowed the privilege of being human.[13]

There was a time when ministers would simply accept this expectation as part of their role. But the image of the minister as professional changes this. The trend is toward giving the minister room to be more human, to define his own goals and identity: "Clergy today are struggling to act much more upon their real inner motives and values than upon ideals imposed by, or assimilated from, church and society."[14]

The minister as professional has the same rights as other professionals: time off, privacy in the home, a fair salary, adequate boundaries. But the wheels of change grind slowly. Social trends may take decades to filter down to some churches and pastors. Despite the trend toward a more professional identity, the older ideal is still very much a part of the minister's self-perception. One minister's wife has remarked, "Too many ministers have a queer 'conscience' that makes them feel guilty if spending time relaxing at home."[15]

Thus to some degree, ministers are driven by their expectations of themselves. These are internal factors that contribute to the minister's role conflicts. We will examine these factors from two aspects: a review of what others have written about the "ministerial personality," and a look at how family history can affect a minister's perception of his role.

The Pastor's Personality

Edward Golden wrote, "It is a common saying that there are three kinds of people—men, women, and ministers."[16] Many researchers have tried to answer the question, Is there a particular type of person who goes into the ministry? There are, of course, no conclusive answers. And in terms of an ecological perspective the question is too narrow.

There is, however, one consistent theme in the literature on the ministerial personality that is of direct interest to us: the theme of psychological boundaries. Using the terms of our discussion in chapter 2, researchers have found two opposite tendencies in the personalities of ministers. On the one hand, some ministers tend to have personal or psychological boundaries that are too rigid; they are disengaged from their congregations. On the other hand, some ministers run to the opposite extreme and become enmeshed with their congregations. Both tendencies are essentially a problem with differentiation.

In chapter 3 we described how idealizing the minister and his family—putting them on a pedestal—can leave them feeling isolated and alone. While some ministers find this isolation frustrating, others may actually seek it. One researcher writes,

Many who enter the ministry seek its authority, isolation, and separateness. . . . There is some evidence to believe that some of those who enter the ministry have difficulty in developing relations of trust with others. Some entrust themselves to God or Jesus Christ, but build walls around themselves and others.[17]

Recall the discussion of differentiation in chapter 2. Some people would rather avoid the anxiety of honest relationships with others. Relationship involves risk, the possibility that others may hurt you. One way to avoid that risk to is build walls around yourself to keep yourself emotionally distant. The ministry can make this possible. The social isolation of the role, which some ministers experience as a nuisance, can also be taken as a refuge. While some pastors keep trying to climb down off the pedestal, crying, "Just let me be a real person," others stay up there willingly. For the poorly differentiated pastor, it may seem safer.

Other researchers have noted an opposite kind of excess in pastors. Some ministers lack a firm sense of identity as individuals. Grasping for crumbs of identity and meaning, they may overinvest themselves in others. One researcher describes it this way:

One may lose himself in people to the extent that his identity is completely dependent on others. "Who I am becomes what others *say* I am. Therefore, I am not really myself, but a reflection of the image that others project on me." This is clearly one danger in the ministry, perhaps more than in any other profession.[18]

Thus, while one pastor may use the isolation of his role as an excuse to keep himself aloof, another may feed on members' images of him as a badly needed source of identity and fulfillment. Both approaches betray a lack of differentiation.

But we must be careful here. It would be foolish to conclude that all ministers are therefore either disengaged or enmeshed. This view is, again, too narrow and just plain incorrect. The point is that there are characteristics of the ministry *as a social environment* that provide fertile ground for certain personal quirks. A minister with exhibitionist tendencies may be a brilliantly inspiring preacher. A person who would be branded as rigid and narrow-minded may flourish in a congregation that needs and admires his "strength of conviction." There are people who have strong needs to be admired, to be in control of others, or to wallow in guilt. The ministry has something to offer all of them. As ministers they can find more or less acceptable social outlets for their personal needs.[19]

General questions about the personality of the "average" pastor should always be put back into an ecological context. It is not so much a matter of individual personality as it is of the *fit between the individual and the environment*. Gotthard Booth has expressed it well:

> If one examines an average "normal" candidate [for ministry], one is bound to find weak spots in his personality structure. . . . Whether a given individual is going to become sick depends on the particular correlation between his personality and the demands he has to meet. The ministry not only makes demands, but also provides for certain personalities a way of living in which they can function usefully and creatively in spite of limitations such as have broken individuals engaged in a different type of work.[20]

Think of it this way. Let's say you had a flower bed outside your home that had never been planted. This year you decide to brighten up the yard a bit by planting some flowers. There is a right way and a wrong way to go about choosing flowers. You could go to the nursery, pick out the most attractive plant, and then return home and place it in the soil. If you're lucky, the plant will bloom. It may, however, be either sickly or dead in two to three weeks time. Why? Because there are other factors, environmental factors, that should have been taken into account. How much sun will the plant get? How good is the drainage? Is the soil soft and porous or hard and clay-like? Does the soil have the kind of nutrients the plant will need? Making an informed choice means trying to find the right plant for the environment, or conversely, changing the environment to fit the plant.

Making value judgments regarding a pastor's personality can also be done in too restricted a fashion. Various personalities fare differently in different settings. Psychological health is not just an individual matter. We cannot reliably distinguish between healthy personalities and unhealthy ones. Instead, we should think in terms of how pastors fit the ministry and their churches. In general, the characteristics of the ministry as a vocation offer ample opportunity for a pastor to be enmeshed or disengaged, if he so wishes. More particularly, the local congregation also has its own personality, which will suit some ministers better than others. Pastors come in as many varieties as plants in a nursery, and congregations offer different "soil conditions" into which the pastor puts his roots. The personality that a pastor brings to his ministry, then, is only half the story. How well that personality works for him will depend, at least in part, upon the congregation he serves. We will look at this idea again later in this chapter, under the heading of *collusion*.

There is yet another piece to the ecological puzzle. Individual personalities do not develop in a vacuum. To a large extent, our personalities are reflections of our family histories. It is important, then, that we ask how the pastor's childhood family may influence how he approaches the ministry.

The Influence of One's Childhood Family

J. C. Wynn, writing to pastors who practice marital and family therapy in the parish, has these words of advice:

> It is not required that you have all your marital and family problems solved before you intervene with some other family's dysfunction. What is required is that you have come to realistic terms with your own marital and family status, that you know both where you stand and how to work on your human condition.
>
> Not to have faced your own family background and condition with honesty can be folly, for it can lead to two gross temptations. On the one hand you may be tempted to project your own family difficulties, ghosts, and worries into the counseling situation and try to solve your own problems through this relationship. . . . On the other hand, you might heedlessly foist your own value system upon another family and attempt to influence them to reconstruct their family system on your own model; that too is bound for failure.[21]

Much of who we are as adults was formed in us when we were children, growing up in our families. The imprint of our family histories colors the way we see things, the way we react to people. When we try to intervene with other families, the influence of this imprint can be especially strong. But the influence of our childhood families, otherwise known as our families of origin, is not limited to the context of family counseling or family ministry in the church. Because the minister's family of origin is reflected in his very personality, that influence is relevant to every aspect of ministry.

There is an important parallel between the pastor's childhood family and his congregational family. We are born into this world as infants with certain potential and predispositions. These inborn characteristics, however, are not yet a full-fledged personality. The child's personality is molded and shaped over the years as his or her potential comes face to face with the encouragement or discouragement of parents and society. The minister's personality, as an individual rather than a minister per se, grows and develops in this family context.

There is a parallel process awaiting those who enter the ministry. In chapter 3 we stressed that the congregation itself should be considered as a family in its own right. The minister's identity is forged in the context of a congregational family, much as the infant's personality is molded by its biological family. Instead of biological birth and entry into the world, there is the pastor's entry into the social world of the ministry. And just as the infant brings certain innate capacities to the interaction with his or her family, so the minister brings a personality—the marks of his family of origin—to the interaction with a congregational family.

Pastors who seek out psychological counseling soon discover the extent that their family background influences their lives as ministers. There is the pastor who grew up under a distant and critical father and who now has trouble submitting to denominational authority. There is the minister who had overly controlling and invasive parents who overreacts whenever he feels the congregation invading his privacy. And of course, there is the P.K. who has become a preacher himself, heir to all the unresolved conflict he had with his own minister-father.

Several studies have searched for patterns in the family backgrounds of ministers who seek counseling. For example, one author noted the following pattern in ministers' childhood families: the minister's father was psychologically absent, and the minister had an overly close relationship with his mother and weak relationships with his peers.[22] Another writer noted that ministers' families of origin tended to be secretive, seeming to be harmonious on the outside, but masking disharmony on the inside.[23] The structure of the family typically looked like this: a dominant mother; ambivalence toward the children; limited expression of feelings, with anger more acceptable than love; and feelings of guilt and shame over sexuality.[24]

Still other studies raised the theme of the minister as the "good" or responsible child in his family of origin.[25] Being the responsible child is certainly not bad in and of itself. Yet some children are "responsible," not because they are confident and mature, but because it is the only way they can have the love of their parents. These children may become the superministers who feel they must personally handle every problem in the church, to the exclusion of their families and even their health.

None of these patterns is unique. They are the kinds of family histories that characterize almost anyone who enters psychotherapy. Ministers are, after all, human. Their family problems are not necessarily any different from anyone else's. What makes the minister's family background so relevant is the uniqueness of the ministry environment. Because the congregation is, practically speaking, a family, the minister is that much more likely to play out family-of-origin patterns in that context.

Is there, then, anything unique about the family histories of ministers? Margaretta Bowers cites case studies of ministers who share one thing in common: a childhood experience with death, usually the death of a family member. In the childhood memories of these men, death in the family brings the minister to their home. In his priestly garb and role, the minister seems to hold a magical power over life and death. As adults we know better. But this is how children think. The impression becomes deeply embedded in the child's unconscious mind and later influences how the minister-to-be perceives his role.

Bowers tells of James, the "good" child of devout parents, a boy who had a close emotional bond with his grandfather. When Grandfather died, James was naturally angry toward him for dying and leaving him alone. But James was also angry with his father and the priest who told him, "Be good while the church takes Grandfather away."[26] This scene was deeply etched in the young child's impressionable mind. Later in life the unresolved feelings from the episode influenced James's approach to the ministry and to God. Bowers writes:

> James's God was a changing concept. As long as his grandfather
> was alive, he had a concept of God who was an extension of this
> grandfather, a very wonderful Grandfather. . . . But then there was
> the terrible anger at God when Grandfather died, and the definite
> decision that James would become the omnipotent, magical priest

of God, that he would do what he wanted to with God and God's will in relation to people.[27]

Bowers's reading of the case is based on psychoanalytic assumptions. The basic idea is that the image of the priest is blown out of proportion in the young child's mind. The boy had little chance to deal realistically with his devastating loss. Rather than being comforted, rather than being told that it was all right for him to grieve, to scream, to cry, James was told to "be good."

The loss of a loved one is difficult for children to understand. It strikes at the very heart of their sense of security. They are, after all, little people in a big world, still dependent on others for their basic needs. How does a small child gain a sense of power in a big people's world? By identifying with the big people. Normally children will identify with their parents. James identified with his grandfather. If Grandfather had lived longer, James would probably have turned out differently. But fate intervened, and Grandfather was literally taken away. James was like a ship without an anchor, no longer having a strong tie to an adult to give him a sense of security. What was the young boy to do?

The loss of his beloved grandfather made James feel small and powerless. In his anger, pain, and fear he latched on to the most powerful adult on the scene—the priest. In young James's eyes, the priest seemed to be the gatekeeper between life and death. Unable to mourn properly for his grandfather, James handled his loss the only way he could; he unconsciously identified with the mystical, powerful priest of God. Unfortunately for James, the circumstances were too traumatic for that identification to be a positive one. In a sense, unconsciously identifying with the priest was a desperate measure for a desperate situation.

Is Bowers right? Not everyone who enters the ministry has had an early experience with death, but this is not the point. The essential insight for our purposes has to do with how a child understands the heavy symbolism of the ministry. For example, what is a child to think of a person who prays over bread and wine, or even crackers and juice, and declares them to be Christ's body and blood? And it isn't as if the child could dismiss the minister as some kind of crazy person, because when he performs these magical deeds, everyone in the congregation sits in silent reverence. It is particularly in his role as priest and liturgist that the minister takes on a mystical quality in the eyes of the very young. These impressions are not formed by the rational deliberations of an adult, but by the emotional reactions of a child. For someone like James, the symbolic power of the priesthood held out the only anchor for a boy caught in an emotional tempest. Grandfather's death was an accident of family history. That accident, however, endowed the ministry with grave emotional significance for James.

Not everyone has to deal with this kind of childhood tragedy. But the essential point remains. The minister occupies a position of great symbolic power. This may be even more true in High Church traditions, where clergy wear liturgical vestments and perform sacerdotal rituals. To a child who looks for heroes to worship, the minister may seem to be a magician or a superman. These childhood impressions are hard to change because they are more emotional than rational and are deeply rooted in the unconscious mind. Like James, children with such impressions may grow up to be ministers who believe they can work magic with a congregation or who are driven to be superministers.

Have we then found general principles which apply to all ministers? Perhaps. It is always dangerous to overgeneralize. There seem to be two broad principles, however, with regard to the importance of the minister's family of origin. First, the minister's personality takes shape within his family. This is nothing new. What is important is that the church, too, is a family. This means that the strengths and weaknesses of a minister's relationship to his family of origin will also come to bear in his new family setting, the church. Second, encounters with the church and its ministers in childhood may have formed deep, long-lasting impressions. Depending on circumstances, these impressions can be positive or negative. Whether good or bad, they are carried into the minister's adult life, where they can influence how he perceives his role.

The same argument could be used to show that the family background of every single member of the congregation is also important. Like the pastor, each member brings a unique personal history to the life of the church in general and to the definition of the pastor's role in particular. These expectations can either conflict with or complement the pastor's. And even if expectations do mesh, this does not guarantee a productive and growing relationship; collusion can be as harmful as collision. Let's investigate this idea.

Internal/External: Collision and Collusion

Where is the line between internal and external role conflicts? It depends on your point of view. The way we have used the terms reflects the minister's vantage point, that is, they distinguish between what is internal to the minister from what is external to him. If you are trying to sort out the sources of role strain, the distinction can help you get your bearings. It is the kind of distinction, however, that is meant to be discarded once it has served its usefulness. There are three reasons for this.

First, we have taken the minister's point of view because we are writing a book about ministers and their families. But it is just as valid to discuss these matters from the parishioner's point of view. Because each person's family history has some bearing on how one perceives the minister's role, the distinction between internal and external begins to lose importance. Consider Mr. Clarke, a hypothetical parishioner. His family history and personality are internal issues for him, but external issues for the pastor. But the pastor's family history is internal for the pastor and external to Mr. Clarke.

The second point is implicit in the first. The minister's role does not exist in a vacuum. The title and role of "minister" are meaningless without a congregation. Here's a more commonplace example. If you have children, think back to what it was like before you had them. For many of us there is a tremendous difference between what we thought we would be like as parents and how we actually behaved after our children were born. We are not really parents until we have children, no matter how many books we have read about parenting, no matter how well prepared or trained we are. Parents and children are two sides of a single relationship. We can discuss either side separately, but we must remember that one cannot exist without the other.

In the same way, we should remember that the minister's role is only one side of a pastor-congregation relationship. To take the viewpoint of the parishioner we have to go beyond simply asking how he or she perceives the pastor's role. Instead we must ask how the parishioner views his or her own role in regard to the minister. Our hypothetical Mr. Clarke may see the minister as a powerful, somewhat more-than-human person. But how does he view his own role? Is he supposed to submit to the minister's authority? Or is he supposed to agree with the minister on the face of things while simultaneously trying to undermine his power? The point is that our expectations of others do not exist by themselves. Role expectations are two-sided coins. On one side is what we expect of others in relationship to ourselves; on the flip side is what we expect of ourselves in relationship to others.

There is a third limitation to the internal versus external distinction. All of us have sets of expectations that we have learned to associate with certain roles. Yet all these expectations arise from our interaction with others and therefore have an external root. In their day-to-day work, pastors constantly revise and adapt their expectations of themselves in response to others' expectations of them. The same is true of parishioners. Thus what begins as external becomes to some degree internal. In the ongoing interaction between a minister and a congregation is a give-and-take process by which role expectations are gradually modified.

This assumes, of course, that there *is* interaction and that both the minister and the congregation are willing and able to adapt to each other. The most difficult and destructive kind of role strain happens in a stand-off situation where clergy and parishioners disagree but neither is willing to give any ground. If by contrast there is adequate communication and a cooperative spirit between them, differences can provide an opportunity for growth. Where there is give-and-take, people eventually lose track of whose expectations are whose.

Thus there are three closely related reasons for looking at the interaction of internal and external sources of role conflict. Each reason stresses an ecological view of roles, as being part of the minister-congregation relationship. First, when studying the roles of the minister, it is just as valid to use the parishioner's standpoint as the minister's. Parishioners' family histories are just as relevant to expectations as the pastor's. Second, there is no parish minister without parishioners. Thus we must turn the tables and ask about parishioners' internal expectations of themselves in relation to the minister along with the minister's expectations of his parishioners. Third, when there is continual interaction, expectations are traded and modified. After a time it is no longer possible to distinguish what began as internal and what was external.

This is an ecological orientation. We need to be reminded that both parties bear responsibility for a relationship. If a minister is experiencing role strain, it could be a result of the congregation's giving double messages; however, it could be due to the minister's personal issues. It is most likely a combination of both.

We should not think of internal role conflicts as something happening inside the skin and of external role conflicts as something "out there." The point is that ministers learn gradually through their life experiences what it means to be a minister: how to behave, what goals to have, how parishioners are expected to respond. Similarly, parishioners learn their own sets of expectations. Before a minister even sets foot in a particular church, he and the congregation have both developed a host of values and expectations for their respective roles. There is, so to speak, a history to their interaction before they ever interact!

Let us consider, then, how what we call external and internal sources of role conflict interact. When a minister's expectations differ from a congregation's, there is obviously role conflict. In other cases there may be a fair degree of correspondence. But even where minister and congregation agree, this agreement may serve to perpetuate an unproductive or even unhealthful relationship. We will look first at some examples of what happens when clergy and parishioners disagree, and then consider the notion of *collusion*, when clergy and congregation mutually support a destructive relationship.

When Worlds Collide

Because there is so much social interaction in the ministry, it seems likely that few of the conflicts that a minister experiences will be either purely internal or external in origin. Even if a conflict seems to be external in origin, it will interact with the minister's own sense of what he should do in the situation. As one team of researchers has put it:

The roles a minister performs in society today are basically subject to two or more interpretations. On the one hand, the church has a traditional set of norms by which [the minister] is expected to be guided. On the other hand, the church member has a set of functional expectations by which the minister's performance is to be judged. *This is the minister's dilemma. The clergy face basic ambiguities concerning which roles they are to perform.* To add further confusion to the issue, there are the various roles with which the clergy feel most comfortable or enjoy the most, and roles in which they feel particularly effective. Not only that, but the clergy possess a set of expectations about which roles they are to play.[28]

This is clearly illustrated by Samuel Blizzard's classic study of clergy roles.[29] Blizzard surveyed 690 Protestant clergymen regarding their attitudes toward six "practitioner" roles of the minister. These six roles were the following:

1. Administrator: the minister's role as manager of the parish, involving such activities as church planning and denominational assignments.
2. Organizer: involving leadership and planning in local church associations, community organizations, and the like.
3. Pastor: the minister's interpersonal functions, including counseling and visitation.
4. Preacher: having to do with the preparation and delivery of sermons.
5. Priest: the minister's role as liturgist.
6. Teacher: including church school, Bible study groups, etc.

Blizzard asked the ministers to rank order the six roles from highest to lowest in response to four questions:

1. How important is each role?
2. How effective are you in each role?
3. How much do you enjoy each role?
4. How much time do you spend in each role?

The results, which may come as no surprise to those in the ministry, are shown in table 5.1.

The most glaring discrepancy is in the administrative role. These ministers rated the role as the least important of the six and an aspect they neither feel effective in nor enjoy. Despite this, they spend more of their time in administrative tasks than in any other role.

Table 5.1
How Ministers Ranked Blizzard's Six "Practitioner" Roles

Role	How important?	How effective?	How much enjoyed?	How much time spent?
Preacher	1	1	2	3
Pastor	2	2	1	2
Priest	3	4	4	4
Teacher	4	3	3	6
Organizer	5	6	6	5
Administrator	6	5	5	1

(Note: *1* reflects highest ranking, *6* lowest.)

Blizzard's study was published in 1956. Has anything changed since then? Another team of researchers did a similar study nearly ten years later, using seventy-seven ministers in the Washington, D.C., area.[30] Compared with Blizzard's group, these ministers rated administration more important and they felt more effective in the role. One finding had not changed, however: the administrator role was still their least favorite while placing second in the amount of time it required. Furthermore, when the researchers asked the ministers to describe their weekly activities in more detail, they found that pastors consistently underestimated the amount of time spent in administration.

Our own pilot study of Doctor of Ministry students still shows administration as the role that consumes the largest share of their time. These ministers estimated that on average more than 27 percent of their work week was devoted to administrative tasks. We think it is safe to say, however, that nowhere close to that percentage of their seminary training focused on administrative skills.

Ministers come to their profession with their own ideas about roles. There are those they view as important, those they enjoy and feel comfortable in, and those they feel equipped to handle. The pastors' histories and training lead them to expect a personal but vaguely defined picture of parish ministry. They may be surprised to find, however, that their expectations clash with reality once they have settled into a church. The more adaptable minister will find ways to learn the skills he needs and to impart some of his own vision to his parishioners. The less adaptable minister may become seriously disillusioned.

This is a simple example of internal/external role conflict. What the pastor is required to do externally may conflict with what he wants or likes to do. Does this mean that the pastor should simply seek to be joined to a church whose expectations match his own? Yes and no. In one sense it is helpful and necessary to have some basic areas of agreement. There must of course be some compatibility between a pastor and congregation on matters such as basic doctrine and vision for ministry. Beyond such explicit and conscious issues, however, there can be a multitude of less conscious factors. Unless recognized, these factors can draw a minister and congregation into a relationship that is unhealthy even though their expectations mesh. This brings us to the subtle notion of *collusion*.

When Pastor and Parish Collude

A dictionary definition of *collusion* is "a secret agreement for fraudulent or illegal purpose" or "a conspiracy." The term has been borrowed by therapists to describe how married couples conspire together to keep an unhealthy relationship intact while at the same time refusing to acknowledge that it is indeed unhealthy. The marriage is based, not on mutual strengths, but on a dovetailing of mutual weaknesses: you have what I need, and I have what you need. But instead of the spouses learning from each other, they use each other to fill the holes in their personalities. The "secret" is that they are usually not aware they are doing this. Their "purpose" is to feel whole. By colluding in this way, however, they are defrauding themselves; the relationship may be "whole," but the individuals are not.[31]

Jim and Jenni Shapiro, for example, each brought a sackload of unresolved family issues to their marriage. Jim grew up in a family that placed a strong emphasis on achievement and success, but not on personal relationships, love, and acceptance. As a child he learned quickly that if he wanted approval from his parents, he had to perform. And perform he did: he walked early, talked early, and seemed to outstrip his peers in every aspect of development, much to his parents' delight.

Of course, much of Jim's rapid progress can be attributed to a level of inborn potential that not every child has. But more important is the kind of response he got from his parents and the type of relationship it helped to create. Jim received little attention from his parents except when he did something remarkable. His parents took great pride in showing him off to visitors. Obviously, though, he could not be a prodigy every minute of every day. His parents lavished him with attention and praise only when he was performing. Between performances they did little to make him feel loved and wanted simply because he was their child. He was largely ignored during the more routine times of the day.

This may seem harmless enough on the surface. But it left a large gap in Jim's sense of his own worth. He was an intensely driven man in nearly all aspects of his life. It was as if he feared that his entire sense of identity would fall to the ground unless he kept performing and succeeding. Jim started his own business and poured himself into it as if his life depended on it. The business turned a tidy profit the first year and continued to grow. He was known throughout the community as a tireless entrepreneur. In the eyes of his neighbors he was someone to be admired for his energy, stamina, determination, and talent for making things happen. Thus Jim's overzealous and intense way of life was constantly rewarded and praised by his peers. No one thought to ask how this was affecting him physically or emotionally.

In his personal relationships Jim continued to have a need for someone who would love and accept him. The problem was that he didn't know how to find and receive love for just being himself. All he knew how to do was to perform for praise. So Jim set out in search of a wife who would admire him, look up to him, idolize him. This wasn't a conscious decision. He did it because it was the only thing he could do.

Jim found a perfect complement in Jenni. She was born into a family with fairly traditional values. Her father was a successful businessman who traveled frequently. Her mother did not have a job and did not want one. She was content to raise Jenni and take care of her husband as her job.

Unfortunately, Jenni's parents divorced when she was still young. After the divorce, Jenni lived with her mother, who, lacking valuable job skills, had to struggle to make ends meet. Jenni's mother spent nearly every waking hour trying to keep their small household together. She worked odd hours at whatever job she could find. At home she tried to keep a clean house and to make sure Jenni was properly clothed and fed. But spending personal time with her daughter was a luxury she felt she could not afford.

Jenni found little to admire about her harried and frustrated mother. She was too young to fully appreciate her mother's struggles. What she needed was someone to idolize, and her successful father fit the bill. To Jenni, Dad was a glamorous object of worship. Whenever he came to visit, he entered with a grand flourish, bearing expensive gifts for his girl. He relished her devotion; it made him feel better about leaving her and satisfied his own need to be constantly one-up on his ex-wife. But he was not the father Jenni made him out to be. Though he was allowed to visit every other weekend, he would show up only erratically. Often he would cancel his visitation plans to fly off somewhere to close a business deal and neglect to tell either Jenni or her mother. But this did not tarnish Jenni's starry-eyed image of her dad. She went on daydreaming about how important he must be to have to fly away to distant lands on a moment's notice.

Her inability to see her father's lack of commitment betrayed how much Jenni needed to have a parent she could admire. Jenni was never really encouraged to develop a sense of worth and identity. Her mother was always too busy to be encouraging. Her father was so wrapped up in his need for success that he was ineffective at helping his daughter feel successful in her own right.

Jenni's major source of self-worth, then, was her basking in her father's reflected glory. As an adult she sought to marry someone who would have enough success and glory for both of them, someone through whom she could experience the fullness of life. When the handsome and ambitious Jim Shapiro breezed into her life, Jenni was swept off her feet. They had dated barely three months when Jim proposed marriage. To their friends they seemed an ideal and happy couple.

What their friends could not see, however, was that their perfect union consisted of two half-people making one whole. Jenni idolized her new husband because she had no sense of her strengths or her worth as a person. And Jim needed her reverent adoration to assure him that he was worthy of someone's love. Their respective needs dovetailed perfectly. But their marriage could and should be more than this.

Meeting a strong emotional need, making up for losses in one's personal history, may be a precondition to growth. But it is not identical to growth itself. It is like a person dying of thirst. All he or she can think about is that life-saving drink of water; but beyond that critical moment of survival it would be wrong to believe that water is all one needs to live. So it is for Jim and Jenni. They are enmeshed in a relationship where they depend on each other for emotional survival. Their relationship is stable in the sense that they are highly motivated to stay together. But this is a relationship of weakness, not of strength. In a healthier, more differentiated marriage, the couple unites by choice rather than necessity.

The story of the Shapiros illustrates the nature of collusion. And it requires only a small step to apply the notion of collusion to the relationship between a minister and a congregation. Suppose Jim is a minister rather than a self-made entrepreneur. Do you know any ministers whose careers have the same quality of drivenness that Jim's does?

Is it difficult to imagine a congregation adoring its pastor in much the same way that Jenni adored Jim? Instead of thinking about Jim Shapiro starting a business, think of Reverend Shapiro planting a church. What does he bring to the task? He has energy and charisma, the power to hold people's attention and motivate them. These are all valuable gifts. But he also brings his personal history and the needs associated with it. It is not the glory of God that Jim is striving for, but his own glory and the feeling of worth that it gives him.

What kind of congregation will Jim draw to himself? If his vision for ministry were clearly differentiated from his personal needs, he would probably try to draw key people from the community with whom he could create a shared sense of mission. The mission, however, is a personal one. Many of those he gathers into his new church will not be looking, if truth be told, for a place to worship God. Rather, they will be looking for a human leader, a powerful person to worship and admire. The congregation's sense of identity will be less rooted in their relationship to God than in their pride of their dynamic pastor.

We don't want to overstate the case or draw a caricature. The essence of collusion in the ministry is not bound to the specifics of this particular example. Others could be created. The point is that just because the minister and the congregation agree on the minister's role, it does not follow that the role is realistic. If we look closely at a congregation that seems to idealize its minister, we may find that the minister idealizes his role also. Pastor and parish collude to maintain an unrealistic role because it meets their own personal or emotional needs.

Nor do we wish to create a false either-or distinction whereby churches can be classified into collusive and noncollusive categories. Any solid interpersonal relationship will have some areas of complementary need. There are pastor-parish relationships, for example, where the pastor has a need to nurture and the congregation has a need to be nurtured.[32] This need not be destructive or growth-inhibiting. As with the concept of differentiation, it is a matter of balance. If pastor and parish are relatively well differentiated, the nurturing relationship can be a positive one. If they are poorly differentiated, however, the roles can become too rigid to the point where it is no longer possible for the congregation to nurture the pastor.

Summary

In summary, the minister plays many roles. Each role may be defined differently according to the minister, the denomination, or various members of the congregation. The sheer number of possible combinations makes it likely that there will be disagreement somewhere in the church. Because there is often such a deep emotional investment in these roles on the part of both the minister and the congregation, conflicts about them may be painful.

Role conflicts may be external, rising primarily from disagreements in the congregation. They may be internal, as when the minister has adopted incompatible expectations for himself. Or they may be a combination of the two where the minister's expectations collide with those of the congregation.

Role conflict, however, is not the only problem. Sometimes there is a tacit agreement regarding the minister's role. At the same time, the role expectations may be idealized and unrealistic, or may serve to perpetuate a parasitic kind of relationship between pastor and parish. This is the notion of collusion in the ministry.

As always, we have attempted to keep a consistent ecological thrust. The role of the minister does not exist in a vacuum, but in the ongoing relationship between the minister and the congregation. Moreover, role expectations are often forged in the context of one's family history. A complete understanding of the minister's roles pushes out into wider social contexts.

One of these connected contexts, of course, is the minister's own family and marriage. We have used a fictional married couple to illustrate collusion and have applied the concept to the pastor-parish relationship. We believe this is more than just metaphor. Though the names and faces are different, the underlying processes are the same. We gain a hint of that from ministers' spouses, who may complain that "the minister is married to the church" or that "the church is the minister's mistress." It is impossible, then, to appreciate clergy marriage fully without also considering spouses' involvement in the church.

We will return to this theme when we discuss clergy family and marriage relationships in part 3. But in the next chapter we continue to examine role expectations by focusing on the minister's spouse. Let's return to the Miller family at First Church, Kirkdale, and take a closer look at their situation from Arlene Miller's point of view.

6

Married to the Minister

Arlene Miller, you will recall, bore the distinction of being married to the pastor of the First Church of Kirkdale. As far as the church members were concerned, this was virtually the sum total of her identity. Parishioners referred to her as either "Arlene" or "the pastor's wife," and they used the two terms as if the latter completely described the former. It didn't really matter that she had her own goals. She had a master's degree in education and hoped to go on to doctoral work. Eventually she wanted to teach other teachers. These aspirations helped to shape her true identity. But to the congregation she was simply the pastor's wife. And Arlene was never comfortable with this, even though she was enthusiastic about her husband's ministry and was otherwise devoted to the church.

Living in a parsonage was a constant source of stress, for it made it more difficult for Arlene to find an escape from the confines of her churchly role. But even when things were going well with the ministry, the parsonage never quite seemed like home to her. It always seemed like somebody else's. In an effort to create a sense of ownership, Arlene proposed a few items of redecorating. The board politely turned down her request, saying that the church budget for the year was too tight. Then she suggested she could pay for the modifications herself by taking a part-time teaching job if the church would simply give permission for the changes to be made. This request was turned down also and, Arlene thought, a little less politely than the first one.

Inwardly Arlene realized that the parsonage was not the only issue. What she really wanted was to work, and she hoped that the money needed for the modifications would provide a good excuse for getting a job. But she knew, even before she asked, that the request would be denied. Thus she decided to take a teaching job anyway. Some members of the congregation, and of the board in particular, took her decision as a personal insult. Nobody, however, wanted to provoke an open conflict. The only outward signs of the congregation's discontent were the hushed conversations around the church grounds on Sunday mornings.

Then Arlene decided to sign up for evening classes at the local community college. This would not have been a problem in itself except that one of the class sessions met on the same night as the women's group that Arlene was supposed to chair. She gave the group ample advance notice and appointed a capable woman to lead the group in her absence. They nodded and seemed to accept her announcement graciously, making broad and innocuous comments about the value of education and so on. Privately, however, some of the women wondered where this streak of independence would take her. Soon, they predicted, the pastor's wife will abandon her responsibilities altogether.

At first, Arlene ignored the murmurings and trusted that the discontent in the congregation would gradually subside. What she couldn't see was how her refusal to face the situation more squarely was helping to fuel the fire. Eventually she realized that certain parishioners were simply not going to adjust to her diminished involvement in the church. Arlene felt trapped and resentful. So she decided to confide in Bonnie, the wife of one of the church's lay leaders. Arlene was understandably cautious at first, allowing only a little of her anger to show. But Bonnie was understanding, and Arlene began to open up more and more. Soon the two women were having coffee together every week, and Arlene looked forward to those times as therapeutic.

Then her worst nightmare came true. The emotional triangles that had been silently proliferating erupted into a church split, and Bonnie sided against her. Everything that Arlene had revealed in her weekly gripe sessions now became public knowledge. She was betrayed and humiliated.

The Miller family eventually left Kirkdale to take up another ministry at a parish in a distant state. Arlene never fully understood the role conflicts that had brought her grief at the Kirkdale church. She never recognized her lack of differentiation or the way that she had triangled Bonnie into her problems. She learned only one thing from her experience: that she would never be close friends with a parishioner again.

*   *   *

Obviously, the parish pastor is not the only one who feels the pressure of congregational expectations. Much of what we said in the previous chapter about ministers can also be applied to the minister's wife.[1] She too must deal with external definitions of her role. And like her husband, she has internal expectations that may conflict with what others expect of her. Although in many cases expectations placed on the minister's wife will be less intense than those for the pastor, she may not receive the compensation of support and role status that her husband enjoys. Often it is simply assumed by all that the minister's wife is part of a package deal with the minister, without recognition that she may have personal goals independent of her husband's ministry. As one frustrated minister's wife has written: "Are we just his wife? Or also his unpaid assistant?"[2]

It is just as important for clergy wives to understand their sources of role conflict as it is for their pastor-husbands. In this chapter we will try to build on the foundation of previous chapters while introducing issues relating more specifically to pastors' wives. We will first reexamine "the glass house syndrome" from the wives' perspective. Second, we will show how congregational expectations can lead to loneliness and social isolation. Finally, we will take a broader view and show how the clash between traditional and modern expectations creates role conflicts for clergy wives.

Clergy Wives in the Glass House

Clergy wives, like their husbands, are confronted with strong expectations of their roles. Such expectations are neither good nor bad in themselves. For some women the role of minister's wife is rewarding. For others it is suffocating. Wallace Denton has written:

The role of the minister's wife has built into it certain potentiali-
ties which can be an asset to mental health. But the role can be
equally devastating. Most wives find the role deeply meaningful.
However, the wife who seriously feels that she is trapped in a role
with rigid expectations from the church, community—and possibly from the husband and herself—is the wife who is likely to
need and seek counseling. This person may feel whatever individuality she possesses being squeezed from her.[3]

We agree with Denton that most clergy wives find their role
meaningful. In our own research we asked both ministers and
their wives if they wanted to stay in the ministry. Of the 117
wives who responded, 52 percent indicated they were eager to
continue and an additional 29 percent said that although they
were willing to leave, they preferred to stay.

But what of the others? Nineteen percent of the wives, nearly
one out of five, was either neutral on the matter or actually
preferred to leave. This is a much higher figure than for the
pastors, where only 4 percent of the 124 men in our survey
wanted to leave the ministry. This suggests that although most
clergy wives seem relatively content, there are important
differences between how they and their minister-husbands
experience their roles.

This is essentially an ecological question. To approach the
matter of the clergy wife's role ecologically means that we must
pay attention to the sources and kinds of expectations and how
they interact. It is not enough to make generalizations about
whether it is good or bad, easy or difficult, fulfilling or
restricting to be a minister's wife. The role can be all those
things in different degrees, in different ways, with different
women in different congregations.

There are many possible reasons why a clergy wife who fits
Denton's description may feel her individuality being choked.
First, it may be that the congregation has unreasonable and
inflexible expectations. Second, her husband may put pressure
on her, either because of his own narrowly defined expectations
or because of pressure that the congregation is putting on him.
Third, she may have unrealistic expectations of herself that were
acquired earlier in life.

These are some of the different sources of expectations. As we
argued in the last chapter, however, there is also the ecological
question of *fit*. Congregational expectations may be more rigid

for some aspects of a wife's role than for others. If she is fortunate, expectations in these areas will not conflict with her own understanding of her role. If she is less fortunate, the congregation will be least flexible in the areas that are most sensitive to her. Let's say, for example, that there is a clergy wife who is adept at social organization and handling congregational business, but because of her childhood experience she lacks confidence as a mother to her young children. She and her husband have received offers from two churches and are trying to decide which offer, if any, they will accept.

Congregation A wants the pastor's wife to be virtually a co-minister. She is expected to oversee the educational ministry, the women's auxiliary, the missions program, and so on. The previous minister's wife in that church had spent a great deal of time educating parishioners about family life and had been very open about her struggles. Congregation B has a larger pastoral staff and thus they need a senior minister more than a pastor-wife team. Informally, however, the spouse will be expected to be a model wife and mother.

This minister's wife would have very different experiences in the two congregations. This is why the ecological view is important. Whether the question is which church to choose or how to understand the one she's already in, the pastor's wife must think in terms of how her personal characteristics fit with the demands of the social environment. This requires that she evaluate herself and her environment honestly and accurately.

The stresses of the clergy wife's role can be thought of in terms of the problems of idealization, intrusion, and impoverishment that we introduced in chapter 3. Idealization means that the pastor's wife is expected to be superhuman, an ideal role model for the women in the church. Intrusion has to do with physical and/or psychological violations of the family's boundaries. Impoverishment is the condition of a clergy wife's being constrained from developing personal friendships within or outside of the congregation.

When we asked clergy wives to identify the greatest disadvantage of being in the ministry, many cited a lack of privacy. One wife wrote more specifically, "I have the feeling that we're being watched." This intrusiveness can be joined with idealization so that a clergy wife feels the congregation watching to see whether she is living up to their expectations. Another wife wrote, "I don't like the feeling of being in the fishbowl, especially worrying about whether people will be scandalized if they see me doing things they don't approve of."

This double problem of intrusive idealization is a common theme in our survey responses. We had given a list of problems common to clergy families and asked the wives to rate the degree of severity in their own family.[4] We found that one problem in particular—the lack of freedom to be themselves— was closely related to clergy wives' wanting to leave the ministry. We asked the wives to name the most difficult thing about being a clergy wife. Here is a sampling of their answers:

Living up to the image people expect you to be.

Not having a life apart from the church, and living up to members' expectations.

Fighting feelings that I must be a certain type of person.

People who feel I am a little more than human.

Feeling that I'm always on display, that I can't be myself.

The feeling of being under observation in all circumstances.

Again, not all clergy wives experience these pressures to the same degree. In a recent study Duane Alleman asked the following question of 228 pastors' wives from four denominations (Assemblies of God; Presbyterian Church [U.S.A.]; United Methodist Church; and Episcopal Church): "To what extent do you experience pressure to conform to a certain role as a pastor's wife?" Forty-nine percent of the women responded that they experienced at least moderate pressure. The other half cited little or no pressure.[5] Alleman also asked whether they felt free to be themselves. Here 71 percent of the women felt either complete or considerable freedom; 23 percent, moderate freedom; and the remaining 6 percent, little or no freedom.[6]

We do not know precisely what percentage of clergy wives experience these role pressures. The information we have does indicate that while the demands to conform to a particular role and the lack of freedom to be themselves are not universal, they are common experiences. Each clergy wife must try to understand the role demands within her particular social context. We will consider the content of that role toward the end of this chapter. For now, we must also address another consequence of being idealized: the clergy wife's isolation from the supportive friendships she craves.

The Social Isolation of the Pastor's Wife

A prevalent theme in the literature on clergy wives is *loneliness and social isolation*. Ministers' wives consistently express a desire for close friends with whom they can be honest and open and with whom they can share the emotional burdens of the ministry. More than anything else, some clergy wives want to be accepted for who they are: real people with real struggles. Because of the idealization of their role, however, they feel cut off from the informal social fellowship that other members of the church enjoy. Asked what one thing the church could do to improve her family's life, a survey respondent answered:

> Love us more and invite us into their homes. I grew up wanting to be a pastor's wife. But it's a lot different than I expected. My biggest frustration is that it somehow makes a spiritual life at home difficult. When we don't feel like going to church, we have to, and we can't talk to anybody about it. We aren't close friends with members. I'd like to be involved in a prayer-study group, but with people with whom I could be totally open, people whom I could ask, "Am I a Christian?" I met once with a group of ministers' wives, but they all seemed to have it together. No one opened up and said, "I'm a frustrated, confused Christian." I may anonymously join a study group outside of my denomination so that I can be open. I need it so badly. I want to be a Christian, but am dying from a lack of open fellowship and nurture. Help!

This minister's wife wants to be treated as an equal, nothing more. But in her idealized role she appears to others as "the pastor's wife" rather than a flesh-and-blood person with the same spiritual struggles other Christians face. Without supportive friendships in which she feels free to be honest she may lack the resources she needs to cope with the stresses of ministry. Marietta Hobkirk wrote:

> [The minister's wife] is always making a choice among goods; and no matter which she chooses she is likely to meet some criticism. Now other wives have similar problems; but most women have an emotional outlet of some kind. . . . Ministers wives seem singularly lacking in this respect.[7]

This lack of an emotional outlet leads to the loneliness that many clergy wives experience.

In chapter 3 we identified impoverishment as one of the boundary problems faced by clergy families. These families often find themselves in a dilemma: because of their social position they cannot make friends within the congregation, while the time and energy demands of the ministry prevent them from making friends outside it. This is especially true of the wives:

> The loneliness of the minister's wife is partly attributable to an attitude expressed by many of them that there should be no close friendships among parishioners. Since church people provide the main social contacts outside the home for most of the wives, they simply have few close friends.[8]

This quotation gives a clue as to why many minister's wives have a rule against forming friendships with parishioners. Yet not every woman responds in the same way to the idealization of her role. We suspect that the other clergy wives appeared to "have it all together" because they *wanted* to appear that way.

This is the notion of the *pseudo-self*, which we discussed in chapter 2. To an extent, the pseudo-self is like a character played by an actress. The character is a fictive creation, designed to fit the environment of the story. Although an actress may give her best performance when she can identify with the character she portrays, it is still a portrayal. The character may represent some unexpressed portion of her personality, but it is not identical with her true self.

All of us are performers; all of us have some level of pseudo-self. We are given roles in each of our social contexts, and we learn to play them with a certain degree of finesse. This need not be a problem unless one of two things happens: (1) we can learn to play a role so well that others will confuse the performance with the performer and refuse to acknowledge any behavior that is out of character, or (2) the performer herself may lose the boundary between the stage and real life. For her, life itself becomes a performance, and she becomes nothing but a character in a story.

Either situation makes it psychologically possible for the clergy wife to accept the idealization of the congregation. These undifferentiated responses have dire consequences. Consider the first instance. If parishioners expect her to have it all together, then that is how she will behave. So she may fool others into thinking that she really is the ideal image they want her to be and in this way reduce the pressure of their expectations. Once she does this, however, the other people will not remove her from the pedestal no matter how much she insists that she was just play-acting. Once she performs the ideal role in earnest, the other characters in the play will not let her drop it because they want to keep the play going according to the script.

The second problem can be more severe, for she is fooling not just others, but herself also. Here the minister's wife *wants* to be the ideal that others set for her, and she suppresses all evidence to the contrary, keeping the truth even from herself. Lacking confidence, she creates an aura of confidence. Feeling insecure in her own spiritual life, she affects ultraspirituality. She creates the character she believes she should have, and then she lives as if the character were real.

Either way the wife reinforces the idealization that separates her from the honest relationships she needs as a human being. The clergy wife who has a rule against being friends with a parishioner should ask herself the purpose of it. Is it to maintain a more separate, ideal role? That purpose itself may explain some of the stress she experiences in her ministry.

There are other reasons for avoiding friendships with parishioners. Some clergy wives have become emotionally guarded because of negative experiences. One minister's wife wrote the following:

> A couple in the church we attended before we went into the ministry became very involved with their pastor and his wife. They went out together every Saturday . They were so close that they excluded and neglected others in the church. It caused much jealousy and resentment. Eventually the problem became so intense that it caused the pastor and his wife to leave the church. Seeing this happen made me very cautious in forming friendships in our own church.[9]

Another minister's wife recorded a more direct experience:

> Not long after we had come to the church, I formed a great friendship. Something inside me said not to get too close, but I was hungry for a close friend, so I did anyway. We talked a lot; she

> knew when someone in the church offended me, and she knew my
> personal feelings about the church. Later, we had a split in the
> church, and she went with the other side. She betrayed *all* my
> confidences. Only if you experience this personally can you
> imagine the pain it brings.[10]

This pastor's wife is unlikely to take a parishioner as a friend
again. Unfortunately, the healing of the betrayal requires the
kind of openness to relationship in which one risks being
betrayed again.

Here, however, we must interject a word of caution. It is one
thing for a clergy wife to lament her misfortune when a friend
betrays her secrets. It is another to realize that she has been
triangling her friend all along and thus has contributed to the
split that led to the betrayal.

We recognize that everyone needs a sympathetic listener;
there is nothing wrong with that. But having someone listen to
our problems is not a solution in itself. The trap comes when we
use others to vent our emotions because it makes us feel better,
but then avoid actually taking a hand in solving the problem. A
person with a severe illness may find a drug that alleviates his
pain. It may be helpful or even necessary to use the drug to help
him tolerate the therapy needed to cure the disease. It would be
a drastic mistake, however, to rely on the drug alone, for then he
will have both an addiction and the illness. Similarly, we must
beware using friendships in ways that perpetuate triangles and
support a lack of differentiation.

So we see that clergy wives have different reasons for being
guarded about friendships. But due to the very nature of the
clergy wife's role, other people will be guarded toward her.
Clergy wives are treated differently *because* they are clergy
wives, a different species of humanity. Outside the church, their
status may be a social stigma, as this story from one minister's
wife shows:

> I worked in a hospital in Indiana for three years. While I was there,
> a nurse returned to work after fifteen years away. I was assigned to
> help her become oriented again to nursing. We had some good
> times together. Then one day as we were working, another nurse
> asked a question about my husband's ministry. The look that came
> over the face of the new nurse was almost comical. "Your husband
> is a minister? Oh, I had better be good now!" Even though we
> were still friends, there now was a reserve in her attitude. She no

longer was relaxed with me because she had some preconceived idea of the level of spirituality a minister's wife must have.[11]

Within the church, their role elevates clergy wives above the common fellowship. This theme surfaced clearly when we asked wives what the church could do to improve their family life. Here are some of the responses:

Be our friends and do not exclude us from fellowship apart from church activities.

Accept us as real people just like themselves.

Spend time just visiting us.

Accept us as fellow members of the church.

Socialize with us outside of church functions.

Have more fellowship with us outside of church.

Accept us for who we are and ignore the roles we represent.

Accept us as one of the church members with *love*.

Despite the great difficulties in making friends either within the congregation or without, not all clergy wives feel obstructed in this way. Alleman asked the women in his study, "How free do you feel to develop close friends within your church?" About one-fourth of the women responded, "Totally free," and another fourth answered, "Fairly free." The most common response, however—35 percent—was that they felt "some constraint." The remaining wives, just under 14 percent, said they did not feel free to make friends in the congregation.[12] Overall, Alleman found the following patterns:

— 21 percent of clergy wives surveyed, or more than one in five, had no close friends in the parish;

— 44 percent had only one or two close friends;

— 35 percent had three or more;

— about 58 percent had at least one close friend who was also a minister's wife in the same denomination;

— fewer than 19 had friends who were pastors' wives of other denominations;

— more than 80 percent had close friends outside the parish.[13]

Thus, not all clergy wives find themselves at a loss for friends. For those who do, we have a final word of caution. One study of how clergy wives cope with the stresses of their role unearthed an interesting pattern: they tend to use coping strategies that keep them isolated. The authors of the study, Theodore Hsieh and Edith Rugg, wrote:

> It seems that the evangelical ministers' wives tend to refrain from those activities that are relatively more tangible or concrete in their involvement of people. . . . She tends to consider helpful those activities that she can do alone. She desires a higher degree of self isolation or insulation.[14]

Among the coping strategies reported as helpful, the four most common responses concerned an individual relationship with God. Other popular responses involved what Hsieh and Rugg summarize as "developing self-reliance and self-esteem," coping strategies that are also individually rather than interpersonally oriented. The coping behaviors that involved other people were limited either to relationships within the boundaries of the immediate family, or to other ministers' wives.[15] Unfortunately, seeking solace from family members is not likely to help clergy wives cope with family problems. And while friendships with other pastors' wives can be helpful, the time demands on both ends may make it difficult to maintain such relationships on a meaningful level.

We are primarily concerned that pastors' wives may trade one source of problems for another. Like their husbands, they may become "people saturated" and seek solitude as a way of replenishing their emotional reserves. If all or most of their coping strategies are directed away from people, however, they may encourage a self-perpetuating cycle of social isolation.

Thus the triple threat of idealization, intrusion, and impoverishment can plague the life of a pastor's wife. These are matters of her relationship to the congregation and mutual expectations of her role. Other members of the clergy family may face similar difficulties. One aspect of the wife's role difficulties, however, does not apply to her husband nor her children. As a woman, she alone is subject to the ambiguities surrounding the recent evolution of women's roles.

The Changing Role of the Minister's Wife

The consciousness-raising effect of the women's movement in this country has created a dilemma for many ministers' wives.

On the one hand, they may find themselves in situations where significant aspects of their role are still as they were thirty years ago. On the other hand, they may have more alternatives available that have little to do with their role at the church. In other words, they may find themselves trying to fulfill both traditional and modern expectations.

Traditionally the role of the minister's wife was seen as part of a two-person career.[16] That is, the minister's wife was automatically assumed to be part of a two-person ministry team along with her husband; she is hired when he is hired. This is illustrated in a 1964 panel discussion in which ministers' wives were asked, "Is it possible to be just an ordinary wife and church member, or would one's husband's work be affected by this?" One woman responded:

> Certainly it is possible but it is not pulling one's weight in the team and does not make for happiness. If you are not interested in what he is doing, and he has little time to be interested in whatever it is you are doing instead of helping him, what sort of basis is this for a happy marriage?[17]

At least three assumptions in her reply help us to see the traditional role more clearly. First, the minister's wife is expected to share in her husband's ministry. To do otherwise is viewed as a moral failure, a refusal to "pull her own weight." Second, her failure to support her husband in this way will cause her marriage to suffer. Third, there is clearly a double standard. The focus is entirely on the importance of the minister's role, and the wife is expected to follow along. The ministry is, of course, important; but the resulting attitude is that unless his wife is working beside him, it is to be expected that the minister will be too busy to take any interest in what his wife is doing.

Similar traditional assumptions of the role of the clergy wife seem to undergird the widely known study of ministers' wives conducted by William Douglas, published in 1965.[18] Based on their attitudes and patterns of behavior, Douglas classified ministers' wives in one of three types: teamworker, background supporter, or detached.

Teamworkers exhibited the essence of the traditional clergy wife's role. They engaged in side-by-side ministry with their husbands and shared his sense of calling. Because they were intrinsically motivated to share in the responsibilities of the ministry, they experienced little or no strain associated with their roles as ministers' wives.

Wives labeled as background supporters could still be enthusiastic about the ministry, but did not see their roles as working side-by-side with their husbands. Those who were satisfied to remain in the background often viewed their family responsibilities as their top priority. This emphasis on the family, too, fits the traditional expectations for a clergy wife. If she cannot be both a co-minister and an exemplary wife and mother, let her be the latter. In general, the background supporters were just as motivated to participate in the church's ministry as any other involved layperson.

Other background supporters wanted to be helpful, but felt frustrated and inadequate. These women, according to Douglas, took longer to feel content in their roles as ministers' wives. Reading between the lines, it seems as if they believed they should be traditional teamworkers, but the role was like an ill-fitting garment. Their frustration and sense of inadequacy came from the gap between what they were and what they felt they were supposed to be.

As the label implies, the detached wives did not participate with their husbands in ministry. Some were detached on principle: the principle that a minister's wife should be no different from any other Christian. Douglas found that these women were still strongly committed to the church. Other wives, however, were detached in rebellion. They found the role of minister's wife to be frustrating and confining, and they were in constant competition with the church for their husbands' time. When these wives participated in parish ministry at all, the motivation was to gain more time with their husbands.

The point is that a clergy wife in rebellion is rebelling against the traditional role. The role expectation that she will minister at her husband's side still makes itself felt. Even those who consider themselves detached on principle may do so defensively against the intrusive expectations of others and their own discomforting doubts.

The typology therefore reflects a traditional understanding of the role of the minister's wife. In his more detailed discussion of the three types, Douglas notes that teamworker wives are psychologically better adjusted than detached wives. This view was criticized by sociologist Mary Taylor in a 1977 issue of *Christian Ministry* magazine.

> [T]he wife's failure to accept the two-person career is viewed as pathology requiring therapy. . . . Given the changes that have occurred in American society and within the churches in the past decade, this view may be less common today. Nevertheless, lacking convincing evidence to the contrary, one can probably safely assume that the ministry as a two-person career is still an ideal as well as the norm and that churchly orientation persists.[19]

Yet another decade has passed since Taylor made those comments. Has society changed even more? Undoubtedly. But have the role expectations of the minister's wife changed?

The recent study by Duane Alleman indicates that a majority of pastors' wives view themselves as either teamworkers or background supporters. Alleman asked clergy wives to categorize themselves according to Douglas's typology. A full 82 percent of the women responding labeled themselves as either teamworkers (29 percent) or background supporters (53 percent).[20] This is similar to Douglas's own results from 1965. Of 4,777 clergy wives surveyed, 21 percent rated themselves as teamworkers, while 64 percent saw themselves as background supporters.[21]

There has been change, however, in the number of clergy wives who take jobs outside the church. The issue of whether or not the pastor's wife should hold her own job helps to highlight a subtle shift in her role. Robert Rankin wrote that the clergy wife who seeks employment becomes guilty of three transgressions against her traditional role.[22] First, she violates the expectation that she will exemplify to other churchwomen the maxim that "the woman's place is in the home." The second area of conflict, obviously, is that working outside the church will make her less available for the duties that she and only she is expected to fulfill.

Third, her pursuit of a separate career may lead parishioners to the disparaging conclusion that the minister's wife is more concerned about money than spiritual matters. This may result in conflicts over the pastor's salary. Parishioners may resent any request that may appear even remotely materialistic. This condition underscores the fact that in some congregations, what the clergy family say they need is less important than what the congregation thinks they should need. The minister's wife, moreover, is the one who often bears the burden of negotiating for those needs. This source of stress is captured in one parishioner's comments about her pastor's wife: "I really resent our minister's wife. She just asked our women's association to buy her a new stair carpet, when she almost never uses the parsonage for entertaining."[23] One wonders what criteria the pastor's wife would have to meet to be granted the carpet!

Over the years, however, an increasing proportion of clergy wives have taken jobs outside the church and home. In the late seventies, Taylor and her colleague Shirley Hartley surveyed 448 ministers' wives from six mainline denominations. Their results suggested a gradual shift away from the two-person career and toward a true two-career marriage. Taylor, noting that clergy wives tend to be the type of women who are well qualified for rewarding jobs, wrote, "Approximately 40% of the wives in the survey were employed outside the home, about twice the proportion Douglas found a decade earlier. . . . wives who worked outside the home spent less time in church-related activities."[24] In Alleman's more recent study, about 30 percent of the clergy wives were employed full time while another 35 percent had part-time jobs.[25]

Against the view that this movement of pastors' wives into the work place would jeopardize their marriages, Hartley wrote:

> The individualistic pursuits of the wife need not lead to decreased marital satisfaction. . . . We may expect increased similarity in the role-expectations of clergy and non-clergy wives. There are indications that clergy wives will be less and less willing to play the expected role of "gainfully employed" associate pastor in the "two-person" career.[26]

Both Alleman's study and another by Richard Blackmon would indicate that pastors are generally supportive of their wives who work. When Alleman asked eighty-four employed clergy wives if they felt their husbands supported their work, almost 93 percent responded that their spouses were either "glad" or "very glad."[27] In an earlier study, Blackmon put the same question to the pastors themselves. Of the 178 pastors who responded, 84 percent were either "glad" or "very glad" to have their wives working, while the remaining 16 percent wished their wives did not work, some voicing this strongly.[28]

Whether or not a minister's wife takes a job outside the church, however, is only a secondary issue. What is at stake is her right to define her own role, her own identity. Freedom from one role constraint may simply result in captivity to another, such as when she is "freed" from her ministry obligations to fulfill her family obligations instead or to "minister to the minister."[29]

Thus it is not only her involvement in the church that defines the traditional role of the minister's wife. She is also expected to be an exemplary wife and mother. This may include caring for the children alone while the husband is away evenings, involved in his ministry. Another minister's wife in the 1964 study wrote:

> Don't worry about being lonely in the evenings. Once the family comes along you'll probably spend many evenings blathering to a baby who hasn't learned that he ought to sleep at that time. . . . I've been a minister's wife for nearly 14 years, I've got three children and I don't remember being lonely.[30]

There is an edge of sarcasm to her words that makes us suspect that she silently and unconsciously resented both her role and her husband's absence from the home. We cannot be certain. Consciously, however, she seems to hold her role as a mother as more important than her own needs.

Traditional gender roles require that the husband be the breadwinner, looking after the family's financial needs while the wife cares for the home and family. This is particularly true for traditional clergy wives who have a position of exampleship to fulfill. Even today, when more women have jobs outside the home, there is still a tendency to make the home the wife's responsibility rather than the husband's. In such families, both spouses may be gone all day to work, but the husband will still ask his wife, "What's for dinner?" And more likely than not, she will, in fact, view cooking and other household chores as her responsibility, however grudgingly she does them.

Similarly, regardless of whether they work or not, pastors' wives seem to be more "home-focused" than pastors. For example, as the spouse who is responsible for making ends meet, the wife tends to rate the pastor's salary as less adequate than the pastor does.[31] And as we shall see again in chapter 9, when a clergy family experiences ministry-induced stress, the pastor's wife is much more likely than her husband to want to leave the ministry. We suspect that even the most "modern" pastor's wife will still retain some remnant of her traditional role, related to her family responsibilities.

The role of the clergy wife, then, is a mix of traditional and more contemporary elements. On the one hand, she may be expected to be the teamworker, actively engaged in the parish ministry. Such expectations can come from the congregation, the minister, or herself. If she is not an active part of the two-person career, she will at least be expected to model the ideal Christian wife and mother. On the other hand, the contemporary clergy wife is part of a culture where women enjoy more options. It is acceptable and even respectable for women to pursue more individualistic career goals instead of the traditional roles of wife and mother.

In this transitional era, however, many women are confused over how to balance or reconcile their traditional and modern leanings. The issue is more acute for clergy wives whose behavior is more conspicuous. In essence they cannot make truly individual decisions because others are watching to see what they do. What they decide for themselves becomes the model for other women's decisions. As one pastor's wife wrote to us, "I personally feel inadequate as a 'pastor's wife.' I hate being used as a role model; I don't like people looking at me and I feel very uncomfortable thinking people are looking at me as an example for what to wear, eat, do, etc.—which they do!"

Therefore, as a contemporary American woman the pastor's wife may wish to create an identity apart from the two-person ministry career. This may, but does not necessarily, include the possibility of committing herself to a career outside the church. If she does, she will undoubtedly alienate and displease those who hold to more traditional definitions of roles and duties.

If, however, she conforms to traditional expectations, she runs the risk of being criticized by those who will interpret such behavior as weakness and insecurity. At the very least, to the extent that she has internalized more contemporary values, she may experience a lack of fulfillment and silently denigrate herself for not developing a solid personal identity apart from her husband. She may feel secure only when she is playing the role of the minister's wife while at the same wishing she could be her own person.

We have cited Hartley's view that clergy wives will probably be less and less inclined to be one-half of a two-person career and will seek their identities elsewhere. This is not a question of their devotion to the church as Christian women, but of their expected roles as pastors' wives. When Alleman asked, "Do/did you feel called to be a minister's wife or to full-time Christian ministry?" only a little more than half of the more than two hundred women said yes. Over 34 percent said they did not feel called to the ministry, and just over 15 percent were not sure.[32] This latter group will have to find some way to mediate between their sense of identity and the congregation's expectations.

In summary, the role of the pastor's wife can be as complex as the pastor's. She, too, is often expected to fulfill superhuman expectations. These may both exhaust her and isolate her from the kind of friendships she needs to cope with the stress. Beyond this, the changing roles of women in society in general can add confusion to her already complicated role decisions. The clergy wife must develop ways of coping with her role stress that do not encourage either triangling or social withdrawal.

We have one more member of the clergy family to visit: the minister's child, commonly called the P.K. As we shall see, even the pastor's child must learn to deal with the pressures of social expectations.

7

Perfect Kids:
The Pressures of the P.K.

"People think because you are a minister's child, you have to be perfect and never fail."   —Anonymous P.K.[1]

"If a pastor is worth his or her salt and practices what he or she preaches, the P.K.s must be perfect."   —Anonymous P.K.[2]

Children are born into a world of expectations. Almost from the moment they emerge from the womb they must begin to learn about the world and what it expects of them. That world is not just physical, but social. In the physical world, for example, they will learn that falling down or touching a hot stove hurts. In the social world they will learn that failing to meet the expectations of someone we love can hurt too. As individuals, children are born with certain talents, gifts, and potential as well as weaknesses. Throughout their lives, but especially in their early years, they must learn how to adapt these God-given capabilities to the expectations of their social environment.

Parents are a particularly important source of expectations. There is something special about our children that brings out our most deep-seated convictions and strongest expectations. We want our children to have what we had. Or we want them to have what we didn't have. We want them to be what we are. Or we want them to be what we're not but always wanted to be. And so on. While the precise nature of a parent's expectations will differ from case to case, the point is that we have personally and emotionally invested in our children. For some of us it is difficult to stand back far enough to be able to distinguish clearly between who they are and our image of who we want them to be.

Though all children must learn to adapt to social expectations, the expectations placed on preachers' children (P.K.s) may be more intense than most. We have already seen how ministers can be idealized by their congregations or can even idealize their own roles. Given our emotional investment in our children, such ideals may be easily transferred to them. Because the minister's family is a family within a family, there are potentially many more expectations to which the P.K. must adapt.

In light of the negative possibilities, some of us have almost come to expect P.K.s to be poorly adjusted or to have some deficiency in their personalities. An abundance of negative stereotypes of ministers' children exists. Psychotherapists, for example, are familiar with the image of the P.K. as a tormented soul crushed under the weight of the parents' morality:

> Every experienced analyst is familiar with ministers' children who were never allowed to have so-called bad thoughts and who managed not to have any, even at the cost of a severe neurosis. . . . [The parents] have attempted to stifle or have actually stifled the child's vitality by making impossible moral demands.[3]

Certainly this rather bleak picture will be true in some cases. There are ministers and their spouses who have never experienced any grace from their own parents and thus are unable to show grace to their children. But are all children of ministers raised in such a suffocating environment?

Contrary to simplistic negative stereotypes, there are also some benefits to being reared in a clergy family. In one survey study, for example, a minister's wife wrote the following: "We have had people in our home whom other children have never had the benefit of knowing: African pastors, foreign missionaries, evangelists, other preachers. Our kids have been able to talk to them, play games with them, and find out more about the world and what makes people tick."[4] Thus, though there are hazards that may be unique to the clergy family, there are also unique advantages. P.K.s have access to people, cultures, and experiences that would enrich the life of any child. Indeed, many ministers' children are satisfied with their lives, as this response from a 16-year-old minister's daughter shows:

I'm very glad I am a pastor's kid—they have sheltered me from most of the world's garbage and I have obtained a solid foundation for my future. But there is one thing that I can do for my dad which would show my support for his ministry; it is to love God with all my heart, mind, and soul, and follow him for the rest of my life. My dad is a wonderful, fun, terrific person!

Ups and downs characterize the life of a minister's child. For some, there are more ups than downs. No stereotype, either positive or negative, is sufficient to capture the complexity of a P.K.'s life. We need to get away from one-dimensional questions about the emotional health of P.K.s in general. Instead, we must focus on patterns of interaction and expectation, trying to understand both the positive and negative influences on a P.K. In keeping with our ecological theme, we will examine the life of ministers' children from three perspectives. First, we will look at the role of the minister and his wife as parents. Second, we will focus specifically on the expectations that congregations and peer groups place on ministers' children. Finally, as a model for understanding how the stresses placed on the minister can also cause problems for the P.K., we will revisit the notion of triangling.

Preacher, Pastor, and Parent

As we saw in the previous two chapters, the minister and his wife have many roles to fulfill. They must care for both their own family and the congregational family. Sometimes, in shuttling back and forth between roles, they may lose track of the boundaries between the families. For example, J. C. Wynn tells of a pastor who overheard an argument between his two young daughters. The preacher was brought up short when he heard one girl say to the other, "You'd better be careful or Daddy will mention in a sermon what you've been doing."[5] What the pastor belatedly realized was that in his role as a preacher he had invaded the privacy of his children. On further reflection he also realized that he often related to his girls more as a pulpit-pounder than as a father.

Many other pastors get caught in a similar bind. Paul Haakenson tells of one P.K. who was trying to communicate with his father, but felt that he was being treated like one of the parishioners. The young man exploded, "I'm not some member of the congregation; I am your son!"[6] The pastor had responded to his son from his pastoral role rather than as his father. The son in turn had experienced this as a violation of their special relationship. In that moment, in failing to respond as a father, the pastor made his son feel brushed aside and depersonalized. J. C. Wynn has said it best:

> It is ironical that many a clergyman, long trained in the area of social psychology, still handles family relationships as the pulpiteer. Even though he knows full well that behavior is more effectively altered by relationships that include love and encouragement, he may continue to preach at and preach about his own offspring. He is too likely to get at his own children by means of stern lectures, lengthy precepts, and finger-shaking commands. What Queen Victoria said of Gladstone might well be echoed by many a child of the parsonage: "He insists upon addressing me as if I am a public audience."[7]

Would P.K.s say the same of their parents, particularly of the pastor? In some cases apparently, they would.

As we will see clearly in the next chapter, the ministry can place a great strain on a clergy family's time and energy. A pastor who is emotionally drained and short on family time may occasionally resort to preaching at the children. It is, after all, easier to preach at them than to listen to them. None of us can do what is best for a relationship all the time. When we are under pressure, we often do what seems easiest. For some pastors, preaching at the kids is a quick-fix to regain a sense of control over the household. Realistically, occasional parental quick-fixes are a fact of life. The question is whether or not we know how to do anything else. Do clergy parents distinguish between what is appropriate in their role as ministers versus their role as parents? What is appropriate at church may be inappropriate at home. It is one thing to preach at our kids occasionally; it is quite another matter when preaching is the only way we relate to our children.

Professionals in many fields must learn to keep clear boundaries between professional and family life, between their roles in the office and at home. Marriage counselors and psychologists, for example, can get themselves in trouble by pulling back and analyzing their spouses' behavior in the middle of an argument. Likewise, attorneys may resort to cross-examining their spouses and children rather than communicating in a more balanced fashion. The problem is not that counselors and attorneys can't tell the difference between their clients and their families. It is rather that when we feel anxious or insecure, we slip into the roles that make us feel more in control.

There are times in all family relationships when we feel threatened or unsure of ourselves: when we are arguing with a spouse, disciplining a child, and so on. We feel the force of our unvoiced doubts: Who is right? Am I wrong again? Am I doing the right thing?

It matters what we do with our uncertainty. Do we slip into other roles that give us an edge? There is the counselor who expertly analyzes his wife's behavior but is oblivious to his own. There is the attorney whose swift questioning makes her husband and children trip over their own words while she herself is unassailable. The better approach would be to tolerate the uncertainty and not grasp at the things that would make us feel more powerful than the other person. This kind of vulnerability keeps us in a true person-to-person interaction. To be able to do this, however, requires at least a fair level of differentiation and a willingness to take a risk. Without these, we are more likely to choose the security of the roles that make us feel more in control.

Pastors and their spouses must all learn the difference between being ministers and being parents. Moralizing may work in the pulpit, but it doesn't work at home. Church members may be willing to listen to a long sermon; they may even expect it. But the P.K. needs something other than a sermon from his or her parents. The P.K. needs to see the minister as a real person who understands the foibles of real people and the fits and starts of growing up. We suspect, however, that this separation of professional and family roles is more difficult for pastors. The clients of counselors and attorneys, for example, usually know little about the professional's family life and may not care to know more. The very credibility of a pastor's ministry, however, may seem to hinge on what church members see through the walls of the glass house. There is the added pressure to be a perfect family: to be perfect spouses and perfect parents, and to rear perfect kids.

This makes it all the more difficult for the pastor and his wife to be patient and understanding. In response to congregational pressure they may impose greater restrictions and hope that the P.K. won't rock the boat. But where the personal and religious development of our children are concerned, moral rules are poor substitutes for a solid parent-child relationship.

Consider, for example, the research that relates parenting style to the religious commitments of children. One study found that when parents (and other authority figures) are inconsistent and authoritarian, their children are more likely to feel alienated from their parents' religion.[8]

On a more positive note, another study revealed that children who were reared in a warm and supportive environment were more likely to share their parents' religious commitments. This was true over and above the parents' attempts to influence their children's religious values directly.[9] Such research counsels us against the false hope that tightening the reins on the P.K. will insure best behavior. Rather, the spiritual development of our children depends on good parenting. Good parenting in turn requires a good relationship where the child experiences the warmth and acceptance of an empathetic parent.

The apostle Paul once wrote, "Because you are sons, God sent the Spirit of his Son into our hearts, the Spirit who calls out, 'Abba, Father.' "[10] God's love for his Son is now mirrored in his love for us; we are truly the children of God, who by the Spirit are able to call out to God as a child calls to her daddy. But does this not also teach us something about the relationship between the pastor and his children? God responds to us as a father, not as an impersonal deity, nor as someone with whom we must make an appointment to be heard. God has bridged the gap between his divinity and our humanity. We come to him personally, and he responds personally. Can the pastor afford to do less for *his* children?

None of us, of course, is perfect. Parents and children, pastors and P.K.s, share a common and fallible humanity. We are all in need of the grace that God extends to us. Consequently we must also learn to extend that grace to one another.[11] In the family, however, parents have the greater responsibility. If children are to learn anything about grace, they will learn it most deeply from their own mothers and fathers. Once that foundation has been laid, they will be able to show mercy and grace in return. It begins with parents, especially pastors and their spouses, who are willing to be vulnerable with their children. These are parents who can maintain their status as adults without having to deny their imperfect humanity.

This may be more difficult in clergy families, where superhuman perfection is often expected. Perhaps for that reason alone, to make the clergy family a community of grace becomes that much more important. One pastor has poignantly written, "I have learned more about the practice of forgiveness from my long-suffering, understanding children than they have ever gained from me. And I now understand more about the doctrine of the grace of God through family life than I have ever understood from books in theology."[12]

The Burden of Expectations: Congregation and Peers

Of course, it is not just the minister and his wife who may put pressure on the P.K. Ministers' children are often faced with unrealistic expectations from church members and their peers. This may be the case regardless of what the parents themselves expect. One minister's child has written, "I think the P.K.s' parents realize their children are the same as others—but I don't think the community/congregation realizes this—problems are sometimes *socially* imposed."[13]

Like the minister and his wife, the P.K. is somehow expected to be more than human, an example for all. In milder cases this leads to an uncomfortable self-consciousness on the child's part, a heightened sense of visibility that prevents him or her from simply being one of the crowd. A minister's wife wrote:

> One of our daughters used to complain that they would never start the youth group meeting until she was there, even though she wasn't an officer. She resented the fact that although she was usually on time, everyone noticed the times she wasn't. When others were late it didn't seem to matter, but when she wasn't quite on time it was a big deal.[14]

The special status of being the pastor's son or daughter carries with it the expectation of moral perfection. The quotation excerpted at the beginning of the chapter is very revealing:

> I've never liked being labeled a P.K. People think because you are a minister's child, you have to be perfect and never fail. But my sins are the same as everyone's, except when I fail, it's the front

page news because of who I am. You can never get away from it whether you are 12 or 60 years old.

P.K.s are not free to behave like other children because they are to be an example to the rest, as one minister's daughter indicates: "[P.K.s] are forced to be the idol of all children. They are a role model. . . . 'Oh, Lord, the pastor's daughter wore a miniskirt to church!' Seriously—my mother sent me home!"[15] In more severe cases, the expectations can be intimidating, as one minister's wife shows:

> We have a youth leader who expects more out of our teenager because he is a P.K. than the rest of the kids in our youth group. In this man's view, our son is not allowed to experience the temptations, mistakes, or failures that the average young person goes through. He is to be ultra-spiritual and mature at all times. And when he isn't, the youth leader makes it obvious to my son, as well as to those around, how he feels about it.[16]

Children of the parsonage often experience the sense of being viewed and treated as "different" outside the congregation also. Asked what it was like to be a minister's child, a twelve-year-old responded, "It's hard. Kids act like you're 'weird' or 'out of it' because you're born again. I try not to get it in the way of my friendships." Another twelve-year-old wrote, "Sometimes it isn't heaven, but it's okay. Once in a while you get teased. They might call you P.K. or little angel. But not too often do I get called any of these names." A sixteen-year-old answered that being teased at school was the most difficult part of being a minister's child. Overall, however, we must note that only four of the forty-seven children responding to our study reported that they tried to hide their identity at school. Moreover, even these four said they were glad to have fathers in the ministry.

The strength of the expectations that a P.K. must face will vary from case to case. To what extent are such expectations built on unrealistic stereotypes? In chapter 4 we discussed how our own biases can result in narrow stereotypes of what a Christian family *should* look like. This includes our perceptions of ministers' children. To have expectations of a person's behavior is one thing. To have expectations based on a stereotype creates a self-perpetuating cycle: the stereotype feeds the expectations, and our expectations reinforce the stereotype.

Parishioners' stereotypes can become a straitjacket for the

P.K., especially when they become independent of the child's actual conduct. Some people expect nothing but moral perfection from P.K.s, while others assume that they will be moral rebels.[17] The crucial factor is not whether the expectations themselves are positive or negative, but how they are used in relating to the minister's child. We will look at some negative and positive stereotypes in turn and consider what problems they pose for ministers' children.

One negative stereotype is that of the "unruly P.K." whose behavior is an embarrassment to the minister and the congregation alike. Daniel Blain has written:

> The popular concept of the profligate character of the minister's son is evidence of the distortion so common when people occupy the spotlight of prominent position. Frequently, behavior which is considered normal for the average parishioner is regarded as especially sinful when seen in the minister's family.[18]

Blain makes it clear that the stereotypes have some origin other than the child's behavior itself. That is, church members have expectations of the P.K. that are prior to, and to some extent independent of, the P.K.'s actual conduct.

The problem is that such labeling can lead to self-fulfilling prophecies. If you expect to find problems, you will. Once we put labels on a person, they are hard to remove. This is clearly demonstrated, for example, by David Rosenhan's studies of how psychiatric inpatients were evaluated and diagnosed.[19] Rosenhan had eight normal people pretend to have symptoms so that they could gain admission to hospital psychiatric wards. These eight volunteers, including three psychologists and one psychiatrist, called various hospitals for treatment. During the intake interview they falsified only three pieces of information: their names, occupations, and the claim that they had been hearing voices. All other questions, including those regarding their personal and family histories, were answered truthfully. Once diagnosed and admitted, they stopped faking any symptoms.

The hospital staff never detected the bogus patients. The staff continued to relate to the eight volunteers as actual psychiatric patients even though the pseudopatients had ceased faking symptoms. Embarrassingly enough, many of the real patients could tell the difference. At times they voiced their suspicions strongly: "There's nothing wrong with you; you must be

checking up on the hospital." Rosenhan's point was that once
the pseudopatients had been diagnosed and labeled, the psychiatric staff related to them as if the diagnoses were true, despite
any evidence to the contrary. Even normal behavior was
reinterpreted to match the clinical diagnosis. In a sense the
label took on a life of its own.

All of us are prone to the same error of forcing reality to fit our
preconceived ideas. Suppose someone were to tell you that John
Doe is a devious and hostile person. "Oh, he seems nice
enough," your confidant tells you, "but once you get to know
him a little, you'll see how cunning and manipulative he really
is." The next day you meet John Doe for the first time. He
extends his hand to you and with a warm smile says, "Hi, I'm
John. It's a pleasure to meet you." How will you react? Most
likely you will be wondering at some level, "What does he want
from me?" You may even read ulterior motives into his smile.

Suppose now that your confidant comes back to you and says,
"Hey, it was all a joke. John's really a nice guy. I was just
kidding." Can you completely erase your suspicions about John
Doe? Probably not, for two reasons. First, you may reason to
yourself, "If the first time it was a joke, how do I know he's not
kidding me now? Better be cautious just in case." Second, the
more contact you have had with John, the more likely he has
already behaved in ways that confirmed your suspicions. Being
told that it was all a joke does not change the "fact" that you
have independently "verified" the "truth" about John.

This is what makes stereotypes so dangerous. Whether they
are true or not is less important than the fact that they create
their own truth. Stereotypes resist change because they help us
to maintain our prejudices. They allow us to feel a little better
about ourselves compared with someone else. Racial bias and
racial pride, for example, go hand in hand with racial stereotyp-
ing. We can support our prejudices against certain races
different from our own by believing that they are less intelligent
than we are; they are heathens, and we are religious. We can
then relate to them as if the stereotypes were true, whether or
not they have any basis in fact. We thus create the reality that
verifies what we already wanted to believe.

In less extreme cases we may find ourselves unable to change
our perceptions for a more simple reason: we have a hard time
admitting that we were wrong. The person who was duped into

being suspicious of John Doe may take the attitude, "Fool me once, shame on you; fool me twice, shame on me." He may continue to be suspicious to avoid being fooled again. Even if he accepts his gullibility, his wounded pride will make him wary, and he will be all too ready to seize on any evidence that he was right all along.

We have taken the long way around to a simple but important point. From our ecological point of view, it is unhelpful and even dangerous to relate to P.K.s on the basis of negative stereotypes. They can become self-fulfilling prophecies, driving a wedge between us and the real person. We can leave the P.K. feeling misunderstood, trapped, and alienated.

In extreme and, we hope, rare cases, there is a further danger. Ministers' children who find themselves hemmed in by negative stereotypes may develop what Erik Erikson has called the *negative identity*.[20] The basic idea is that every human being needs to have a coherent sense of identity that pulls together the various strands of one's personal history. Most children have a chance both to see and to imitate numerous role models. It is the task of their teenage years to weave meaningful identities out of these experiences. Some children, however, have never been given a positive vision of what they could become; their formative years have been marked by continual scorn and criticism. Instead of being directed toward positive roles, they are told they will never be any good, but will turn out to be bums, prostitutes, drug addicts, or the like. These negative predictions may be the only consistent roles held out as possibilities to the child. Such prophecies will be self-fulfilling. The child is faced with a no-win choice: to have either a negative identity or no identity at all.

Some pastors and congregations are asking themselves, "What happened to the P.K.? How could the child of a minister have gone so wrong?" What they must also ask is whether they consistently related to the P.K. on the basis of negative stereotypes. This is not an all-or-nothing question. It is not as if congregations either do or don't have negative stereotypes or that P.K.s simply develop either negative or positive identities. But to the extent that we relate through negative stereotypes, we give the P.K.s the option of taking that role into their developing sense of self. It is, if you will, like giving them the ammunition to shoot themselves.

Not all expectations and stereotypes, however, are negative. The positive expectations we place on P.K.s can be just as confining. Often it is simply assumed, for example, that the pastor's son will also be a pastor one day. Church members do not necessarily try to impose this role on the P.K. in any direct way; they simply behave as if it were an obvious truth. This may happen especially when there is a long line of ministers in the family background. No one in the church even doubts that the pastor's son will follow in the footsteps of his father, his grandfather, his great-grandfather, and so on. When it comes time for the P.K. to make career choices, he may find himself in a bind. He knows that no one is forcing him to be a minister, yet he may feel guilty for even considering other options.

Positive expectations can bind the P.K. in other ways. Many children are familiar with a pattern of expectations that can be called "the tyranny of the best." No matter what they do or how well they do it, we tell them they could do better. On the face of it, there is a great difference between direct criticism and what seems to be benevolent encouragement to strive for higher goals. But encouragement can be constructive or destructive. The difference is whether or not we realistically know and accept the child's own desires, talents, and limitations. If the child feels that we accept her for who she is, she can also accept gentle encouragement to stretch herself beyond her usual limits. If we present the goal without the acceptance, however, she will feel the despair that she will never be good enough, and she may spend the rest of her life running after a goal that will always be just out of reach.

We suspect that congregations, ministers, and religiously minded people in general are capable of translating their expectations into religious language, adding an additional burden of guilt to the child. The point is not that all such expectations are invalid or that religious language has no place in a child's training. Rather, we must return to our earlier point: it is absolutely crucial that the key word in this training should be *grace*. Spiritual maturity is not guaranteed by a child's ability to meet external standards, even religious ones. Some congregations have been shocked and disillusioned at seeing P.K.s who seemed near to saintly perfection eventually rebel and leave the church. What had looked like spiritual maturity was only a shell, a role adopted by the minister's child to cope with other people's expectations.

Maturity is not something that can be donned like a coat: it must be built from the inside. For children to live a life of grace, they need to experience grace from those who care for them.

We have spent some time looking at expectations and stereotypes. Expectations can come from the minister and his spouse, the congregation, and the P.K.'s peers. Positive and negative expectations alike can be experienced by the P.K. as unrealistic or restrictive, with possible dangerous consequences for his or her emotional adjustment.

It is important to note the sources and types of expectations and pressures put on the minister's children. If we recognize the consequences of our expectations, we can do something about them. But we must push further than this. To look only at expectations and their consequences can focus our attention on a symptom and away from other underlying problems. Ecologically, we must ask what it is that keeps these expectations alive and what purpose they serve. We will argue that the pressures put on the P.K. may reflect poorly differentiated relationships, with the result being an ongoing process of triangling among the pastor, the P.K., and the congregation.

Triangles and the P.K.

As we have seen, the pressure put on the pastor may make it more difficult to be an effective and understanding parent. It is hard enough for some parents to be patient and empathetic, given their family histories and the expectations they have for their children. This is made doubly difficult for clergy parents, who are subject to the additional pressure of a congregation's expectations. Wynn has written,

> It's a pretty sure bet that the clergyman-father suffers from enough anxiety about his professional status that he projects his feelings of concern upon his sons and daughters. Evidently he has a feeling that the parishioners peer into the parsonage windows and judge him by the behavior of his family.[21]

The clergy family lives in the midst of a larger congregational family. As we will see in the next chapter, this can be good news or bad news, depending on the quality of the relationship between the two families.[22] For the moment, ask yourself the following: how can your parents make life easier or more difficult for you when you have your own children? New mothers and fathers need their parents' support, but also need to be encouraged to rear their children in their own way. It creates stress for new parents to feel that their own parents are constantly peering over their shoulders, watching their every move with the baby.

A similar feeling is true for clergy parents trying to rear children in a congregational setting. In some ways clergy parents are no different from other parents. They have the same strengths and weaknesses, the same capacity for love and patience or for anger and irrational behavior where their children are concerned. But their context, living in the midst of a congregation, makes a difference. Some congregations can be supportive and encouraging and offer a great deal of solace. Other congregations can behave like intrusive in-laws, making clergy parents feel that they live in a glass house. In such situations, how clergy parents rear their children will to some extent be determined by the kinds of pressures they face from the congregation.

Paul Haakenson provides an example. One P.K. responding to his study wrote, "We were not allowed to skip church unless we were sick or gone, not because it was such a big deal to [my parents], but I lived in a small town and *everyone* was watching and noticed when we were gone and many didn't approve."[23] Three parties are involved here: the P.K., the parents, and the congregation. The P.K. seems to be saying three things: (1) the parents didn't allow the P.K.s to skip church, (2) not because of parental displeasure, but because (3) certain members of the congregation disapproved. In this case the threat of congregational disapproval influences, if not overrides, the parents' opinion. At the very least, on an issue where a minister and spouse may be neutral regarding their children's behavior, pressure from the congregation may tip the scales.

Congregational influence is very real and should be taken into account in understanding P.K.s. The question at hand, however, is not whether the congregation should have such an influence. Nor are we trying to ask how much influence is too much. What concerns us is whether the relationships among the clergy couple, the congregation, and the P.K. are relatively differentiated and whether there are tendencies toward forming triangles. In what kinds of triangles do P.K.s get entangled? We shall address a few possibilities.

Sometimes members who have a conflict with the P.K. will triangle the minister or someone else in the congregation. Remember the quotation from the minister's wife who complained that the youth pastor had unrealistic expectations of her son? The youth pastor would not only criticize the P.K. directly, but also publicly air his criticisms to others. If this youth pastor were genuinely concerned about the P.K.'s behavior, the more appropriate and biblical approach would be to confront the child in private. Voicing his complaints publicly is an inappropriate attempt to triangle others into the conflict.

But often the P.K.'s behavior is not really the core issue. The real sticking point is that certain church members may have a conflict with the minister. Yet because it feels too threatening to confront the minister directly, they may pick a more indirect avenue of complaint: the P.K.'s behavior. They are implicitly criticizing the minister's ability to be a good parent. The clergy parents, listening to a church member complain about their children, may hear another message between the lines: "So you're not so perfect after all."

Clergy parents should suspect such triangling when church members seem to be unreasonably picky about a P.K.'s behavior. This is more than just a double standard. The congregation often does expect more from the clergy family in general and from the P.K. in particular, as we have already seen. But in some cases it seems as if the double standard itself has become an excuse for complaining to the pastor. It is triangling because the underlying conflict is really between the parishioner and the pastor, and the P.K. should not be involved at all. If you are a clergy parent and you suspect this kind of a triangle, ask yourself whether you have any unresolved conflicts with the church members who are complaining about your children. To answer the question, you may need to look more closely for subtle (or even not so subtle) signs that the parishioner is dissatisfied with *you*. If the P.K. is in fact being triangled, clearing up the parishioner's conflicts with you should help take care of the complaints about the children.

As we have said, people who find themselves being drawn into triangles are not just passive victims. This means that how clergy parents respond to the triangling of their children is important. It's like two kids having a fight. When the parent walks into the room, they both point and scream, "He started it!" But the parent knows that beyond a certain point it doesn't matter who started it. What matters is that both children were responsible for keeping the fight going. In a similar way, when it comes to the triangling of the P.K., clergy parents cannot simply opt for the excuse "the congregation started it." To the extent that parents keep the triangle going, they too are responsible.

Let's say certain members of the congregation are dissatisfied with Pastor Guilford's ministry at their church. Instead of dealing with their dissatisfaction directly, they triangle the minister's children and frequently call the parsonage to complain about the P.K.'s latest escapades. How do the parents respond? Even if they have some dim awareness that the children's behavior is not the real issue, it may be more expedient for them emotionally to take up criticizing their children. They may have an unconscious hope that tightening the restrictions on their children will bring them into line, thereby shutting off the complaints from the congregation and easing the pressure. It is not that they wish to be cruel or demanding with their children. Rather, they are trying to find some way to survive the pressures they are experiencing.

Based on his vast experience counseling clergy families, Howard Clinebell has written, "It's hard for many ministers to listen to their own kids because they feel so vulnerable in terms of status in the congregation—which again emphasizes the need for a strong sense of self-worth and personal identity."[24] The children can be drawn into an emotional triangle where the conflict between pastor and congregation is deflected into the pastor's increased expectations of the children. The pastor's attempt to resolve conflicts in this way is an empty hope, because the P.K.s' behavior is not the real problem.

There is a passive and more subtle form of this triangle. This is when the clergy parents, unwilling to be more direct with the congregation, simply accept the complaints about their children. Consider again the parents who did not seem to think that it was a big deal for their P.K. to skip church. Because the congregation seemed to think it was, the parents imposed the rule that skipping church was not to be allowed. They may have given their children the message, "We know it's unreasonable, but it's a small thing. Let's not rock the boat, okay?" The problem is that the parents have allowed their own anxiety about congregational disapproval to dictate how they will rear their children.

Under pressure, all parents will sometimes choose the expedient over what they know to be a better way of handling a situation. If your two-year-old throws a tantrum in the grocery store, you probably wouldn't handle it with as much grace as you would if he or she threw a tantrum at home. You feel as if every eye in the store is on you, and you want to get out of that situation as quickly as possible. It becomes a problem, however, when parents get into the *habit* of doing what is expedient, of parenting "defensively." Trying to avoid rocking the congregational boat is hardly a solid foundation for parenting. Some P.K.s may grow up with the sense that the church members, not the clergy parents, are the ones who define the limits, who decide what is right or wrong for them.

Again, as a clergy parent you may occasionally choose to accept some of a congregation's expectations just to avoid creating unnecessary conflict. The important question is, Could you have chosen otherwise? Can you set and keep boundaries with complaining parishioners? If parishioners put pressure on you to discipline the P.K., could you tell them that the P.K.'s behavior is your responsibility and not theirs? How you handle individual complaints will depend on the situation. In general, however, there must be clear limits as to how much and in what ways congregational pressure should be allowed to influence the way a clergy couple rear the children. If you find it difficult to set such limits, then you may be vulnerable to passive triangling of the P.K.

Still another possibility is that the actual conflict may be between the P.K. and her parents, but the parents triangle the congregation. Suppose the parents do in fact object to the P.K.'s behavior, but are uncomfortable with making direct demands. Instead, they use the congregation as a convenient excuse for imposing rules that they would have wanted to impose anyway. These clergy parents may deny personal responsibility for the rules, always pointing a finger back at the congregation. The message from the parents is, "Don't blame us; it's the congregation." Unable to penetrate this emotional shield, the P.K. may become frustrated because her attempts to deal directly with her parents are continually deflected.

To make matters even more complex, there may be more than one kind of triangling occurring simultaneously. Gary and Virginia Sterling, for example, were ministering to a small suburban church in Southern California. The Sterlings were generally amiable and unassuming folk. Their parishioners described them as self-sacrificing servants. Those who knew them well, however, also knew that their "servant" orientation covered for an inability to say no even when it was appropriate to do so. Gary and Virginia worked hard to keep their environment conflict-free and thus said yes to every request that was made of them. Deep inside, however, they resented always having to take care of others while no one took care of them.

The Sterlings adopted a similar approach toward their children. They were giving parents, but at the same time they feared direct conflict with the kids. Whenever they imposed limits, they would quietly reason with the children, giving the perennial excuse, "What would the church say?" In this way they denied responsibility for their own limit-setting. In essence they were communicating to the children, "If you're going to be mad about it, get mad at the church, not at us."

Two kinds of triangles operated at the same time. On the one hand, the Sterlings were unable to be honest with their feelings toward the congregation. Expectations of certain church members were too intimidating to confront, and they passively triangled the children to diffuse some of the tension. This meant that even unreasonable expectations of their children were simply passed along because they were afraid to stand up to the congregation on either their own or their children's behalf. On the other hand, the Sterlings also tended to triangle the congregation when it came to the awkward task of making demands of the kids. Thus the children grew up with two strikes against them. First, they were left emotionally unprotected with no parental advocate to filter the congregation's demands, and second, they had no target for their frustrations. Both parents were adept at sidestepping their part in any conflicts with their children. What could the children do? To nearly everyone, Gary and Virginia were nice Christian people. And who can get mad at nice people without feeling guilty?

There are many forms of triangling and many possible responses to them. The constant factor is a lack of differentiation. Triangling is a way of avoiding responsibility for our feelings, a refusal to take a stand and say, "This is who I am and what I feel." Unfortunately, when there is a lack of differentiation in the clergy-congregational relationship, the P.K. may end up taking the brunt.

Differentiated clergy parents, however, can affirm the autonomy and individuality of their children. They trust their own parenting, which means that they also trust their kids to make the right decisions or to take responsibility for themselves when they make the wrong ones. Here are some quotes from grateful P.K.s with differentiated parents:

> I felt no resentment toward my parents because they felt it was up to me to make my own decisions, but they always let me know what they would want me to do. I had no reason to rebel because of this. If I did do something wrong, they would let me know they felt bad, but wouldn't punish me, so I respected and loved them.[25]

> They have never not allowed me to do things even though they may not agree (e.g., attending parties, etc.). They have let me create my own judgment from my own opinions and they *never* try to make me see things *one* way. They are incredible people, and I feel very lucky not to be a typical P.K. with "holy" parents.[26]

Not every minister or minister's spouse is able to do this. Every parent has a personal, emotional investment in his or her children. Children represent their parents, and many parents find it difficult to draw a line between their children and themselves. As Wynn has written, "The minister who cannot accept his own child's weaknesses because they seem to reflect painfully upon himself tends to have the greatest trouble."[27] One minister's daughter, already past her teenage years, wrote the following in response to our study:

> Other families in the church seem to be less strict on views such as movie-going, dress, makeup, drinking, etc.—but my father has very strong beliefs, almost to an extreme, in my opinion. He seems to watch my behavior constantly and if he suspects anything, he gives me speeches. I feel I'm old enough to make my own decisions and he makes me feel guilty.

The long-term effects of such a situation may vary. The poorly differentiated P.K. may internalize unreasonable expectations and the conflicts that go with them. This comment was given by another post-adolescent P.K. responding to our survey:

One of the biggest things I faced was overcoming the feeling that I had to suppress my true feelings. If I (we) didn't like something— or didn't have enough—we couldn't be ungrateful—that's OK— but it carried over into other areas of my life—like not being honest in relationships—expressing my unhappiness—or anger— was not existent for a long time and produces many emotional problems. . . . The pressure to perform—to be perfect really gets to you.

In this case, the conflicts of being a minister's child have been taken into the P.K.'s developing sense of self. It can begin with a consistently negative response to the child's emotions by either the parents or church members. The child can quickly learn, for example, that it is sinful to express or even feel anger. Or perhaps the P.K. learns that expressing her own unhappiness creates too much tension for her parents as they try to maintain the image of the model Christian family. Either way the P.K. finds that honest expression of certain emotions is discouraged or punished. These emotions, then, will be excluded from the child's growing sense of self. By the time the basic elements of the P.K.'s personality are in place, there will no longer be any need for negative responses from others. The P.K. will have an internal monitor, an overindustrious conscience, that will not allow her to experience these emotions no matter how others respond.

In other instances, the child may grow up seeking an external outlet for her frustration. She may then attempt to resolve the internal conflict by putting the same rigid expectations on other people. In this way the P.K. identifies herself with the internal censor and punishes others for their feelings the way she herself feels punished. Recall the youth leader who constantly held the P.K. under close scrutiny? That is just one example of what we are discussing here.

There are still other possibilities. The P.K. may externalize the conflict by relating to others as if they expected too much. He experiences others as controlling and manipulative regardless of how others actually behave. Or the minister's child with a more differentiated sense of self may see all too clearly the discrepancy between his parents' public and private selves. When he is old enough to decide for himself, he rejects his parents and the church in disillusionment.

Triangling is a matter of degree. But even without triangling, pressures on the minister are bound to affect the family at least to the extent that (1) there is a shared sense of family identity, of bearing one another's burdens, and (2) other family members know of the problems. Thus P.K.s may simply react to the pressures their parents face. One fourteen-year-old wrote, "We have a small, loud group of power-hungry people in our church who have been heavily criticizing my father. This really gets to the members of our family, and it is especially hard on my mom." Should a young teenager have to deal with this kind of emotional pressure? A twenty-one-year-old respondent to our study wrote, "People do not usually complain to me directly, but I hear about people who have criticized my Dad. The problem in this kind of situation is with my attitude towards those people. I kind of want to protect my Dad."

Louis McBurney notes that these forces may hinder communication within the family. "Often P.K.s recognize the tremendous stress and expectations the church puts on their parents, and so they decide just not to cause any additional problems. They go along quietly and keep their own stress inside."[28]

The pressures put on P.K.s can be enormous. This does not mean, however, that P.K.s therefore are an unstable or psychologically deprived lot. We must learn to get away from unproductive stereotypes that isolate ministers' children from their social context. When the boundaries between the clergy family and the congregational family are adequate, where triangling is kept to a minimum, P.K.s can grow up with a full appreciation for the value of the parish ministry.

We have looked at the role expectations of the minister, the minister's wife, and their children. In the next chapter we will focus more broadly on the clergy family as a whole.

PART THREE

THE FAMILY, THE
MARRIAGE, AND BEYOND

8

Stress and the Minister's Family

In the three previous chapters we have looked at the roles of the minister, his wife, and his children. Although we focused on the roles of individual family members, it was always with an eye toward understanding these roles in their larger social context. In part 3 we move forward from this emphasis on individuals. In this chapter we broaden our focus to the family as a whole and ask about the kinds of stress a clergy family experiences. How do these stressors affect the quality of family life? What is the connection between a clergy family's stress and their relationship to the congregation? We will try to answer such questions by reporting what clergy families have told us.

Understanding Stress

"Stress" has become a catchword in our pop-culture psychology. What does it mean? If you ask someone how he or she is doing, you may get the response, "I'm really under a lot of stress these days" or "I'm feeling stressed out." For some, it is simply a psychologized way of saying, "I'm tired." But there is more to it. Usually when someone says he or she is feeling stressed, it is a shorthand way of saying, "I have a lot of demands on me, I'm not sure I have the resources to meet them, and that makes me tired and anxious." The stressed person stress may not be thinking in these terms, but if we were to examine his or her situation, we would probably find the longer statement to be accurate. There are three elements here, and it is important to keep them distinct: the *stressor* itself, the *resources* available for coping with the stressor, and how one *perceives* the stressor.

First, stress involves some kind of pressure or demand, which is called the *stressor*. It can be physical, as when we have to work long hours without rest. It can also be financial; people who have had to work their way through college and struggle to pay the rent have an intimate knowledge of financial stress. Stressors can also be emotional demands. How do you feel when someone angrily accuses you of something? Your face flushes, your heart rate increases, and you may clench your teeth and ball your fists. And of course, a stressor may be all three. When a loved one is hospitalized, the family experiences physical, financial, and emotional stress all at the same time.

The clergy family faces these same three kinds of demands. The long hours of a minister's schedule can be a physical burden. The requirement that a pastor place his children in denominational schools can be a financial stressor. And of course, the clergy family encounters many emotional demands—and this has essentially been in view in our discussion of triangles, boundary problems, and role expectations.

Second, how a family responds to the stressor depends on its *resources*. The process is like using a checking account: stressors make demands on a family's physical, financial, or emotional "account," and how the family reacts depends on its current balance. If the balance is high, the stressor makes little impact. If the account is low or overdrawn, even the slightest of stressors may precipitate a crisis.

How you respond to physical stress depends on your level of health. If you are in peak physical condition, exercise is invigorating. If by contrast you are out of shape, the same exercise program will exhaust you. In terms of financial stress, how you react to your bills at the end of the month depends on how much money you have. Emotional stress can be either constructive or destructive, depending on whether or not you have a secure sense of identity and a supportive network of friends and family. Thus physical health, income, and supportive relationships are all examples of the resources that families need to cope with everyday stress.

What resources does a clergy family have? While many families recharge their physical energy by going on vacation, some clergy families complain that they can never get away; the children are free on weekends, the minister is not, and so on. Financially, many clergy have trouble meeting the high cost-of-living on meager salaries; while the pastor and the parishioners may both agree that ministry is a self-sacrificial calling, this does not in itself make the family's bills vanish. The clergy family's relationship to the congregation can be either an important emotional resource or a burdensome emotional drain; suppose a pastor receives a phone call from the school principal complaining that his son faces possible expulsion because he has been getting into fights at school. An understanding and empathic church can be a great help during this potential crisis; yet the congregation could take this event as an opportunity to criticize and say, "I told you so," thereby increasing the emotional load carried by the clergy family.

Therefore, whether or not you experience stress in ministry or in family life depends on more than just how many pressures you face. It is a matter of balance between these demands and your available resources. When your resources are adequate, demands can challenge you to grow and develop. When resources are scarce, however, each new demand can seem like another millstone around your neck.

There are no universal rules for deciding what is a stressor and what is a resource. Different people experience events in different ways. One spouse hates parties and meeting new people; the other loves parties and finds new people fascinating. The same party is a stressful demand on the first spouse and a resource of emotional energy for the other. Similarly, families differ in the meaning they give to events. The marriage of the oldest child can be seen as a tragic loss or the joyful uniting of two families. The clergy family can experience church members' intrusions as invasions of privacy or as an indication that the members feel welcome in the pastor's home.

Thus we confront the third element of family stress: how family members *perceive or attach meaning to* the events in their lives. To some extent, whether or not an event is stressful depends on how we view it.

Our findings indicate that living on church property is generally a stressful experience for clergy families. But it depends on how we look at it. One minister's wife said, "Living on the church grounds has been a rewarding experience for me because I am a very public person. It has been almost devastating for my husband who is a very private person. He is under a great deal of stress and has developed problems with his health." So, while living in a parsonage can be a source of stress, the impact will vary from person to person.

Minister A and Minister B have identical schedules. For both, weeknights are the only times they have to spend with their families. But they must attend some church functions that regularly meet on weeknights. Minister A finds the meetings a drain; Minister. B does not. Why? The difference is in the meaning they attribute to this responsibility. Minister A places a high value on time with his family, and he believes that the church should be more self-sufficient. He views his attendance at weeknight church functions as "putting in an appearance," a gesture he feels unnecessary. By contrast, Minister B does not see the meetings as competing with his family life. He and his family enjoy a somewhat more random lifestyle; the other family members are not jealous of his time. Minister B actually enjoys attending church functions and sees them as an honest display of his solidarity with the congregation. Thus one minister sees the meetings as an extra, unnecessary demand on his time; the other sees them as opportunities. It is not a question of which perception is "right." They are simply based on different assumptions and values about ministry and family life.

To cope with stress, clergy families must learn to see how stressors, resources, and perceptions work together. It may be possible to make productive changes in any or all of the three areas. First, there may be ways of reducing the demands on the family. In Acts 6 we read that the Twelve decided to delegate a portion of their ministry in order to devote themselves to "the ministry of the word of God" (v. 2, NIV). The initial step is for the clergy family and the congregation to recognize when the demands are too heavy. Once this has been admitted, they can work together to find creative ways of sharing the load.

Second, the clergy family's resources can be increased. The family's physical vitality can be encouraged by allowing them more time to relax and be free of responsibilities and expectations. Their financial resources should match their economic demands. This may mean increasing salaries or benefits, paying the spouse for work done in the church, or allowing or helping the spouse to find other work. Emotional resources are also important. Church members should remember that the minister's family needs their continued personal support. Parishioners can find numerous creative ways to communicate that support if they would take the time to think of it. For their part, members of the clergy family must learn to reach out for that support. It is too easy for them to buy into the myth that because of their status in the congregation, they must rely on God and not others for their emotional support.

Third, the clergy family can learn to look at things differently. This book is devoted to helping clergy families learn a new way of thinking about their ministry and their social environment. Some disgruntled clergy adopt a victim attitude: "I did everything for them, and look what they did to me." Some congregations do victimize ministers; but there are also ministers who victimize congregations. Wherever there is overwhelming stress, bitterness, or mutual antagonism in a clergy-congregation relationship, the chances are that both have contributed to the problem. All of us as members of a local church, the minister's family included, must break out of narrow persecutor-victim perceptions. We must learn to see our own part in keeping painful patterns going. While we may come from many different experiences and life histories, while we may differ in some basic values, we must also learn to appreciate that, under the skin, each of us is motivated by a need for love and acceptance.

Thus a clergy family under stress can try to reduce the demands placed on them, increase their resources, change their perceptions, or find some combination of the three. Whatever strategy the family adopts, however, it must always be kept in an ecological context. Particularly in more poorly differentiated congregations there is an inherent motivation to maintain the status quo. Any change that a clergy family tries to make can be essentially a stressor or demand on the relationship between the family and the congregation. The less differentiated that relationship, the more likely that stress reduced in one area will simply pop up somewhere else.

For example, Pastor Stone feels frustrated and powerless. His efforts to get his congregation to assume greater responsibility for themselves have repeatedly met defeat. Therefore he delegates many of his ministerial duties to his wife. Now in addition to being a model homemaker and mother, she must also visit the sick, help lead the youth group, and organize the women's society. The minister and congregation have in es-

sence transferred their load to the minister's wife. The strain of
trying to be a super minister's wife eventually wears her out,
and she becomes less and less able to handle the duties
assigned to her. So the stress comes back full circle to the
minister and the congregation, and nothing has been resolved.

Reverend McGee's family offers another example. Immediately upon coming to the church, they experienced the pressure
of the congregation's high expectations of the McGee children.
The minister's first reaction was protective. He felt confident of
his children and didn't want them subjected to criticism. The
congregation's high level of expectations became a chronic
source of stress for the McGee family. Eventually the pastor
found a way to deal with his own stress regarding the children;
instead of viewing the expectations of church members as
intrusions, he relabeled them as loving counsel. His children
were not convinced. While he did not actively side with the
congregation against his children, neither did he do anything to
shield them. In one sense he succeeded in reducing his stress
by sidestepping the issue.[1] The success of his solution, however, was short-lived. Because the children felt betrayed by
their father, they soon rebelled openly from the unrealistic
expectations that had been dumped on them. Rather than
reducing stress, in the long run more stress was created for both
the minister and the congregation.

In an ecological sense, the experience of stress is a signpost,
an indicator, of a problem rather than the problem itself. The
problems have to do with imbalances in relationships: triangling, a clash of core family values, conflicts of role expectations,
and the like. In our own pilot research we have asked ministers
and their families to help us understand what kinds of problems
they normally face. Here's what they told us.

Typical Problems in the Lives of Clergy Families

What kinds of stressors and problems do clergy families
typically face? In one study we approached the question two
ways.[2] First, we gave several open-ended questions to a group
of ministers and their family members.[3] In particular we asked
them to complete these sentences:

"For our family, the greatest disadvantage of being in ministry is . . ."

"In terms of our family, the most difficult thing about being in ministry is . . ."

The responses to the two questions were, of course, highly similar, as we will see shortly.

Second, we consulted the literature on ministers' families and compiled a list of eleven typical problems. We then asked each family member to rate how severe each problem actually was for the family. Comparing the ratings of ministers, their wives, and their children is quite revealing. We will look first at the problems and disadvantages the families listed, then at how they rated those problems.

The Disadvantages and Difficulties of Ministry

If you were to ask clergy families to describe the greatest disadvantages of being in the ministry, what would they say? The families we surveyed gave a wide variety of responses, but there were five broad, recurring themes that ran like colored threads through their answers. From most frequent to least, these five themes are not enough family time together, high expectations, low pay, moving, and lack of privacy.[4]

By far the most common response was that *clergy families do not have enough time together*. Two subthemes are present. The first is, the minister's busy schedule doesn't allow for enough time with the family. There simply aren't enough hours in a week. The second subtheme is more specific: peculiarities of the minister's schedule take away the times most families would spend together, namely, weekends and evenings.

The most general responses cited time pressures as the greatest difficulty or disadvantage of the clergy family. The responses of the wives in particular pointed directly to what one wife called "the bottomless pit": the fact that the minister's work is never done. Another wife complained of the constant reminder of pressures at church. Still another wrote, "There is always too much left to be done." And one minister's child poignantly wrote, "Our father is always too busy to be with us." The sheer volume of responsibilities that some clergy face can become a serious problem when it leaves no time for building family life. As we noted in chapter 1, most ministers are aware of their need to spend time with their families. Their frustration lies in trying to clear more time in their schedules.

The ministry is not a nine-to-five, forty-hour-per-week job. Both regularities and irregularities in the minister's schedule make it difficult for the clergy family to have time together.

What are the irregularities? For most people, work ends when you walk out the door of your workplace. But the minister and, to a lesser degree, the minister's wife are never off-duty. Just when they think they have an evening free to spend together or with the family, their plans can be instantaneously short-circuited by a phone call from a parishioner in need. This is not to say that parishioners have no right to call a minister at home or that the minister must selfishly guard his evenings. In one sense it is a problem of boundaries. The predictability of a nine-to-five schedule means that there is a clear distinction between being at work and being at home. Without that predictability, there is no way to guarantee a time when the minister can truly be at home with his family and free of church-related responsibilities. If it is legitimate to assert that clergy families need time together just like any other family, then what can be done to ensure that they have that time?

The regularities of a minister's schedule can be troublesome as well. In a society where the five-day work week is the norm, evenings, weekends, and holidays are important times for families, especially where there are school-age children. For the clergy family, however, these times are often taken up by important church responsibilities. There are evening services and special events over which the minister is expected to preside. Some churches schedule events for nearly every night of the week, and weekends are not available for family times. And while holidays mean vacation for the secular world, they are holy days for the church. The minister may give extra preparation to that special Easter sermon, particularly if he anticipates a larger attendance than on ordinary Sundays.

A closely related problem was mentioned by several of the ministers' wives: the inability to go away for the weekend. This entails more than just a need for family time. It involves family time that is completely free from church responsibilities, and that means going somewhere else. Many parents feel similar urgings. Though they love and cherish their children, they long for that one night or weekend where they can steal away, leave the kids in someone else's care, and just be a twosome again. Such mini-vacations can have a rejuvenating effect on their commitment to and love for their children.

Taking a vacation is one way that families replenish their resources or, if you will, recharge their physical and emotional batteries. But there is an energy crisis in clergy families created by the busy life of the ministry. As one pastor put it, "The church seems to dominate my free time and energy; when family time comes, I'm pooped." This means that even if family time were available, there is no guarantee that anyone—especially the minister—would have enough energy to enjoy it.

Researchers Nick Stinnett and John DeFrain have noted that spending time together is one of the secrets to a strong and vital family life.[5] If the church wants the clergy family to thrive, it will have to find ways to encourage and preserve their time together, above and beyond the rest and relaxation they need to replace their depleted energy reserves.

The second biggest problem cited by clergy families has to do with the *high expectations* placed on them. This comes as no surprise, given our earlier discussions. One pastor said the greatest disadvantage to being in the ministry is "the unrealistic expectation to be the model family." Another pastor's response reflected more emotion: "The people want a perfect family, and each one is a judge." The ministers' wives gave similar responses. One wrote, "We are not allowed the same mistakes as most people." Another complained that she did not fit "the stereotype church members have of pastors' wives." A teenage son wrote that all the members of the clergy family "seem to be put on a pedestal, different from anyone else."

The expectations expressed for the children were a common concern. One young minister's wife lamented the emotional "pressure and expectation to be perfect" that church members and the wider community place on P.K.s. One clergy wife with four children wrote, "The outside community watches the children's actions and expects certain behavior of them." Many of the P.K.s who responded to our survey agreed that much was expected of them. A bright twelve-year-old asserted, however, "You can't please everyone."

These ministers' families underscore the concrete reality of the high expectations they must face. We will see later that clergy family members disagree on how severe this problem is.

The third most commonly cited disadvantage is *the minister's salary*. Every family has certain financial demands, and its level of income is the resource it uses to meet these demands. Quite simply, if they don't have enough money, their financial obligations become burdens and a certain source of family stress. Thus, when asked for the greatest disadvantage of the ministry, one pastor simply replied, "$." David and Vera Mace tell of the pastor who was asked, "If you had to take a ten percent reduction in your salary, where would you make the first cut?" The pastor replied, "Across my throat."[6]

We mentioned in chapter 6 that the wives tend to be more concerned about salary than the ministers are. There are probably two reasons for this. One is that the minister's wife often manages the household finances and has the responsibility for making ends meet. But more directly, a shortage of funds may mean that the minister's wife is forced to work outside the home even if she would prefer not to. That in turn gets entangled with other family difficulties such as their need for time together. This is clearly shown by the responses we received from one clergy couple. Asked what the church could do to improve their family life, the wife answered, "Increase our income so I could quit work, or allow more time off so we could spend time with our children." The husband's response struck a similar chord: "Raise my salary so my wife can stay home."

A fourth area of concern for clergy families is *the stress of moving*. The difficulty is more emotional than physical. The key word here is "roots." The problem with moving, as one minister's wife told us, is "not being able to put down roots." Clergy families, as with other professionals who must move frequently, may adjust by refusing to become too close to people outside their immediate family. They have learned that if they sink their roots too deeply, their pain will be greater when they are uprooted to another community. The congregation can be an important emotional resource, but if the members of a minister's family are afraid to form close ties to the congregation, they will effectively cut themselves off from this valuable resource.

A fifth difficulty of clergy family life is *a lack of privacy*. This is particularly true for families who live in a parsonage or other property close to the church grounds. Clergy families whose congregations respect their privacy may find it difficult to understand how intrusive church members can be. One pastor wrote that the greatest disadvantage for his family was "no privacy due to the parsonage being located next to the church. Some members are so comfortable with us, and so used to being in our home, that they enter without knocking, and come clear back to the master bedroom where we are." Here the lack of privacy is expressed positively as showing how comfortable the clergy family and the congregation feel with each other. Yet all families need clear boundaries to maintain their sense of identity as a family. We will explore this further when we discuss the effects of intrusion on clergy family life.

The comments we received from clergy families confirm and enlarge what we already knew from other sources. In summary, members of ministers' families point to five broad disadvantages in the ministry: lack of family time, high expectations, low salary, emotional rootlessness, and lack of privacy. These are some of the issues that affect the balance of demands and resources in the life of a clergy family. But how a family member perceives the situation is just as important. Does each family member experience these problems in the same way?

How Clergy Family Members Rate Their Problems

To get a more detailed picture of the way various stressors affect the life of the minister's family, we listed eleven potential problems and asked each family member to rate their severity for their own family. The problems were (1) a lack of family privacy, (2) church members criticizing the minister, (3) church members criticizing the minister's spouse,[7] (4) church members criticizing the minister's children, (5) inadequate income, (6) lack of freedom to be oneself, (7) loneliness from not having a close friend, (8) church members' becoming jealous when a family member becomes too close to another church member, (9) not feeling the freedom to buy what one wants to buy, (10) unrealistically high expectations, and (11) lack of time for family life due to parish demands. After compiling the ratings from ministers, wives, and children, we constructed a composite picture of how family members differ in the way they rate the eleven problems.[8] The result is shown in figure 8.1.

The table shows some striking similarities and contrasts. On the whole, the ratings of the ministers and their wives are in high agreement. The children's are quite different. Let us first highlight the similarities and then explore the contrasts.

Figure 8.1
How Members of Clergy Families Rank Various Problems

Type of Problem	Family Member Responding		
	Minister	Wife	Child
Time spent in church leaves little time for family life	1	2	6
Inadequate financial income	2	1	2
Loneliness from not really having a close friend	3	3	8
Unrealistically high expectations of me	4	8	1
Church members criticizing minister	5	4	7
Lack of family privacy	6	5	3
Not feeling the freedom to buy what I want to buy	7	7	4
Church members becoming jealous when I become too close to another member	8	9	11
Lack of freedom to be myself	9	6	5
Church members criticizing minister's wife	10	10	10
Church members criticizing minister's children	11	11	9

(A rating of "1" indicates the most severe; "11" is least severe.)

The matter of money is given a high rating by all family members. Three items are given consistently low ratings: jealousy from church members, criticism of the minister's wife, and criticism of the minister's children. All family members also agree that criticism of the minister is a much more important problem than criticism of either his wife or his children.

The contrasts are perhaps even more instructive. Together with the matter of income, both the minister and his wife view the lack of family time and loneliness from not having a close friend as important problems. The children, however, seem to have a different perspective, ranking these two issues sixth and eighth respectively. Ask yourself why.

Most of the children who responded to the survey were adolescents. Think of your own teenage years or of your teenage children. Adolescence is a time when children turn their emotional energies away from families and begin to wrestle with the question of who they are with respect to peers. They must establish a firm sense of personal identity that is grounded on but differentiated from their families. Pragmatically this means that while teenagers may still see the lack of family time as a problem, it is less so for them than for their parents.

Loneliness from not having a close friend is a much greater problem for the minister and his wife than it is for the children. Again, this is probably because the children have a network of friends outside the church. Recall the discussion of idealization and impoverishment in chapter 3. Idealization, you will remember, has to do with the ideal images and superhuman expectations placed on the members of the minister's family. Such expectations can come from themselves or from parishioners. Whatever their source, these expectations can create a barrier to forming peer relationships between the clergy family and parishioners. This is complicated by the problem of impoverishment, in which the demands of the ministry can prevent the clergy family from establishing peer relationships outside the congregation.

What the present findings suggest is that impoverishment is more of a problem for the minister and his wife than for the children. Even if idealization were to prevent every member of the clergy family from having close friends within the congregation, the children at least have other relationships to fall back on. The minister and his wife, then, share a common problem of loneliness.

What do ministers' children see as the most difficult problem, if not a lack of friends? The most severe problem is parishioners' unrealistically high expectations of them. There seems to be a common theme of intrusive expectations in the P.K.s' responses, in line with our discussion in chapter 7. Note that the children rated these problems higher than did either the minister or his wife: lack of family privacy, not feeling the freedom to buy what they want to buy, and lack of freedom to be themselves. This is all the more striking when we consider that none of the family members seems to regard direct criticism of the minister's children as a great problem. What does this mean?

There are two possibilities. First, recall that in chapter 7 we showed how the pastor's children face expectations from several sources: their parents, church members in general, peers in the congregation, and peers outside the congregation (such as at school). It may be, however, that not all these sources are experienced in the same way. The high ranking given to unrealistic expectations and the low ranking of the congregation's criticism of the P.K. suggest that the most keenly felt expectations come from parents and friends. These are the people who have the greatest influence on the formation of the child's character and identity. They are therefore sources of both the greatest sense of security and confidence and the greatest sense of insecurity and pain.

This situation is complicated by the question of triangling among the parents, the congregation, and the minister's children. If a congregation begins to put more pressure on the minister and his wife, they in turn may put more pressure on their children. The triangle can also work the other way: instead of confronting the pastor, the congregation may step up its demands on the P.K. Direct and indirect expectations and criticisms can come from more than one source at one time, making the situation very confusing for the minister's child. More detailed study is needed to understand how the social influences of parents, friends, and congregation interact in the lives of clergy children.

The second explanation for the clergy children's ratings moves us away from looking for the source of expectations to asking how expectations are communicated. The survey asks P.K.s to rate how severely they are criticized by church members. But is criticism the only way to communicate expectations? Earlier we discussed what we call "the tyranny of the best." Even what seems to be well-meant encouragement can feel like a crushing weight when a relationship is not characterized by grace. Thus there are two probable explanations for the ways a pastor's children can experience unrealistically high expectations without a great amount of criticism from the congregation: (1) the expectations and criticisms come instead from family and friends, and (2) the expectations are communicated by some means other than criticism. We suspect that both are true to some extent; again, such questions can be sorted out only through further study.

In summary, let us make two related points. First, the similarities in how family members rated problems suggest the value of looking at the clergy marriage and family as a collective unit. Certain kinds of stress and pressure are common to all members of the minister's family. Second, the differences in the ratings underscore the value of understanding how family members differ as individuals. In ecological terms, it is important to recognize that the various family members have somewhat different social networks. This fact alone can change the way the members experience life as a clergy family. A truly ecological perspective will need to move back and forth between individuals, marriages, families, and social groups, paying close attention to how these interact with each other.

We could make other observations and speculations regarding table 8.1, but we will leave that to you and encourage you to share your thoughts with us.

Thus far we have looked at clergy family stress in two ways. At a general level we asked clergy families to tell us about the greatest disadvantages and difficulties of being in ministry. Their responses helped us both to reinforce and to develop what was already present in the literature. A lack of family time, the presence of high expectations from the congregation, the inadequacy of the minister's salary, the upheaval of moving, and a lack of privacy are all common themes.

More specifically, we asked the families to rate the severity of various problems. Their responses confirmed the importance of the five main problems. Furthermore, the similarities and differences in the family members' responses gave us a clearer understanding of how each potential problem actually affects the minister's family. Ministers and their wives seemed to order the problems differently from their children. This warns us against assuming that all members of the clergy family experience the same emotional pressures.

The Relationship to the Congregation: Intrusion or Integration?

Problems, problems, problems. Is that all a congregation has to offer a minister's family? Of course not. When we discuss problems, it is always with an eye toward focusing on patterns and relationships. We want to see how the stresses of clergy family life can help us understand their social ecology. Nevertheless, a continuing emphasis on stress and problems can give a negative cast to our discussion. Are there any strengths? What does a healthy, supportive relationship between a minister's family and a congregation look like?

We have explored this question by distinguishing two factors in the relationship between a clergy family and a congregation. We call these factors *intrusion* and *integration*. To get a sense of what we are describing, think about your own family and other families whom you know. Some families can be very intrusive and demanding. But whether or not this becomes a problem depends on how supportive the family is. The children in one family, for example, may openly resent their parents' high expectations; in another, however, the children may accept these expectations even if they are just as demanding. Why? Because the children in the second family also experience their parents' love and support. In the first case, if the parents do not temper expectations with genuine support and encouragement, the children have the feeling of being thrown to the wolves. In the second case, the children feel more like emissaries sent out into the world from a strongly supportive home base.

It is the same with ministers' families. Expectations must be balanced with a sense of belonging. In terms of stress theory, as we discussed at the beginning of the chapter, intrusion is a stressor or demand on the minister's family. It can be both physical and emotional. Physically, parishioners may actually disrupt the clergy family's privacy by inviting themselves to their home unannounced, calling them unnecessarily during dinner, and so on. Emotional intrusion is somewhat more subtle but no less real. The minister's family can feel an ever-present watchfulness, a sense of pressures and expectations that are hard to escape. This can lead them to feel that the needs of parishioners compete with their own, or that there is no place for the clergy family to express their needs. In short, they may feel that they are not allowed to be human.

Integration, by contrast, describes a feeling of belonging. The minister's family experiences the congregation as a truly supportive and benevolent extended family. It is the same kind of balance that a newly married couple must find in relationship to their respective families. The newlyweds must be recognized as a separate unit with their own lives and their own goals. All too often, new couples tend to get absorbed into one family or the other. Indeed, many conflicts in the first years of marriage are over which family they should be absorbed into. The answer is neither one. The couple must learn to create their own family unit and sense of identity. Their families in turn must affirm and encourage them without abandoning them. The couple must feel that they belong to both families and have the support of both families without being absorbed into either one.

The same is true for the relationship of the minister's family to the congregation. The clergy family needs the loving support of the congregation. This is evident in the responses to our survey. We asked the family members to complete the following open-ended sentence: "The greatest advantage of being in ministry for our family is . . ." By far the most common response centered on the family sense of the congregation's support. One minister wrote, for example, "We have a built-in support group who constantly encourage us." Another pastor wrote that for his family, the congregation was a "built-in extended family which shares love and support quite freely." Even the children appreciate this. One child wrote, "We have made a lot of super family friends that are church members." Every member of the minister's family can enjoy the support and friendship of a caring congregation.

At the same time, the support should not be intrusive. There is a vast difference between the kind of support expressed in "we're here to help" and in "we're here to do it for you." A high level of integration means the clergy family feel that they are part of the congregation but that their separateness as a family is recognized and affirmed.

Integration, then, is an emotional resource. It contributes toward a positive balance in the clergy family's emotional account that they can draw against in times of stress. Conceptually at least, intrusion and integration are closely linked. If we think of intrusion as a stressor and integration as a resource, we should expect that (1) the more intrusive the congregation, the higher the clergy family's stress, and (2) the more the minister's family feels integrated into the congregation, the lower their stress. Is this true?

As part of our study we measured the congregation's intrusiveness, the clergy family's sense of integration into the local church family, and the level of family stress.[9] First, intrusiveness was measured by asking all clergy family members to rate how well each of the following statements applied to them:

It is difficult for family members to take time away from the church.

Family members feel pressured to spend most of their free time in church-related projects.

It seems that there is never any place to get away from church matters at our house.

Family members find it hard to get away from church matters and/or church members.

Second, the level of integration into the congregation was similarly based on family members' responses to the following. (Note that higher scores on the latter two statements contribute to a lower score on integration.)

Family members have little need for friends outside the church membership because the church is so close.

Most personal friends for our family are not church friends.

Family members find it easier to discuss things with persons outside the church.[10]

Scores from each family member on each item were tallied to create that family's scores for both intrusion and integration.

Third, we needed a measure of the clergy family's overall stress. We asked the ministers and their spouses to rate how being in the ministry had affected their family life. Specifically, each spouse was given five incomplete sentences, such as "Being in the ministry has made our life as a family . . ." and "Being in the ministry has made my role as a partner to my spouse . . ."[11] They were instructed to complete each sentence with one of five options, ranging from "much more difficult" on one end to "much easier" on the other. The scores from both spouses on all five sentences were added together and labeled "family stress."

We found what we expected to find. First, the families that rated their congregations as more intrusive also scored higher in family stress. This means that intrusive congregations have a negative impact, making various aspects of clergy family life more difficult. Conversely, families that felt more integrated into their congregations reported lower levels of family stress.[12] When the minister's family can feel the love and support of church members, family life is made easier.

This should not come as a surprise. In retrospect, the results seem obvious. We must emphasize again, however, that these findings point strongly to the need for an ecological perspective, a way of understanding that is difficult to maintain in practice. In other words, if you want to find out how a minister's family is doing, you have to look at more than just the family itself. You need to ask what kind of relationship the family has with the congregation.

The local church can help or hinder the quality of a minister's family life. Both clergy families and church members need to recognize this. Parishioners must realize that their expectations can be an intrusive burden on the clergy family, especially when such expectations are not balanced by appropriate support and encouragement. Ministers, too, must avoid the pitfall of thinking of the congregation and family as separate areas of concern. This can lead to the folly of trying to improve family life by itself, when what really needs to be changed is the way that the family and the congregation relate to each other.

*   *   *

When we speak of stress in the minister's family, therefore, we are not talking about a family that exists all by itself, experiencing its own internal tensions. The minister's family is a family within a family, and stress is an indicator of how these two families interact.

The minister's family and the congregation must work together to create a manageable balance between demands and resources. Many demands strain the minister's family: claims on their time and energy, intrusive expectations, and the like. To cope effectively they need adequate resources. Time together and time away, enough money to make ends meet, and the loving support of the congregation are just a few factors.

The same argument, of course, could be made more specifically for the minister's relationship to his wife. How does relationship to the congregation affect the quality of the clergy marriage? As we will see in the next chapter, the minister's marriage, too, needs to be kept in ecological perspective.

9

Are We Married
to the Congregation,
or to Each Other?

Pastor George Jacobs and his wife Kathy have been married for eighteen years. They have a fourteen-year-old daughter, Carla, and an eleven-year-old son, Brad. Pastor Jacobs has been in the ministry for sixteen years and is now pastor of his third church. Although George and Kathy appear to have a good marriage, it is one in which Kathy has experienced very little freedom or emotional closeness.

George grew up under an alcoholic father. When he was drunk, his father was authoritarian and controlling. When he was sober, he was permissive and emotionally distant. George became a Christian at age fifteen. The church offered him the love and acceptance he sorely needed. He went to every service and volunteered to help in any way he could. Church members continually praised George's involvement. To George, their encouragement was like water to a wilting flower. At age eighteen he decided that God was calling him into full-time ministry.

During his junior year in college George met Kathy, who at that time was a waitress in a restaurant near the college. She had run away from home a year earlier during her senior year in high school. George took an interest in her, led her to a personal Christian faith, and proposed marriage to her, all within a year after they met. They married as soon as George was graduated.

Then it was off to seminary. Kathy worked to support them while George studied. During these early years of marriage, Kathy was content to be dependent on George, who was older, more educated, and more experienced in the faith. For his part George could be controlling at times. He forbade her to work as a waitress because it was "beneath her." He was also very selective about whom she could have as friends and how much time she could spend with them.

To Kathy, George's behavior was annoying, but it seemed a small price to pay compared with the family she had left. Her major disappointment was that George almost never talked with her about what was on his heart and mind. He seemed reluctant to talk about feelings.

George did well in seminary, and a church position awaited him when he was graduated. He worked hard in that first pastorate in much the same way as he had worked for acceptance as a teenager in the church. Kathy felt left out. She began to confront George about his tendencies to control as well as her disappointment with the lack of any real intimacy in their relationship. She pointed out that he rarely asked her how she was feeling and never expressed his own feelings, even if she asked. George dismissed Kathy's complaints as "just a male-female thing."

Kathy continued to express her needs, but the situation didn't change. Occasionally, after much nagging on her part, George would mutter condescendingly, "All right, let's talk since you need to." But when Kathy tried to express herself, George would intellectualize what she said and avoid discussing feelings. Sometimes he would end the conversation abruptly by labeling her complaints a spiritual problem. As Kathy became even more desperate, she would start to cry. This made George feel both guilty and angry, and he would then accuse her of having emotional problems. Kathy tried for years to get George to change. Eventually she gave up and met her emotional needs the best ways she could, mostly through her children and a few close friends.

George became a good preacher. He seemed free to reveal his feelings while behind the pulpit, in ways she had never experienced in their marriage. Many women in the church would comment to Kathy, "It's wonderful to have such a sensitive pastor who isn't afraid to talk about his feelings. You sure are lucky to be married to him." Kathy would bite her tongue and think to herself, "If only you knew." She played the role of the perfect wife in the perfect marriage while secretly resenting George and her own hypocrisy. At times she wished she could be free from her marriage.

As Kathy saw it, George appeared to be warm, caring, and sensitive with parishioners but not with her. She saw his involvement with the congregation as meeting his personal needs in two ways: his need for acceptance and his need for control. Because of this, she found it hard to think of George's endless hours at the church as "working for the Lord." She felt trapped in a vicious circle: the more that George's needs for acceptance and control were met by the congregation, the more time he would devote to the church and the less time he would spend with her. She was now beyond being resentful, for she had already given up on her marriage and was determined to find fulfillment elsewhere. Nevertheless, she never dared to let their marital problems show because, after all, who would provide the model for the congregation?

*   *   *

In the title of one of their books, David and Vera Mace ask, "What's happening to clergy marriages?"[1] Ministers, just like other human beings, have marital problems and sometimes even get divorced.[2] They can suffer the same kind of frustration, anger, and despair as embattled married couples everywhere. But is the clergy marriage like any other marriage? Yes and no. As a couple, ministers and their spouses have problems that look a great deal like those of other couples. They bring old hurts and unresolved family issues with them into marriage, and they spend a good deal of their married life trying to solve emotional problems that really originated somewhere else. The difference lies not so much in the marriage itself, but in the unique social context of the marriage.

We have discussed the minister's family at great length, repeatedly emphasizing that the family itself is not unusual or different, but rather the environment. Being the "royal family" within the context of a larger congregational family poses unique advantages and disadvantages. So does the minister's marital relationship. William Douglas has written of clergy marriage, "The relationship between husband and wife can only be understood in the context of their individual and joint relationship to a particular local congregation."[3] Some of George and Kathy Jacobs's problems are virtually the same as those of other married couples. But you cannot fully describe their marital difficulties without also describing the role that the ministry plays in their relationship. In some ways George is more married to the church than he is to Kathy, and both spouses feel obligated to keep up the charade of the model marriage.

Clergy marriages, like clergy families, must find a balance between their connectedness with the congregation and their separateness from it. In this chapter we will probe the relationship between marriage and the ministry. In the first section we will look at studies that assess how well clergy marriages are doing. The second section explores some of the general advantages and disadvantages of clergy marriage. Third, we will specifically discuss the problem of idealization as it applies to the clergy couple. Finally, we will once again broaden our ecological horizons and, looking to our own research, will show some ways in which being in the ministry affects the quality of a minister's marriage.

The Quality of the Minister's Marriage: How Are We Doing?

There are many ministers who are deeply dissatisfied with their marriages, and many whose marriages are in serious trouble. But the same could be said of the state of marriage in general in Western society. It is important for us to recognize that ministers can have marital problems so that we will be able to deal with them with openness and honesty. But this does not mean that all or even most ministers are unhappily married. As with the P.K., it is much easier to make generalizations and stereotypes about clergy marriages than it is to back them up. How satisfied are ministers and their spouses in their married lives?

One way to find out is to ask them directly. In one study we asked a multidenominational group of doctor of ministry students and their wives to tell us how happy they were in their marital relationships. Each spouse was to rate the degree of marital happiness on a seven-point scale ranging from "extremely unhappy" on one end to "perfect" on the other.[4] The results are shown in figure 9.1.

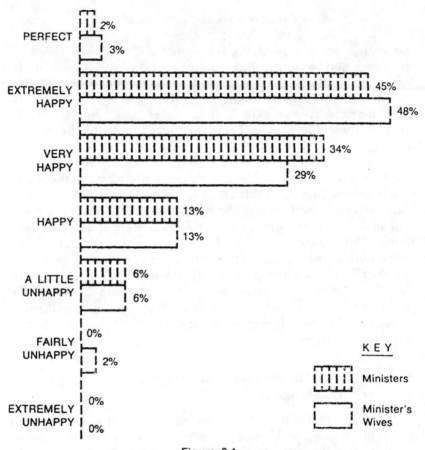

Figure 9.1
How Happy Are Clergy Marriages?
Results From a Multidenominational Group (102 Couples)

As the chart shows, a large majority of both ministers and wives rated their marriages as either very happy or extremely happy.

We wondered whether the results were skewed by our surveying a specialized group of ministers, namely, those engaged in doctoral studies. With the cooperation of denominational authorities we were able to put the same question to two other groups of clergy couples: Southern Baptists and Seventh-day Adventists.[5] These two groups provided a broad sampling of couples in various age groups and levels of education. These results are shown in figure 9.2. As you can see, the percentages are similar across all three groups. Again, the majority of both pastors and their wives rate themselves as either very happy or extremely happy in marriage.

Figure 9.2
How Happy Are Clergy Marriages?
Reports From Two Denominations

Rating	Southern Baptist (164 couples)		Seventh-day Adventist (57 couples)	
	Husb	Wife	Husb	Wife
Perfect	5%	5%	5%	7%
Extremely happy	47%	46%	33%	36%
Very happy	33%	26%	26%	36%
Happy	12%	15%	23%	13%
A little unhappy	3%	7%.	2%	7%
Fairly unhappy	0%	0%	5%	0%
Extremely unhappy	1%	1%	5%	0%

What can we make of these results? Generalizations can be dangerous. Some researchers argue that religious people will say they are happily married because they feel they have to, whether it is strictly true or not.[6] Other researchers, however, reply that such an argument cannot explain away all the studies that show a positive relationship between religiousness and marital satisfaction.[7] Another pitfall stems from the fact that not all the surveys that were sent out were returned. Did most of the people with unhappy marriages throw away the surveys because they were too embarrassed to send them back? We cannot know for certain.

If it is wrong to say that most clergy couples are unhappy in their marriages, it is equally wrong to conclude that most of them are happy. We simply do not have enough information to make such a sweeping claim. But if we take the findings at face value, we can at least say that they give us no basis for a negative stereotype of unhappy clergy couples. In other words, at present we have more reason to believe that the majority of clergy couples are happy rather than unhappy.

We also asked the couples from among the doctoral students to rate the minister as a companion and a lover to his wife. Each spouse was asked to rate the minister's behavior on both counts, using a scale that ranged from "very unsatisfied" to "very satisfied." The vast majority of the responses from both spouses were either "satisfied" or "very satisfied." The wives, in fact, rated their husbands slightly higher than the husbands rated themselves.[8]. These are particularly important findings, considering the time restraints placed on clergy couples and families.

Thus we find no basis for believing that clergy marriages are generally in trouble. The couples who responded to our surveys report that they are both happy and satisfied. This should give at least some small encouragement to those about to enter the ministry!

But we must go further. Even if it is true that most clergy marriages are happy and satisfying, this does not eliminate the ecological question: does the quality of the marriage depend on other factors? It is not enough simply to ask whether or not ministers and their spouses are happy. While having a happy marriage is a worthwhile goal, what can you do about it? One useful strategy is to find out what influences a marriage and think of ways to keep these influences within reasonable bounds. For the clergy marriage in particular, this means understanding how a couple's relationship to the congregation affects their marriage. A general survey of the advantages and disadvantages of clergy marriage will help us to see the marriage in its proper context: the congregational ministry itself.

The Advantages and Disadvantages of Clergy Marriage

To discover what makes clergy marriages unique, David and Vera Mace surveyed groups of clergy couples who came to their retreats and conferences. They asked the couples to think of the advantages and disadvantages of clergy marriage and to take fifteen minutes to write them down without collaborating with their spouses. The Maces sorted the written responses into categories and came up with nineteen advantages and nineteen disadvantages.[9]

The Maces' list of advantages can be condensed into a smaller number of themes. We find five overlapping themes in the couples' responses: (1) spiritual wellness, (2) integration, (3) professional status, (4) opportunities for growth, and (5) pragmatic considerations.

Spiritual wellness is a term used by Stinnett and DeFrain to describe one aspect of strong families: a sense of purpose, a shared conviction. The family are drawn together because they are apprentices to a cause that transcends the family itself.[10]

This is captured in the two advantages cited most frequently by clergy couples: "shared Christian commitment and spiritual resources" and "unity of purpose in ministering to others." This unity is also expressed in the advantage of "the wife's close identification with the husband's work." A less frequent response picks up the sense of both calling and cause: "being change agents in church and society." The call to minister to others provides clergy couples with a strong sense of purpose, uniting them in a common cause, serving under one God.

The second theme has to do with the quality of their relationship to the congregation. This is the notion of *integration* that we discussed in chapter 8. These clergy couples cited the "nurturing support of the congregation" and the "ready-made community of friends" as important advantages of being in the ministry. Concretely, the couples cited "gifts and services from the congregation" as tangible evidence of that support.

Clergy couples also appreciate the *professional status* that the ministry offers. This applies especially to ways the couple relates to groups outside the congregation. First, clergy couples enjoy a certain amount of "respect in the community." Beyond this, they are also part of a larger social network and need the "support of colleagues [and their] denomination." The advantages of the ministry, therefore, are not limited to the couple's relationship to the local congregation.

The ministry offers clergy couples a number of challenges and *opportunities for growth*. There are the horizon-broadening experiences of meeting new and interesting people and of traveling. There are opportunities and sometimes incentives for additional study and training. Interestingly, couples also listed the "challenge to model a Christian family" as an advantage. We surmise that this depends on the nature of their relationship to the congregation; if they feel integrated into the church family, then modeling a Christian family can be experienced as a positive challenge to growth rather than a negative intrusion.

Last, there are purely *pragmatic considerations*. While living in a parsonage can be stressful, it can also be a relief not to have to worry about finding other housing or making mortgage payments. And though there are many demands on the couple's time, their overall flexibility of schedule can be helpful when trying to plan family events.

These clergy couples, then, show clearly that there are several benefits to being in the ministry. A joint sense of calling provides the couple with a common ground and a feeling of unity. They can be blessed with both supportive parishioners and peers in the ministry. They can take advantage of many opportunities to stretch and grow in their faith, education, and skills. And other considerations, such as flexible hours and having their housing provided, can make ministry an attractive occupation.

What are the disadvantages? Again, the Maces list nineteen factors distilled from the responses of their clergy couples. The areas they cite are virtually identical to those we have already discussed as idealization, intrusion, role expectations, and family problems. Here is a sample of the disadvantages: marriage expected to be a model of perfection; time pressures; lack of privacy; financial stress; no in-depth sharing with other couples; expectations of children; role expectations that suppress humanness of pastor and wife; frequent moves; "belonging" to the congregation.

Although the items listed by the Maces are intended to show the advantages and disadvantages of clergy marriage, they seem to apply almost equally well to the clergy family. Indeed, much of what we have said in previous chapters about clergy families applies to the married couple. It is important, however, that we keep a clear distinction between the marital relationship and the family. Even if there are clear boundaries protecting the family, this does not guarantee that there will be adequate boundaries for the spouses. Some couples, for example, are so focused on their children's needs that they pay no attention to their marriage. Each and every relationship within a family must be nurtured, especially the husband-wife relationship. As family therapists are often fond of pointing out, much of the problem behavior in families can be traced to unacknowledged marital tensions.

What then, specifically, can we say about the clergy marriage? One common characteristic deserves special attention: the idealization of the minister's marital relationship.

Clergy Couples and the Ideal Marriage

As we saw in chapter 3, clergy family members are often idealized by their congregation. They are either implicitly or explicitly viewed as something more than human and more nearly perfect than the common lot of humanity. In some cases the clergy family experiences these ideals as confining and unrealistic. Elsewhere the family consciously or unconsciously accepts this double standard and tries to live as if the family were indeed flawless. Either way, the minister's family becomes isolated from authentic interpersonal relationships within the congregation.

This same kind of idealization affects clergy marriage. The clergy couple are expected (or expect of themselves) to show the rest of the congregation what an ideal marriage should be. In such an emotional climate, the couple feel hard-pressed to keep their problems to themselves.

All marriage relationships have ups and downs. The mere presence of stress or disagreements is not a sign of a troubled marriage. Rather, it is the inability to resolve the stress that is a problem. The minimum requirement for resolving marital difficulties is that the couple be able and willing to face their problems realistically and communicate clearly about them. (It sounds easier than it is.) However, for some Christian couples, including clergy, high expectations of happy marriages may interfere with this much-needed realism. The problem is that in our lack of differentiation, in our inability to deal with conflict, we tend to equate a "good" marriage with a conflict-free marriage. Instead of accepting and working through a conflict, we deny its existence.

Many factors contribute to the choice of a mate. Some are conscious, most are not. Anxious to believe that we have made the right choice, we invoke "God's will"; we want to believe that the person we have chosen is the special mate that God has designed especially for us. If we look a little more deeply, however, we would probably find that *God's* will is not the real issue. Instead we say that something is God's will so that we can deny the discomfort of having to be responsible for exercising *our* will. Lederer and Jackson wrote:

> The idea that there is only one possible mate for each [person] originated more or less in the church, which long has regarded marriages specifically as created by God. . . . The idea that a marriage was "made in heaven" is certain to be harmful. The thought that each of the spouses selected each other with divine inspiration, from among the three billion people in the world,

makes them intolerant of the imperfections of marriage, which are always present. More important, it eliminates the notion of personal *responsibility* both in selecting one's mate and in making the marriage workable. . . . Some spouses strive too hard to maintain the illusion of perfect marriage. If one starts out believing that one has chosen the perfect spouse, one becomes too readily disillusioned when the inevitable discovery of imperfection occurs.[11]

Whether these writers have correctly interpreted the church's view of marriage is beside the point. God can and does bless our choices.

What Lederer and Jackson have pinpointed is a common misuse of the notion of the marital sacrament in which we use God's blessing as an escape from responsibility. We try to keep up the appearance of perfection because we cannot tolerate our own imperfections. And when the burden of evidence makes it impossible to keep up the charade any longer, we blame our spouses or we blame God—anyone but ourselves.

For the clergy couple there is an additional complication. Like other couples, they have their own reasons for wanting a perfect marriage. The expectation of perfection, however, is also external: the congregational family expects them to be the model Christian couple. At the very least, this can make it much more difficult for the clergy couple to be honest about their marital struggles, even if they want to be. At worst, the congregation and the clergy couple collude to deny that there are domestic problems. This can lead to the stable but unsatisfactory kind of marriage that Lederer and Jackson call "the Gruesome Twosome":

> The members of a Gruesome Twosome live in accordance with the old proverb "People who live in glass houses shouldn't throw stones." Neither spouse dares to comment on the other's behavior or on the nature of their marriage except to forgive and offer unrequested succor. Each is afraid of what the other may do or say in response to a critical or openly attacking remark. . . . These couples form a rigid coalition on one point only—that they will not admit the condition of their marriage or of their true feelings—but that point they defend against all intruders.[12]

By virtue of their social environment, the clergy couple already live in a glass house. Therefore they may fear that showing anything less than perfection in their marriage will bring that house crashing down around their ears.

In some clergy marriages neither spouse is fully aware that the roles they are trying to maintain are unrealistic. Such couples often develop religious rationalizations that may prevent them from recognizing and dealing with normal marital stress. When the unresolved stress leads to marital problems, the problems are interpreted as symptoms of a lack of faith. Other clergy couples attempt to rationalize away marital problems by redefining them as normal trials that Satan is inflicting upon them. Again, whether or not such ideas are theologically valid is a moot point. The important thing is that these ideas are being used as ways to sidestep personal responsibility in the marriage.

The example of George and Kathy Jacobs at the beginning of this chapter demonstrates one way in which a clergy marriage may be idealized. Kathy was at least aware of the idealized image she and George were trying to uphold. George, however, was too wrapped up in his personally gratifying ministry to face the issue. The more his needs for affirmation were met by others in the church instead of by his wife, the more time he devoted to church work instead of spending time with his family.

Parishioners saw the pastor as sensitive and caring, and they shared more and more of their private selves with him. Many women in the church sought him out for spiritual counseling because of the understanding way he talked with them. Unhappy in their own marriages, these women idealized the pastor. And George was only too willing to be idealized in this way.

If he had been more attentive to what was happening, George could have easily anticipated what came next. But his need to collude with the ideal role that was thrust upon him prevented him from being so realistic. It was almost imperceptible at what point George crossed the line with one of his female counselees. But once he crossed it, there was no turning back. He had an affair. Even then, he managed to rationalize his behavior, saying that it was in the woman's best interest. But that argument soon fell flat when Kathy learned about it.

Kathy was hurt, but not shocked. The pain of the infidelity seemed a logical next step in her ongoing feelings of being emotionally abandoned. Now, after years of pretending to have an emotionally intimate relationship with George, Kathy was tired of living a lie. She couldn't quite articulate it, but somehow she sensed that their marital charade in front of the congregation had played a supportive role in George's affair.

She confronted him. Although he felt some twinge of remorse for neglecting his marriage, his most immediate response was one of panic: what will happen to my ministry? He agreed to stop the affair and hoped that that would be the end of the matter. Kathy, however, felt that George's promise carried an additional implied contract to pretend the affair never happened. She was not willing just to look the other way any more. Through much cajoling and eventually through threats, she convinced George to go with her to a marriage counselor.

In the counselor's office, George was the picture of cooperation. He would do anything he could, he said, to help the situation. As the counselor began to work with the Jacobs, she began to feel their "stuckness." George's cooperative attitude seemed to lack genuine contrition; it was more as if he wanted to find some way to make Kathy happy again so that he could bury the affair and go back to his ministry. Kathy wanted more of a resolution than that, but also feared what might happen if the congregation found out that they were seeing a counselor. Thus, even in the therapy room, trying to focus on their relationship to each other, George and Kathy found themselves unable to shake the presence of the congregation and its expectations.

The Jacobs may seem like an extraordinary case. Certainly few clergy marriages would match their story at every point. It is important, however, how the congregation and the spouses collude in idealizing the pastor's marriage. George and Kathy each had a personal need to be more than he or she was, to be someone whom others would admire. When their personal needs fused with the congregation's idealization of their marriage, they found themselves in a downward spiral of denial and self-deception. Idealization is unrealistic and competes with the realism and honesty needed to iron out marital difficulties. While wanting to have a better marriage is not a problem, wanting to have a perfect marriage usually is.

Ministry and Marriage

Whether or not the pastor's marriage is strongly idealized, the other pressures and demands of parish ministry certainly have an impact on the quality of the clergy marriage. The study of ex-pastors by Gerald J. Jud and his colleagues shows clearly that parish ministry can place a great deal of stress on a couple.

> When we asked the open-ended question, What difference has it made in your marriage and family life to be out of the pastoral ministry? the answers were surprisingly congruent. . . . [The results] showed that even ex-pastors whose marital relationships were good found their family situations happier or greatly im-proved. The change of occupation, not the individual family situation, is the cause of this improvement.[13]

Earlier in this chapter we saw that many clergy couples report themselves as both happy and satisfied in marriage. Now we must go one step further. Instead of asking how satisfied these couples are, we need to find what factors can cause their satisfaction to increase or decrease.

In chapter 8 we discussed *intrusion* and *integration* in the clergy family's relationship to the congregation. We saw that intrusive congregations can increase a clergy family's stress, whereas a sense of integration into the congregation is an emotional resource. The same is true of clergy marriages. The clergy couple whose congregation is more intrusive tend to be less satisfied and less happy in their marriage. Conversely, if the couple feel integrated into the congregational family, they report greater satisfaction in their married life.[14]

By far and away the most important factor, however, is *marital cohesion,* or the degree of emotional closeness a couple share.[15] Highly cohesive couples are in strong agreement with state-ments like these:

> "We are supportive of each other during difficult times."
>
> "We spend time together when we are home."
>
> "We know each other's close friends."
>
> "We are very close to each other."
>
> "We share interests and hobbies with each other."

In our research with doctor of ministry students we found that marital cohesion was the single most important factor related to marital happiness and satisfaction. The more cohesive the couple, the more satisfied they were in their marriage.[16]

Our statistical analysis, furthermore, indicates that congrega-tional intrusion and integration affect the clergy marriage through marital cohesion rather than as separate factors. What does this mean in pragmatic terms? There are four possible interpretations of this result:

1. On the positive side, clergy couples who are already more emotionally close are less affected by congregational intrusion.
2. Integration increases the couple's marital satisfaction by benefiting their sense of closeness to each other.
3. Negatively, couples who are less close emotionally to start with are more susceptible to the effects of intrusion.
4. Intrusion decreases the couple's satisfaction by interfering with their marital cohesion.

These interpretations are interrelated, and all of them may be true. This is a chicken-and-egg question to some extent. The influence from intrusion/integration and marital cohesion is undoubtedly a two-way street. Once the cycle is under way, the question is not "How did it start?" but "What can we do about it?"

Many clergy marriages need a high degree of marital cohesion to face the onslaught of congregational demands. Where marital cohesion is low, congregational intrusion can act like a wedge to drive a minister and spouse apart. The demands of parish ministry may cause the minister to be both physically and psychologically absent from the marriage, leaving the spouse in a void. One wife described this as her husband's "being married to his job," while another expressed the wish that her husband would "realize that his wife and family are *as* important, if not *more* important than the church people." Another wrote, "I don't feel I can have a claim to his time and understanding when I emotionally and physically need his support and nurturing." Still another wife commented, "I feel like a 'married single.' He delegates to me all the household responsibilities: finances, the cars, lawn, trash, children, repairs, etc. When he is home, he prefers not to relate to our family, or he'll watch TV or read or study. He becomes 'people saturated.'" Thus the demands of the parish ministry can leave the pastor emotionally drained so that he is unable to invest himself properly in his marriage or his family.

There is one final point we would like to cite from our research. It concerns how ministers and their wives differ in their reaction to family stress. First, we asked ministers and their wives how eager they were to stay in the ministry. Most of them were eager to stay. Second, we asked the couples how satisfied they were with several aspects of their ministries. We totaled these scores into an overall measure of satisfaction.[17] Again, most were quite satisfied in their ministries. It is less informative, however, to ask how satisfied clergy couples are in the ministry than to ask what would make them less satisfied. As you may recall from chapter 8, we took a measure of the impact of ministry on the family, a variable that we labeled "family stress." We guessed that clergy families who experience more stress would be less satisfied with the ministry and more eager to leave.

We found that we were only partially right. The responses from ministers' wives were clear: the higher the level of family stress, the more they desired to leave the ministry. It was also clear that ministers who experienced higher levels of family stress were, overall, less satisfied in their ministries. The difference, however, was that unlike their wives, this stress on the family did not make them want to leave the ministry.

This means that ministers' wives are probably more greatly affected by family stress than their minister-husbands and are more likely to view leaving the ministry as a solution. This is not unreasonable; as we saw in Jud's study of ex-pastors, leaving the ministry generally resulted in an improvement in the quality of family life. For the ministers, however, leaving the ministry is less of an option. This may indicate that even if the minister is dissatisfied with various aspects of his vocation, he finds more personal rewards in the ministry than his wife does.

The question we want to raise is this: How might this difference affect communication between spouses? This is particularly important when the clergy couple sit down to discuss how things are going or their future plans. Each spouse needs to understand the situation from the other's point of view. The minister must be able to identify his personal reasons for staying in the ministry and then look beyond them to understand realistically how the ministry is affecting his wife and family. The wife's desire to leave may be a sign that the minister has wedded himself to the church and that she wants her husband back. Or perhaps she feels tired of being taken for granted as the second half of the package deal. Whatever the feelings, they must be clearly understood in order for the couple to work toward a creative and accurate solution.

*   *   *

In summary, clergy marriages do not seem to be in any greater trouble than other marriages and may even be doing a bit better. Even so, an ecological approach suggests that it is more important to look at the ways the social environment affects a minister's marriage. A strong idealization of the marriage by the congregation, or even by the spouses themselves, makes it more difficult for the clergy couple to maintain the kind of realism they need to deal responsibly with marital problems.

Intrusion and integration can also influence the clergy marriage, largely by affecting the spouses' level of cohesion or emotional closeness. As with the family as a whole, it is important to keep clear boundaries around the marriage. The spouses need time alone together, free from churchly concerns, to keep alive their sense of identity as a couple.

Finally, the spouses' different responses to family stress can create a barrier to communication. Such stress may cause a wife to want to leave the ministry while the pastor would prefer to stay. In such a situation, patient attempts at empathy by both spouses are needed to keep their communication productive.

Our survey of the minister's family has taken us through an examination of individual roles as well as family and marital relationships. At each level we have tried to keep an ecological focus on the family's relationship to the congregation. We must now broaden our horizon even further and look beyond the local church.

10

Beyond the Local Church

In the first nine chapters of this book we have emphasized the need to understand the life of a minister's family life in its proper context, namely, the family's relationship to the congregation. These chapters taken by themselves form something of a whole. We could stop here. But while it is true that the congregation is the clergy family's most immediate social environment, this identifies only one level of the social ecology. Beyond the local congregation is a complex social world that we generally call modern culture or society. As we suggested in chapter 6, the differences between traditional and more modern or contemporary values form the background for the role struggles of clergy wives.

The term *modern* suggests that our present era is unique due to the massive impact of technological advance on family and society. The pressures that a clergy family faces are more than just a function of their relationship to a local church. To some extent they also have their source in the wider culture. To complete our survey of the ecology of the clergy family we must look at these larger cultural and subcultural patterns.

You may be used to pondering wider social issues. If so, this chapter should help you to clarify how social change affects ministry and family life. If you are not used to thinking in these broad terms, the concepts in this chapter should help you to identify social processes that you have probably taken for granted. Our assumption, of course, is that in the pragmatic world of daily social interaction, knowledge is power. If you

know what is happening, you can do something about it. We are
not counseling you to become a social activist for its own sake.
We merely hope to provide still more conceptual tools to help
you be more active with respect to your own churches and
families.

Our goals in this chapter are both general and specific. On the
general level we will examine how modern culture influences
the religious life of the church. Our specific focus is on how
these general trends are reflected in denominational structures
and in the lives of clergy families. As you read, we encourage
you to broaden your horizons beyond what you have read thus
far; ask yourself how your own family and congregation are
affected by events beyond the boundaries of the local church.
This will give you a foundation to be actively involved in
ministering to your family and to others through interaction with
larger social issues.

As a starting point, we ask what makes society "modern."
Beginning in the eighteenth century and continuing into the
present, people have found ways to apply machine, electronic,
and computer technologies to every facet of human life. The
rapid growth of knowledge in these areas and their widespread
application have literally shaped the course of history. Sociologists attempting to describe these trends use a mind-spinning
array of technical terms: modernization, secularization, plurali-
zation, bureaucratization, industrialization, urbanization, privatization, routinization, individualization, rationalization, subjec-
tivization, dehumanization. One might think that sociologists
have been gripped by an "-ization fixation.'" But what are these
terms trying to explain? Let us look first at how sociocultural
trends affect the life of the local church.

How Does Modern Culture Affect the Local Church?

Why is it sometimes difficult for one person to fulfill the role
of minister today? One general reason is that modern culture
and society affect the local church in a great many ways.
Sociologist John Coleman has reviewed what other sociologists
and historians have written on the subject, and he has distilled
five common themes from their work:[1]

1. *Religious pluralism*. The freedom to hold one's own
religious beliefs is guaranteed by the U.S. Constitution. This

was intended to prevent one person or class from dominating another on religious grounds. What it creates, however, is a social environment where it is difficult to maintain any kind of uniformity of doctrine. All beliefs are judged relative in value, and the door to doubt is left wide open.

2. *Secularism.* Whereas in past centuries the church provided society with a moral anchor, today it has lost most of its hold over the religious and moral dimension of society. Science has in a sense become the new religion of the people.

3. *Complexity of communication.* The old bywords of faith have lost their significance for many. Modern religions want to find new words and symbols for their faith. In so doing, creeds are reinterpreted and the traditional roles of clergy and laity are redefined.

4. *Disintegration of community.* Modern society is highly mobile. Urban "commuter churches" have members who drive long distances to attend. Unless the church can maintain a strong sense of community, congregations turn into mere audiences.

5. *Dominance of economic values.* Nonreligious, economically motivated institutions have become the driving force in society. Religion has been relegated to the private domain, and as a result it is hamstrung in its ability to have public influence.

It is clear that each of these themes describes an area of concern for the church in the modern world. Let us examine each theme more closely.

Making Faith Believable in a Pluralistic Society

The first trend that affects the life of the church is the trend toward religious pluralism. What is pluralism? The general idea is that the world is much too complex to be described on the basis of any single principle. Applied to religious belief, this means that there are numerous belief systems, each with its own interpretation of the divine. No single system is allowed to lay claim to being the best or most nearly true. This attitude reflects the American values of freedom and individual rights and thus of religious liberty: you are free to believe whatever you want to believe, provided someone else's rights are not infringed or compromised. Ultimately religious pluralism makes belief a pragmatic issue: if it works for you, if it helps you to achieve whatever it is that you call spirituality, then that is sufficient reason to believe it.

One of the major tasks of the minister in the local church is to make faith believable. This can be difficult in a modern, pluralistic society. Everyone is exposed to many religious alternatives. The modern religious attitude is "why not explore my options?" Tolerance of religious differences entails a suspicion of any religious system that claims to have the corner on truth. Religion is a matter of choice and personal preference. But is this enough? We still want to believe that our particular faith is the right one. Religious pluralism gives us no assurance, only doubt. The local church finds itself to be just one of many "faithing" communities struggling to create and maintain the plausibility of its belief system. In a sense, every religious group in the United States experiences itself as a minority forced to defend its views in the midst of a religious smorgasbord.

The task of making faith believable falls upon the local minister, who is consequently called on to become the intellectual leader in the church. In the confusion created by competing religious views, members of the local church look to the minister to provide a sense of meaning, centeredness, and religious reality. How can ministers meet this need? Some are tempted to create a sense of security by searching for airtight rational arguments for their beliefs. Although this is not necessarily a problem in itself, the kind of security it generates is shallow, vulnerable to being overturned by better arguments or stronger logic. Clergy may soon find themselves in the position of leading the congregation in sniffing out and eradicating doctrinal impurity and heresy.

In the face of religious pluralism, many clergy may try to protect parishioners from false beliefs by closing the boundaries around the church and insulating it from the contaminating influence of modern society. This can be done in varying degrees. A group can split off from society and envelop itself in a religious world of their own making. This can happen when disillusioned, would-be worshipers pin all their religious hopes on one doctrine or one persuasive individual. An extreme example of this is the ill-fated totalitarian sect founded by Jim Jones in Guyana.

Usually, however, the response is not so extreme. Established churches and denominations try to sort out which aspects of modern culture are less threatening than others. This means that churches and denominations differ in the extent and the way they allow modern culture to infiltrate their lives. It is a matter of balance. The problem comes when one is both a member of a largely separatist church and simultaneously embedded in the broader culture, say, through one's occupation. In such cases the only way to function may be to separate one's life into religious and secular compartments. When life is split into separate sections like this, there is no dialogue, no integration of worldviews. Defending oneself against pluralism by isolating one point of view only allows pluralism to feed on itself.

The challenges of religious pluralism, then, require that ministers be able to provide guidance and leadership to parishioners who are confused by competing religious beliefs. This must be done in a way that does not isolate the church from the world. If it does, ministers may inadvertantly create an anxious double-mindedness in their parishioners.

Religious Faith Versus Secular Society

The term "secular" is commonly understood to mean "nonreligious." It makes sense to us modern folk to have such a word to distinguish what belongs to the domain of religion and what does not. We forget that there was a time when people would have questioned the need for such a distinction. In previous centuries, nearly all facets of social life either were imbued with religious significance or were directly under ecclesiastical influence. Today, however, religion is relegated to a smaller and smaller sphere of authority. Education and the doctrine separating church and state are good examples of this. The entire system of formal education owes its roots to the medieval scholastics of the church. In the political realm, too, the church once held great power and authority. In the eleventh century the Holy Roman emperor Henry IV stood barefoot in the snow for three days to ask forgiveness of Pope Gregory VII, who had anathematized the emperor as a rebuke.[2] In the modern world, however, such images are no longer meaningful. Education and state government have been secularized, removed from the domain of church authority. The ministry itself has adapted secular standards so that candidates for ministerial positions are evaluated not only according to their sense of calling, but also by their professional and academic credentials.

For any society to remain stable, it must maintain some moral absolutes that are not generally questioned but taken for granted by consensus. Throughout human history such absolutes have usually been provided by religion. In a secular and pluralistic society, however, moral certainty gives way to moral relativism. Instead of turning to religion, modern humanity turns to science as its authority. Recently philosophers of science have taken great pains to point out the ultimately religious character of science itself.[3] Yet their arguments have yet to filter down from the academic setting to the "real'" world. With secularization, science replaces religion even for those who have only a vague idea of what science is actually about.

The church has recognized the need to challenge this secular trend, but has tended to respond in unhelpful ways. In their hunger for religious certainty, some churches seek to impose their own moral system on an unbelieving society. As examples of this, sociologist Peter Berger cites liberation theology, the Iranian revolution, and portions of the contemporary American fundamentalist movement such as the Moral Majority. Berger himself opposes these movements because of their politically and theologically restrictive nature. He recommends instead milder, nonsectarian responses that would not impose their values on the whole of society.[4] We will neither refute nor defend Berger's position here. The point is that much of what is happening on the contemporary religious scene is, in fact, organized religion's attempt to respond to secularism. Ministers face a dilemma: how can they cushion their congregations against the corrosive effect of secularism while avoiding making them into negativistic, intolerant communities?

Another false solution is to turn inward for answers. Much of contemporary Christianity has supported this unfortunate turn by becoming subjective and private. Faith becomes "a personal matter." Instead of having an outward impact on public morality, this type of private faith results in an inward preoccupation with the self. Competing faith systems are not evaluated for their truth, but for what good they can do for the individual. The evangelistic Good News no longer centers on grace and the forgiveness of sin, but on solutions to emotional and psychological problems. People of a modern age are more ready to hear about personal benefits than the need for repentance. One need only note the excesses found within much of televangelism in this regard.

Yet a third unhealthful reaction to secularism taken by some churches is the attempt to create purified identities. Such churches seek to establish clear-cut boundaries that distinguish the in-group from the out-group. This is usually done by identifying those who have the "right" doctrine. Churches rally together under the common banners of "inerrancy," "infallibility," "inspiration," "reliability," "authority," and the like. The theology behind the terms is not what is at stake here; our interest is in how such theological terms become almost political slogans. Debates about religious language are not just matters of academic theology; the language itself is used to establish symbolic boundaries around the community of those who speak "the true faith." The problem with attempting to purify the church in this way is that dialogue is prematurely closed. The practical result is a dependence on authority, with a fear of and antagonism toward others with different convictions.

The Complexity of Communication in the Church

Another challenge raised by modern culture and society for the local church is that they have called the significance of traditional religious language into question. Words and symbols that were full of meaning for past generations of believers are found empty today. The irony is that this trend began within Christian liberalism, which sought to save Christianity from the onslaught of modern secular culture. In the hands of theological liberalism, a seemingly clear Bible verse such as Acts 16:31 ("Believe in the Lord Jesus and you will be saved") can be interpreted to mean, "By accepting the truths that Jesus taught, you will be a whole person with an integrated personality." How did such a conception make its way into the church? Consider these words of the famous liberal preacher Harry Emerson Fosdick:

> To be a person is to be engaged in a perpetual process of becoming. . . . The basic urge of the human organism is toward wholeness. The primary command of our being is, Get yourself together, and the fundamental sin is to be chaotic and unfocused. . . . When at last maturity is reached . . . the whole organism can be drawn together into that "acme of integration" which appears in creative work. . . . in modern psychological parlance

the word "integration" has taken the place of the religious word "Salvation."[5]

When words come to have so many different meanings in the modern church, for practical purposes they become meaningless. This is especially troublesome when even the most important linguistic symbols of faith, such as "God," "sin," and "salvation," are interpreted in different ways by different people. Here the gap between clergy and laity can be particularly wide. As others have observed, some ministers stay out of hot water by using traditional Christian vocabulary because then people in the church will interpret the sermon according to their own meanings. This is despite the fact that what they think they heard is not what the preacher meant!

Difficulty also arises when standard religious expressions become viewed as empty clichés. As a result, many individuals choose not to speak of their religious beliefs and experiences because no available "language" seems right. For some people, "Praise God!" is a legitimate expression of faith and reverence; for others it is a religious substitute for "Gee, that's great!" When the phrase itself becomes stigmatized as a cliché, those who use it legitimately are left searching for new words. Local churches, wanting to have a shared language of faith, may standardize a new set of expressions. But these modern expressions are often more subjective, focusing on individual conversion experiences, personal growth, and declarations of private revelation such as "I feel led" or "The Lord is telling me ..." God can and does, of course, speak directly to individuals. This should not distract us, however, from seeing that traditional religious symbols that once had meaning for the community are being replaced by the catch phrases of a more private, individualized religion.

In response to the increasingly murky relationship between religious language and meaning, the church has intensified its efforts in the interpretation of Scripture. These efforts have not always been constructive, especially when the influence of the interpreter's own cultural context is ignored. More often than we care to admit, we interpret Scripture in such a way as to support what is already believed.

To a greater or lesser extent, all interpretation will involve some level of self-interest. In particular, as human beings, we are members of various groups, each with its set of values. Each of us carries an assortment of conscious and unconscious religious, economic, social, and cultural values, and we bring these with us to the process of interpretation. They are reflected in the variety of competing interpretations of passages relating to the roles of women, the structure of the family and church, the morality of war, the socioeconomic aspects of faith, and so on.

To what extent do we interpret such texts according to what we *want* to find? How do we approach someone who interprets them differently? It is imperative that we strive to keep the lines of dialogue open, intentionally interacting with Christians of other cultures and subcultures. It is only then that we will be able to see clearly enough to sort out how our own value assumptions influence our interpretations. Without such corrective dialogue we will simply create a multitude of unconnected and provincial interpretations, a situation that would only make matters worse for recapturing a sense of meaning in our religious language.

Another limiting factor in current interpretive efforts is our tendency to rely too heavily on experts. Much of this has to do with the acceptance of secular standards, so that only those with the appropriate academic degrees are allowed to have anything to say on a given subject. Coupled with the tendency toward pluralism, this creates confusion for nonexperts who have no way of deciding which experts they should believe.

The real problem here, though, is that a reliance on expertise creates a gap between clergy and laity. Many preachers and writers are guilty of making the process of interpretation seem too heady and mystical for the average layperson. When the Sunday sermon contains continual references to the original Greek or perhaps uses detailed geographical expositions, the faithful in the pew can be disheartened about their abilities. There is no doubt that diligent study of Greek and biblical geography are helpful. But we question to what extent such emphases may reflect a typically modern reliance on the mastery of technique, with the resulting division between those who are experts and those who are not. The tools of interpretation go hand in hand with the work of the Holy Spirit. Ministers need to guard against placing themselves in a mediating role of expert where they stand between the Scriptures and their parishioners.

The Vanishing Community

It used to be that if you lived in the same vicinity as another person or family, you automatically were members of the same community. Television shows such as "Little House on the Prairie" depicted farm-based American life where small communities dotted the landscape and the next community was a full day's buggy ride away. Much has changed since then. Indeed, even a program like "Little House" often addressed the theme of how much the pace and values of life in the small community of Walnut Grove differed from those of the big city. Whereas community life was once based on geographical neighborhoods, this is no longer the case in an industrial, modern, urban society. The word *neighbor* loses its meaning in areas where people move every two to three years and many can't even remember the names of the people who live next door. In place of the traditional community and the sense of belonging it brings, there are anonymity and superficial relationships. Without the social control and accountability that come from being responsible to neighbors, many modern-day people can become irresponsible, isolated, and vulnerable to moral whims.

This social disintegration is coupled with the fact that economic and political functions have been removed from the local community and have come to rest with more impersonal bureaucratic organizations. Take the example again of a small farm community at the turn of the century. Most of the community needs could be fulfilled by its members. A variety of products and services were exchanged by neighbors in a simple economic system with a minimum of reliance on outside sources. In a more industrialized society, however, products and services are not so much exchanged as they are packaged, shipped, and marketed. The one who grows the food and the one who eats it are total strangers and may live hundreds or thousands of miles apart. The connection between them is an economic and political one only, held together by corporate or governmental machinery. This sets up a society in which most of life is divided into two spheres: the privacy of one's home versus the impersonal economic world of large bureaucracies. The community, which once mediated between the individual and larger institutions, is no longer there.

Is it any wonder that many people are currently searching for a substitute to fill the gap left by the disappearance of the traditional community? The variety of experimental communes and living communities that have sprung up in recent years testifies to this. People are looking for a secure context within which they can build their lives and identities. This presents the local church with a golden opportunity: to fill this vacuum by becoming a real community to its members. But while there are opportunities, there are also barriers to becoming the type of communities they need to be.

Many congregations use the metaphor of the church as community. The word appeals to the desire for a sense of belonging, of commonality and shared identity, and of interdependence. And though local churches may appear to provide these benefits, on closer investigation some are found merely to be what one writer has called "purified communities."[6] In a purified community, members are bound together not by a genuine knowledge of and caring for one another, but by the mere assumption of commonality. They may be alike in some ways, but their shared identity is simply assumed rather than developed through mutual dialogue. Interdependence in such a group is based on maintaining an image rather than on material, emotional, or social needs. The community does not genuinely mediate between the individual and society. The members of the community simply rely on each other for a sense of respectability.

So as not to disturb the image of the community, such local churches do not allow diversity and may actually exclude people who challenge or tarnish the image. Without genuine interdependence there is no room to tolerate nonconformity. There is little basis for the kind of trust needed to build authentic relationships and spiritual growth. The community metaphor becomes an exploitive appeal and an institutional device to avoid facing the true nature of the relationships in the church. Clearly, the use of the language of community in the so-called electronic church is one example. When the metaphor of church as community is widely misused, the true nature of both "community" and "church" is lost.

We are a much more mobile society than we used to be. A day's journey by horse and cart now takes minutes by car. A journey of months by sea is now possible in hours by plane. The

negative side of this type of technological progress, however, is
that the geographical boundaries which used to define community no longer exist, and there is not always something to
replace them. Individuals living in urban areas can choose to
commute to a church far from where they live. This kind of
mobility can seriously affect a church's ability to maintain
commitment from individual church members. Indeed, some
churches may avoid making demands on members for fear that
they will move to another church.

There is something of a continuum here regarding a given
congregation's ability to integrate into the surrounding community. On one end is the community church, where church life is
firmly embedded in the broader community. On the other end is
the commuter church, where the congregation is geographically
more spread out. The commuter church in particular is a child of
our modern age.

Irwindale Lutheran Church, located in a rural area of North
Dakota, is an example of a community church. It is in a county
where 80 percent of the residents are Lutheran and the majority
are of Scandinavian descent. Irwindale Lutheran is strongly
integrated into the life of the surrounding community. School
events are carefully scheduled so they won't conflict with
church life. Announcements about community activities are
given in the church bulletin. Church members interact with
each other all during the week, not only on Sunday. When there
is a need in the community, the church, rather than a social
welfare agency, is usually the first to respond. The congregation
is made up of a community of people whose lives are truly
interrelated.[7]

Second Lutheran Church in downtown Minneapolis, by
contrast, is a commuter church. When it was first established
over a hundred years ago, most of its members lived within
walking distance. Today most members commute to worship
services from throughout the city or from suburban communities
over ten miles away. The membership of Second Lutheran is
still mostly Scandanavian, and they do continue to have potluck
suppers. But beyond the four walls of the church they really do
not constitute a community. Although some members may
gather for church-related activities during the week, they do not
generally relate to each other in their daily lives.

As these examples illustrate, the extent to which a congregation reflects a sense of genuine fellowship in its corporate life depends in part on its larger social environment. In a modern, more urban society, it has become increasingly difficult for a church to maintain a firm feeling of community. But despite this erosion of community life, the local church can still be the *koinonia*-type environment that we desperately need. To be this, however, the church must follow three general guidelines. First, the church must be willing to be a community of diversity, encompassing various social classes, races, ages, backgrounds, and religious experiences (see also chapter 4). Disagreements and conflicts will inevitably arise, but when they do, they should not be feared. Second, the church must be a community whose members have a genuine knowledge of one another. This does not mean that all members must be equally intimate; we are talking about a community based on the honest sharing of both joys and burdens rather than on image. Third, the church must recreate roles for all its participants. Laypersons need to be empowered to share in the ministry. The clergy-laity gap must be minimized so that the pastor role is not simply one more career in society.

Money Talks: The Dominance of Economic Values

One result of secularization in modern society is that economic life has developed independent of religious values. Since religious values no longer dominate, economic values have been substituted. This is reflected in the phrases of everyday speech; we speak of "the bottom line," we "invest" in relationships, and spending time at the driving range "pays off" when our golf score improves. These common expressions reflect our basically economic way of thinking.

This dominance of economic values is reflected to different degrees in local churches. The most obvious cases are those with clear divisions along the lines of social class. This in turn reflects the class, status, and racial polarizations of residential life. Some churches are interracial and interclass, but because of the importance of economic values in our society, people of different ethnic or class backgrounds may have trouble relating as brothers and sisters in Christ. One research study points out how a difference in social class can cause a gap between clergy and their parishioners:

Our somewhat tentative statistics suggest that social class, representing different styles of life and values, creates social and intellectual distance between ministers and their parishioners. Since both partners to the minister-parish relationship react to the other's social class position, their mutual reactions tend to have a cumulative effect, further dividing them from each other.[8]

On a somewhat larger scale, we can note that affluent churches may resist a communal emphasis in their church life when it implies a sharing of economically valued resources, skills, or knowledge. There would be instead a clear separation of economic and church life, with economics entering the church life primarily through offerings, pledges, and fund drives.

Economic values have also resulted in the "selling" of the Christian message. The gospel becomes a consumer item, to be slickly packaged and sold like any other product. Each local church must make its particular version of the product more appealing than the next. Churches compete with one another. Growth strategies resemble Madison Avenue advertising campaigns. And growth itself becomes defined in economic rather than spiritual terms. The successful church is the one that has the numbers: attendance, size of budget, and so on. There is, of course, nothing intrinsically wrong with having a large church or a fat budget; we question, however, the extent to which these may become ends in themselves. When success is defined in economic terms, evangelism of the people deteriorates into marketing research. Needless to say, the gospel itself is altered or oversimplified in the process in order to make it more inviting to the would-be consumer.

As local churches compete, they standardize and tone down the gospel so as to appeal to the widest number of people. As mentioned earlier, the dual message of sin and grace is not a popular one. But it is not enough for a church simply to avoid an "offensive" gospel. It must also be unique in some way. Thus many congregations become "theme" churches. They appeal to some segment of the marketplace on the basis of a unique program such as a vibrant youth group, superior music, a dazzling sanctuary, or a caring counseling center. At the same time, these churches may stress a unique image, becoming known as the "friendly" church, the "entertaining" church, or the "intellectual" church. A particular personality may be highlighted, such as a widely read pastor-author, a scholarly teaching pastor, or a dynamic athletic pastor. Still other churches emphasize some special concern such as drug abuse, Christian feminism, world mission, or inner-city ministry.

Any of these characteristics can develop naturally as an outgrowth of a church's ministry, in direct interaction with those they seek to reach. We must be careful, however, that these same characteristics do not become changed into marketing tools. In becoming thematic a church stands to lose its ability to find significant roles for members whose gifts fall outside these more narrowly defined themes. In more extreme cases, theme churches can begin to resemble just one more specialized audience or interest group in the mass society rather than a community of faith.

Clearly, trends that make modern society unique also have an enormous impact on the life and ministry of the church. It is not possible for us to examine every dimension of this influence; our intent is only to show that the institutional church is very much immersed in the currents of social change. To ignore these forces is to be at their mercy. To give them their proper place in the social ecology, however, is to empower the church to be able to interact more cogently with society.

Modern Culture and the Minister's Family

The clergy family, as part of both the local congregation and the larger society, is influenced by modern society. These influences can be indirect, affecting the congregation as a whole and therefore the clergy family's immediate social context. Or they can be more direct and less involved with how the minister's family and the congregation interact with each other. In this section we move from our general comments about how the modern world affects the church to focus specifically on the clergy family. We will look at three broad areas: differences between urban and rural churches, the effects of social class, and differences among denominations.

The Urban Versus the Rural Church

Picture, if you will, a church sitting on the crest of a hill in rural Iowa. On one side of the church is the parsonage, on the other a grove of trees. A small stream in back separates the church from a cornfield. The 150-member congregation comprises farm families from the surrounding area. Pastor Swanson, along with his wife and two children, has served this congregation for three years. Things are going well for the Swansons; the children like school, and the family feel very much at home in their rural community life.

Now suppose that somehow the church building and the entire congregation, including the Swansons, were transported to the heart of a metropolis such as Chicago, Los Angeles, or New York City. Nothing about the church is to be changed, only the social ecology beyond the church. The family is the same, and they are a part of the very same congregation. But will the quality of their family life be unchanged? Hardly. The Swansons and the entire congregation are likely to experience culture shock, and their families will reflect this.

Sociologists discuss the difference between these environments in terms of the degree of urbanization. What are some of these differences? In a metropolis like Chicago, people are packed together more closely. In rural areas, neighboring houses may be a quarter-mile or more apart. In the big city, one feels more crowded and less able to find a quiet and secluded place. Many urbanites simply get used to going to sleep while listening to their neighbors argue on the other side of the wall or alley. The Swansons will be surrounded by noise and light: traffic noises, sirens, domestic quarrels, street lights, traffic lights, neon lights. The small community, where most or all of the inhabitants are known to each other by name, is replaced by an environment of more anonymous and impersonal relationships. On short walks through downtown areas, the Swansons will pass literally hundreds or thousands of nameless faces, most of whom scurry by with their eyes averted.

The Swansons and their parishioners will also face a more complex and confusing world. There will be ethnic diversity, a hodgepodge of cultural groups, many of which the Swansons may never have encountered. There are scores of radio and television stations. The Swanson family may even subscribe to cable television, only to find later that in so doing they have created a new censorship problem: at the time, they had no idea that movies were being piped in that had never been available to the children before. Beyond cable, of course, there are also many more movie theaters from which to choose and a variety of cultural and sporting events like the opera, the symphony, and ballet as well as professional baseball, football, basketball, and hockey. By living in an urban setting the Swansons will experience a vastly different realm of choice and a much more pluralistic environment. The family rules that may have served the Swansons well in rural Iowa will be strained to their limits in the urban world.

Church size and urbanization seem to go hand in hand. In the main, rural churches tend to be significantly smaller than their urban counterparts. This can create a conflict of roles for some clergy. On the one hand, a minister may be more content to pastor a smaller, rural church. At the same time, however, he may also feel professional or financial pressure to move up to a larger, urban church, with the results we see in the example of the Swansons. Some researchers have discovered that ministers in small rural churches tend to be more satisfied than those from large urban churches.[9] Moreover, our own studies have shown that there is a relationship between satisfaction in the ministry and quality of family life.[10] It would seem a shame for a pastor to leave a satisfying and productive ministry in a smaller church for the primary reason of needing more money for his family. We will look at problems of finances again when we discuss differences among denominations below.

The rural versus urban distinction brings us back to the difference between community- and commuter-type churches. How might this difference affect a clergy family? As might be expected, the glass-house effect is more prominent in the former than the latter. In the community church the minister's children attend the same school as the children of parishioners; the minister's wife shops at the same stores and belongs to the same community groups as other women in the church. The greater overlap between the lives of the clergy family and the other families in the church means that more opportunities exist to scrutinize the minister's family. In the commuter-type church there is much less opportunity to do so. A minister's child may flunk a course at school without the whole church knowing it. The minister's wife can buy T-bone steaks at a supermarket where no one knows her personally and where no one will raise an eyebrow or ask questions about stewardship. The family can go to the movies without worrying about what others may think.

As we have noted, there is a two-sided sword in the relationship between a clergy family and the congregation. On the positive side, when members of a minister's family feel integrated into the congregational family, they are more likely to be satisfied with their lot. Negatively, a lack of boundaries around the minister's family can allow the congregation to intrude in an unhealthful way. The relationship to the wider community must be understood in the same way. There are advantages for clergy families that are part of community-type churches, for they can become truly integrated into the life of the church. The obvious disadvantage is that they may find it difficult to have the privacy they need. Clergy families in community churches may need to make special efforts to create appropriate boundaries.

Clergy families in commuter-type churches, while being less vulnerable to the intrusion of congregational members, may need to take deliberate steps to cultivate relationships with other parishioners. There may be a need to seek out other families in the church who enjoy similar social and recreational activities. This, of course, will also depend on the extent to which the congregation idealizes the clergy family (chap. 3), making peer relationships within the congregation more difficult. Perhaps the most that can be expected in some commuter churches is that the minister's family will develop specialized social networks of friends within the church. These networks will be similar to those of other urbanites, where there is more breadth in terms of numbers of friends and less depth in terms of genuine intimacy.

Social Class and the Minister's Family

Social class, as mentioned earlier, is one of the characteristics that goes beyond the boundaries of the local church, but greatly affects what happens within those boundaries. A basic sociological principle in church growth theory is known as the homogeneous unit concept.[11] The idea is that people will be drawn toward congregations that contain others who are most like themselves. Although we might wish to deny it, this applies to social class distinctions as well. Most churches are made up of people who are similar with regard to income, standard of living, occupational prestige, and level of education. How does this affect the lives of clergy families?

The social status of a family in the United States is mainly determined by the occupation of the primary breadwinner.

Clergy families have generally benefitted from high status. During the last two centuries, however, the overall social status of ministers has declined compared with other professional occupations. How this relates to the congregation will depend on the class makeup of its membership. Clergy families in more economically deprived congregations are likely to have a higher status relative to the parishioners. In congregations with members in a higher class bracket, the reverse is true: the minister's family will have a lower status than most of the church members.

Such class differences will affect how the clergy family and the congregation interact. We must remember that for parishioners, the church is not only a place to worship, but a source and symbol of their social identity. Therefore it is important to parishioners that their minister and his family fit in. In the eyes of parishioners, the clergy family represents the congregation to the larger community. The congregation may feel embarrassed or uneasy if the minister's family is either too far below or too far above them in terms of social class. There is less of a problem of fit in more homogeneous congregations. Where the social status of all congregational members is more or less the same, the minister's family needs only to approximate this status. When the congregation is more diverse, clergy families may find themselves in a bind. If they associate more with one social class than another, those of the other class will feel snubbed and alienated. This in essence creates one more ball for the clergy family to juggle.

There is some evidence that the minister and his family may socially represent the status parishioners would like to have as opposed to their actual status. This is probably more prevalent in churches with low-income families. In such situations the minister and his family are not only permitted, but perhaps even expected to live at a more affluent level. The fact that the minister drives a fancy car or wears expensive suits becomes a source of pride rather than a bone of contention.

Social class, then, is a variable that cuts across other characteristics of denominations and local congregations. Class distinctions reflect certain subcultural values that church members and clergy alike bring to their relationship with each other. Differences in class can be given either a positive or a negative interpretation. For our purposes it is sufficient to note that the relationship between the congregation and the minister's family is influenced by social class, a matter that is not confined to the boundaries of the local church itself.

Differences Among Denominations

Social class is not the only subcultural influence that we must consider. Denominations have their own values and goals that impact the clergy family both directly and indirectly. The religious liberty guaranteed by the Constitution allowed Christianity to take root in American soil in a number of different forms. Christianity in America consists of a wide variety of denominations, far greater in number than in other world religions. This is an important part of the total ecology of the clergy family. The minister's family is part of a congregational family. The congregation in turn is part of a denomination, which influences the pastor's family as a subculture in its own right.

Denominations vary in important ways that can affect the life of the clergy family. One example is the degree of centralization, determined by the body's form of government. The basic question here is, Where is the power and control located—in the denominational offices, or in the local church? The centralized denomination is like a wagon wheel; the denomination is the hub where policies and decisions are made, and local congregations revolve around it. In more decentralized denominations, local bodies are more independent and see to their own government. How centralized a denomination is will influence the relationship between a congregation and its minister.

In decentralized denominations, control rests with the local church. The church owns its own property, calls its own minister, and has the freedom overall to operate the church as it sees fit. This puts the pastor in the position of being directly responsible to the congregation. In decentralized bodies, the denomination itself has little control over local churches, whereas the local church has great control over its minister.

When, by contrast, the denomination is highly centralized, authority resides with the denomination rather than the local congregation. Consequently the local church's authority over the minister is likely to be more restricted. In some cases, denominational authority can serve as a buffer for ministers who take positions on social issues that may be unpopular with local parishioners. During the civil rights movement of the 1960s and 1970s, for example, ministers in centralized denominations were much more prophetic in urging Christians to become involved in the struggle for justice than were ministers in more decentralized bodies.

In some cases, however, investing too much power in a central office can interfere with the relationship between a pastor and congregation. Let's say that Pastor Baldwin is an ordained minister in a denomination that has an episcopal form of government. Over his twenty or so years in the ministry, the denomination has moved him six times. The first few reassignments always seemed to come just when he was beginning to see his ministry bear fruit. Soon after, he lost his zeal. "After all," Pastor Baldwin reasoned to himself, "what's the use of putting in so much energy? I'll just get moved again in a couple of years, and the next pastor will undo or change everything I've started." Moreover, he found it difficult to establish solid relationships with his new congregations, because they also anticipated that another separation, another change in pastors, would be right around the corner. When he ventured comments to his colleagues about his frustration, he found that he was not the only one disenchanted with the system. None of the pastors, however, knew quite what to do. Emotionally they felt caught between their devotion to the denomination and their frustration with its power structure.

A high degree of centralization, then, can create problems for the pastor-parish relationship. Since the quality of that relationship is so closely tied to the life of the minister's family, centralization has an indirect impact on that family. One might speculate, for example, that clergy families in centralized denominations would find it more difficult to be positively integrated into the life of the congregation, especially if the family is reassigned every two or three years.

Centralization has an even more direct impact on the minister's family in terms of salary and compensation. Where there is more local control, there is a greater feeling of interdependence between a minister and the congregation, including a sense of responsibility in the congregation for the financial support of the minister. In more centralized denominations, funds may be channeled to headquarters, which then writes out the check for the pastor's salary.

This is not just a tangential issue. As we have seen in chapter 8, income is a crucial issue for clergy families. Here are three examples of ministers' families, representing three different denominations.

When Pastor Albertson started an Assemblies of God church twenty-three years ago, he was fresh out of Bible college and in his early twenties. Looking back on those early years, he reminisces, "I accepted the call to be the pastor of a small fellowship. Then there were only four families meeting together weekly for prayer. They wanted me to help them start a church. The weekly offering was my salary, and sometimes there was little more than what we needed for rent. Some days we didn't have anything to eat except rice and beans. Sometimes we didn't even have that, and then one of the members would bring us some food. I often wonder that we all made it. But the Lord provided, and the faithful few grew."

From such meager beginnings, both the church and its pastor grew and prospered. The congregation now numbers 3,500. Pastor Albertson has a salary of more than $50,000 a year, a car allowance, and a congregation that regularly sends him to visit the Holy Land and the church's missionaries in Africa and South America. In denominations like the Assemblies of God, the financial well-being of the minister's family depends directly on the minister's relationship to the local congregation.

Pastor Williams is a member of the Seventh-day Adventist Church, a denomination that has a decidedly different philosophy regarding how clergy are paid. When he was graduated from seminary, Pastor Williams was assigned to a rural church in Texas with a membership of ninety. Every Adventist minister is paid the same amount by the conference, and Pastor Williams and his family found themselves financially secure. Over the next two years they even managed to put some money away in savings. In the middle of his third year, however, the pastor was reassigned to a 300-member congregation in one of the more affluent suburban communities in the Los Angeles area. Many of his congregational members were medical doctors associated with the local Adventist hospital, and many others were in assorted well-paying professions.

In moving to the Los Angeles area, the Williams family found that a home comparable to the one they left behind cost three times as much. Denominational policy, however, did not allow for this increase in their cost-of-living. The pastor's salary remained the same because his reassignment was considered a purely lateral move, a shift in locale without a change of status. This was only the beginning of their financial straits.

All three of the Williams children were then of school age. One of the expectations in the Adventist church is that the minister's children will attend denominational schools. Who bears the burden of this added expense? For the most part, the minister's family does. While there was no provision for increased housing costs, some stipend was provided for the education of the Williamses' children. To the family, however, the stipend was minimal in comparison to the total cost. The requirement that the children attend a denominational school simply placed an added burden on the family's finances.

After two years of struggling to make ends meet, the family decided that Mrs. Williams would have to find a job to help support the family. Although this helped solve the money problem, it caused disruption in both the home and the church. At home the family had to reorganize itself drastically to get all the household tasks done. When she was not at work, Mrs. Williams was still doing the washing, ironing, or cooking. The pastor, meanwhile, also had to rearrange his schedule in order to be home when the children came from school. The overall increase in the family's workload meant that they had less time together in the evenings. To complicate matters, some church members began to grumble when they learned that the pastor's wife was out earning money instead of caring for her children at home. Others, of course, also complained that because of her job, the pastor's wife was not free to do the things in the church that they expected of her.

In some denominations, ministers can expect to be relatively free from financial worry. Pastor Elderberry, for instance, grew up in the Presbyterian church, having first felt the call to ministry in his sophomore year of college. During his senior year he placed himself under the care of his presbytery, which supported him financially while he attended seminary. Upon graduation he took a position as assistant minister. He was not only paid well but also had fringe benefits such as life insurance, health insurance, and a retirement fund. When Pastor Elderberry retires, he can have his choice of a number of

Presbyterian-owned ministerial retirement communities in which to live.

How denominations handle finances, salary arrangements, and the like is merely one example of the kinds of differences that directly affect clergy families. We have noted that having to uproot the family to move to another community is also a concern. Ministers in some denominations can expect to face the stress of moving more often than ministers in others. Some groups such as the Methodists and the Southern Baptists have a reputation for frequent clergy moves.[12] Whatever the reasons for a move—whether episcopal decision or congregational call—the event is a stressful experience.

There are, of course, many other ways in which denominational differences affect a clergy family. Ministers in some denominations are more likely to live in parsonages; Duane Alleman found that more than two-thirds of Methodist clergy wives responding to his study lived in parsonages, while only one-tenth of the Presbyterian wives did.[13] Richard Blackmon found denominational differences in the frequency of pastor-parish conflicts.[14] And there are other variables such as level of education, church size, and so on.

If you are already in the ministry, these variables are somewhat "after the fact": you already do or don't live in a parsonage; you already experience a certain level of conflict with your parishioners; your church is of a certain size. These are all factors that you should take into account in an ecological assessment of your own particular setting. Beyond this, however, take a hard look at how your denomination may set policies that affect your family while failing to take family life into account. We can distinguish, for example, between learning to deal with parsonage living on the one hand and reexamining a policy structure that makes no other options available on the other.

Throughout this chapter our goal has been to illustrate how an ecological perspective must include what happens beyond the local church. Every clergy family is embedded in a congregational body to a greater or lesser degree. The congregation in turn is part of a denomination that has its own characteristics. And all of us are part of larger cultural trends that affect our families either directly or indirectly through our relationship to an institution such as the church. We have only scratched the surface and have therefore suggested some further reading in the notes for those seeking more depth.[15]

Gaining a truly ecological understanding of the minister's family requires looking beyond the family itself. We can ask ourselves how the clergy family relates to the congregation and vice versa. We can examine how our values about ministry and family have been shaped by our cultural context. We can take an active stance in reassessing denominational policies to find out where these policies may unwittingly bind families to the detriment of both the clergy families and their ministries. And we must also move back and forth between these levels as we attempt to sift through how we are affected by our complex society. All of this makes an ecological perspective difficult to maintain. But the point is not that we must become supercomputers, able at every moment to keep track of millions of bits of information about our environment; the ecological perspective is precisely that—a perspective, a way of seeing. Whenever we look at the clergy family, regardless of the aspect we have in focus, we must always keep one eye on the horizon and consider how the relationship to the environment may be relevant.

There is one more area to consider before we close the book with some practical suggestions. Much of what we have said so far ignores the elements of time and change. Part 1 emphasized primarily how social systems try to remain the same. While this is a truth about human nature and social interaction, it is only half the story. In any social group, families and churches included, the issue is always one of striking a balance between changing and staying the same, of finding how to cope with the currents of change while preserving a sense of continuity. Chapter 11 addresses this issue by considering how families— and in particular, clergy families—change over their life span. This discussion will add yet another dimension to our ecological model.

11

Moving Through Time:
The Minister's Family
Across the Life Cycle

Our primary focus in the first nine chapters was on the life of the clergy family in the context of the congregation. In chapter 10 we extended the circle, looking beyond the local church to consider the impact of denominational differences and larger social trends. We need but one more element to complete our ecological model: the dimension of time.

All families live and breathe in a complex social environment today. Not all the social factors that shape a family's life are obvious. Often they must be patiently sought out, much as a detective searches for the clues needed to unravel a mystery. If we could actually see the ecological connections between us, we might have a better understanding of why things happen the way they do.

In searching out the social factors that shape our present, however, we must never forget the role of the past. In chapter 1 we described the social environment as including past as well as present relationships. From time to time we have also mentioned the importance of emotional influences from our families of origin. Families have histories. Each generation is intertwined with the generation directly above and below, and all stand in the stream of time that cascades from previous generations. From our ancestors, immediate or remote, we inherit the confidence of challenges faced and conquered, but also the burden of unresolved pain that lingers into the present and sets the course for the future.

In chapter 4 we cited Edwin Friedman's notion that ministers constantly deal with three categories of families: the families in the congregation, the congregation itself as a family, and the minister's own family. Each of these families has a history, and the way they perceive and respond to their histories is part of the social ecology.

Congregations and churches, for example, have histories of their own: of past and present generations of members and their relationships to each other; of relationships with previous clergy and their families; of interactions with past and present denominational representatives; of the waxing and waning of the local community in which they live. Given that fact, it is too simple to say that a pastor is simply called to "a congregation." More accurately, a pastor with a particular personal history comes to a church at a certain point in its ongoing history, and from that point on they fashion a joint history.

The importance of this is captured in expressions about being in the right place at the wrong time. Let's say that a clergy family, the Parkers, are having trouble with the congregation they recently began serving. Pastor Parker accepted the call to the church only one month after receiving the news that his father is dying of cancer. He can't shake the mental picture he remembers from his boyhood of how his grandfather had died of cancer, slowly deteriorating over the course of years. Needless to say, he now fears that the same fate awaits his father. Though he had accepted the call to the church for other reasons, one of the most important was that it was geographically much closer to where his father lives.

The previous pastor, Reverend Waters, had left suddenly. There had been trouble brewing between the pastor and Mr. Mellon, one of the lay leaders of the church, who disagreed with the pastor on several points of ministry. Their relationship had remained generally cordial but strained. In recent months, however, Mr. Mellon had become less and less tolerant while simultaneously becoming more vocal about his dissatisfaction. The pastor, who was not well-differentiated himself, had simply bided his time until a position opened elsewhere and then made a hasty retreat from the conflict.

What neither Pastor Waters nor Mr. Mellon recognized were the environmental factors that precipitated the conflict. Mr. Mellon had grown up hating his father. As a teenager, however, he had been turned around by a former pastor of that church.

Over the years, various pastors had come and gone. Mr. Mellon had been equally devoted to each and equally devastated when each had left. Yet he had never become reconciled to his father, from whom he had remained emotionally cut off for years.

Six months prior to Pastor Waters's decision to leave, Mr. Mellon's father contacted his estranged son. The elder Mr. Mellon, who was not a Christian, had recently suffered the loss of his third wife. Feeling the effects of his age and the shortness of time, the elderly man decided to communicate with the only family left to him, the son who had not spoken to him for so many years.

When his father called, Mr. Mellon was stunned. So many conflicting feelings surfaced in him that he didn't know how to react. On the one hand, he wanted to keep his father at arm's length and have nothing to do with him. On the other hand, his father's tone was genuinely conciliatory. Mr. Mellon knew that if he didn't reconcile with his father, he might not have another chance. His behavior began to reflect his ambivalent feelings. At one moment he would give a little ground, allowing himself to feel his deeply buried desire to connect with his father emotionally. At the next moment, however, his anger and anxiety would get the better of him and he would push his father away.

Less than a year after Mr. Mellon heard from his father, Pastor Parker arrived on the scene, and three streams of family history flowed together. First, Pastor Parker brought with him the stress of his father's imminent death. Second, Mr. Mellon remained confused and angry over how to relate to his father; it was these intense feelings that had exacerbated the conflict with the previous pastor and would now color his relationship to Pastor Parker. Third, the congregation was still reeling from the sudden loss of its pastor and must adjust to a new one.

The stress that the Parkers are experiencing in the church is to a great degree a matter of timing. If the clergy family and the congregation had come together before these important events in the Parker and Mellon families, the men might have had time to cement a relationship before the stressors hit. If they had joined later, there might have been time to work out their separate issues. Their union, unfortunately, comes at a difficult time for all. The Parkers might conclude that they are in the wrong church, or the church may conclude that they have called the wrong pastor. The truth, however, may be that the place is right, but the timing is wrong. It is important, therefore, to know at what point in their respective histories a clergy family and a congregation come together.

Humans are by nature historical beings, and a social ecology that ignores that fact is incomplete. But ecological "detective work"—that is, investigations of connections between people and events in their social context—is complicated enough when we consider only relationships that exist in the present. Adding a historical dimension, where we must also account for connections to previous generations, makes the task complex indeed. Yet family therapists have found a way to give order to this complexity, making the detective's job more manageable. They have done this by marrying the historical, multigenerational understanding of families to the theory of the life cycle.[1]

The notion of the *family life cycle* is simple. The basic idea is that most families go through a sequence of stages of development. Each stage begins with an important event in the family's life such as the birth of a baby, a marriage, or a death. The event triggers a time of transition and change as the family adapts to the addition or loss, and the relationships must flex accordingly. This process of adapting to natural changes can be stressful. Thus it is helpful for families to know the predictable stresses typically experienced at each stage. This has two benefits. First, a family can learn to anticipate and prepare for these changes in advance. Second, when stress occurs, families have the comfort of knowing that to some extent, the stress is normal for families going through similar changes. Without this confidence, families may add to their problems by misdiagnosing themselves as crazy.

Not all families are equally ready to change at every stage. One family may adapt well to having children enter their teenage years; another family may become rigid and refuse to adapt. This is where a particular family's history comes into play. There are many different reasons for wanting to keep things the way they are. At transitional points in a family's life, the present need for change meets the strengths and weaknesses that have been passed down through the generations. If there is a strong conflict between the two, the family will very likely experience an emotional crisis.[2]

We will use the rest of this chapter to show the power of this perspective for understanding the ecology of clergy families. First, we will focus on the need for change and adaptation at transition points in a family's life. Second, we will consider how these may conflict with a family's sense of identity and history and their need for sameness and continuity. Finally, we will survey some of the stages of the family life cycle as we apply them directly to the clergy family.

The Changing Family

Change is inevitable. No family can remain exactly the same forever. In the course of its life, a family will experience several events that require its members somehow to alter their way of functioning.

What events demand that a family change? First come changes in family membership. When children are born, the other family members must make room for them physically and psychologically. A couple having their first child will have to change their lifestyle as they take on the new responsibility of caring for a helpless, dependent child. They can no longer simply come and go as they please at any hour of the day or night. They have to plan either how they will take the baby with them or who will care for the infant in their absence. When the second child is born, the older child must make emotional room for the baby. The older sibling will no longer enjoy the luxury of her parents' undivided attention. Her relationship to her mother and father will have to be renegotiated so both she and the baby can have the emotional sustenance they need.

Family membership also changes through marriage. Depending on how parents look at it, marriage means either losing their children to another family, gaining someone else's children, or sharing both. How parents relate to their adult children must be adapted to include the new in-laws and later the grandchildren.

Membership changes through death. When key family members die, such as the father in a strongly patriarchal family, the rest of the family will be in shock for some time until they figure out how to relate to each other with Father gone. Pathology occurs when the family cannot or will not adapt to the loss. They will either deny that Father is dead or else appoint another family member to take up his emotional role.

Families must also change as their members mature. Being

the parents of an infant is not the same as being the parents of a two-year-old. And neither is quite like trying to rear a teenager. As children grow, parents must grow with them, allowing the parent-child relationship to flex as needed. The helpless infant needs adults to do things for her. But parents cannot do this forever; she must learn to do things for herself. Some parents, however, refuse to adapt in this way. They enjoy their child's dependence and may keep her in a relatively dependent position for the rest of their lives.

All these are expectable changes that occur from inside the family as it grows through its seasons. But there are also accidents of history, unpredictable events that may take a family unawares. The unexpected death or hospitalization of a family member can create a gaping void in the family's emotional structure. One or both parents may lose a job, forcing them to enact emergency measures. Sudden changes like these can throw families into chaos, taxing their flexibility and adaptive capacities to their limits.

Of course, not all demands for change are traumatic or even unpleasant. Many predictable transitions are accompanied by mixed emotions. There is a sense of progress and growth, but frequently also a sense of loss for what once was. Parents of newborns may take great delight in their children, but miss the freedom and intimacy they shared as a childless couple. Later, as the same parents watch their children marry, they may be both happy and sad: they rejoice with their children, yet grieve over this rite of passage that marks the end of childhood. The depth and quality of emotional reactions will vary greatly from family to family. But growth means change, and change means that some things must henceforth be done differently. This compels the family to stretch itself, and the stretching can be stressful.

Whether or not the stress reaches dramatic proportions depends on the nature of the transition and what it means to the family. New parents who were well cared for in their infancy may find it easier to welcome their baby than those who were neglected as children. All else being equal, new parents face predictable changes as they adapt to the baby. Their family histories, however, will shape how they interpret the experience. When facing the temporary strains of adjustment, their general attitude can say either "It goes with the territory" or else "This is awful and I can't take it anymore." As an example from the other end of the life cycle, retirement can be experienced as either a much-earned rest and a transition into the "golden years" or being put out to pasture to live out one's remaining years without meaning or purpose.

As mentioned earlier, there are two benefits to understanding the predictable transitions of the life cycle. First, if a family knows in advance that it will face stressors of a certain kind, it has a chance to prepare for them. Consider childbirth and retirement again as examples. First-time parents can take preparatory classes that will help them through the birth experience. Learning the basics about how children grow and develop will also help them plan ahead, such as "baby-proofing" the house before the infant becomes a toddler. And they can prepare emotionally by talking to couples who have already experienced their first child. For many parents-to-be, this can be a rewarding time to discuss their own childhoods with their parents.

A retiree faces many practical and emotional issues. Finances must be secure with no surprises about the adequacy of one's pension plan. Retirement can be more traumatic for people who have, so to speak, put all their self-identity eggs into one basket labeled "career." These people should begin to cultivate other interests well before the retirement date.

While the retiree suffers an obvious loss of role, often the spouse does as well. The retiree who has no other interests may sit around the house all day, driving the spouse crazy while taking over some of the responsibilities that formerly gave the spouse a sense of identity and purpose. Couples nearing retirement need to plan for their relationship ahead of time.

We will say more about the various stages of the life cycle later. The examples given are meant to show the first benefit of knowing the predictable stresses of the life cycle: preparing for them in advance will make the transitions smoother. There is a second benefit: knowing the stresses that families typically face will help you decide whether or not your family is crazy.

In a narcissistic culture such as ours, emotional distress of any kind is too easily viewed as a problem that must be subjected to denial or to therapy. Families can overreact to what may be a normal period of transitional stress. Some Christians, for example, may have a distorted picture of what it means to have a healthy family, equating spirituality a lack of conflict or stress. Clergy families in particular may feel great pressure to maintain an image of serenity. This works against their ability to deal with stress directly and realistically.

The same problem can stem from a loss of connectedness between generations. Adult children who feel they must be completely independent of their parents potentially lose an important resource: the accumulated wisdom of parental experience. Experience, of course, is no guarantee of wisdom, and obviously not all parents are wise. But children who are willing to hear their counsel will often discover that their parents know much more about life than they ever dreamed. At the very least, without such counsel each new generation must encounter their own transitions as if theirs were the first to do so. The experience can be like trying to find your way in a strange country without knowing the language or using a map.

Having a general map of the life cycle can help families keep a better perspective on their struggles. Clergy can learn both to be more realistic about what to expect of their own families and to have a deeper understanding of the stressors affecting the lives of other families in the congregation.

Changing Versus Staying the Same

Over against both the predictable and unpredictable pressures on a family to change its functioning are demands for continuity, reasons why family members want to keep things the way they are. These can be more difficult to articulate. While predictable stressors have to do with how families are alike, the demands for continuity are more closely related to their particular histories, to the characteristics that make them unique.

Some of these "preservative" pressures have already been mentioned. Individual family members, for example, may resist change because they want to avoid losing a cherished role. Roles and relationships are integral to our sense of identity. Therefore change can be threatening. Parents watching their children marry feel a loss of their parenting role. They may try to compensate for the loss by creating some other form of continuity. The bride's mother, for example, may try to coax her daughter into wearing the wedding gown that she has kept in immaculate condition for years for just that purpose. The mother's need to preserve continuity, however, may clash with her daughter's wishes. The mother may not be aware of the sense of loss she is trying to ward off.

Taking a broader view, we can move up one step and ask, "Why is the role so important?" The question pushes us back one more generation. The bride's mother, for example, may feel estranged from her own parents. Her relationship as a mother to her children thus takes on greater significance. This is starkly symbolized by her daughter's wedding. She recalls her own wedding, when she married against her parents' wishes. In protest, her parents refused to attend, and the couple decided on a simple civil ceremony. Though she may still believe that she made the right decision those many years ago, she grieves that her parents had no part in her wedding and regrets never having had the church ceremony she dreamed of as a girl. This bit of family history thus asserts itself as she and her daughter attempt to adapt to the stress of change.

Roles are also lost when a family member dies. Here, however, we are not talking about a person's losing a role he or she values, but a family's losing a member who serves an important emotional function for other members. If a key person in the family dies, the survivors' emotional structure begins to crumble and a wave of anxiety washes over them. This is particularly true of poorly differentiated families who are held together by a network of interlocking triangles. Some families, for example, have one member who functions as the central switchboard. Virtually all communication is routed through him or her. What happens when that person dies? Rather than accept the change and adapt to the loss, the panicked family will try to find some way to replace their communication center lest they be faced with having to talk to each other directly. The need to preserve their undifferentiated emotional structure is so strong that change is denied and adaptation is impossible.

In short, virtually any aspect of the family's identity or the identities of the individual members can be grounds for resisting change. When families reach transition points in their life cycles, demands for change meet these demands to stay the same. If there is a strong clash between them, the family experiences an emotional crisis. If, however, the demands on one or both sides are relatively mild, the transition will occur more gracefully. The family that can both anticipate the changes that it will face as well as know its own reasons for resisting change will be better equipped to adapt more smoothly.

The clergy family, too, must traverse its own life cycle. Life-cycle theory can be as easily applied to the pastor's family as it is to any other family in the congregation. We encourage both clergy and laity to think seriously about the implications of a life-cycle perspective for their families as well as for family ministry and life education in the church.

We have repeatedly emphasized that the clergy family is a family within a family. Its immediate social context, the congregation, is an important source of life-cycle stressors, including demands for change and demands to stay the same. Moving to a new congregation may require tremendous adaptation for a clergy family. Suppose a clergy family has been living in a house five miles from the church and then moves to a new congregation and into a parsonage right next door to the church. That fact alone can change family life dramatically. How well they adjust to the change of environment will partially depend on whether they are simultaneously facing some other life-cycle transition.

To use an earlier metaphor, the present role expectations of the clergy family are the merging of three streams of history: the congregation's history, the histories of key families in the church, and the history of the clergy family itself. Depending on the fit between the clergy family and the congregation, these expectations can be experienced either as pressures to change or as pressures to remain the same. As an example of the former, some clergy families may feel that the new congregation is forcing them into a mold. In these cases, the congregation's role expectations become demands for change that clash with the family's identity. Other clergy families may experience their idealized role as a straitjacket that prevents them from adjusting to life-cycle changes. A clergy couple, for example, may be willing to allow more freedom to their teenage children, but feel cornered by the parishioners' expectations of the P.K. Here role expectations become preservative pressures that hamper change and adaptation.

Thus, for the clergy family the balancing act between change and continuity includes not only their own life-cycle transitions, but the expectations that the family members experience from the congregation. These expectations in turn are an outgrowth of their history together as a congregation as well as the separate histories of the families making up the congregation.

The clergy family's life history, then, is closely interwoven with those of the congregational family and the church families. The interaction of these three families makes for a complex social tapestry. A knowledge of the life-cycle stages assists the task of unraveling the strands. We will now look at each stage more closely, beginning with the story of the Edwards family.

Stages and Ages in the Clergy Family

It is Sunday morning and the church is packed to overflowing. The occasion is a special farewell service for Pastor Richard Edwards and his wife, Glenda, who are retiring after forty-two years of faithful parish ministry. The couple's four children and five grandchildren are all present, as are several representatives of other congregations that the Edwardses have served. The associate pastor invites the entire Edwards clan to join the honorees on the platform. At the same time smiling and fighting back tears, the couple verbally reminisce about their many years of Christian service.

If we had a time machine, we could journey backward in time to observe the Edwards family at different points in their career. Their first congregation was in a small, rural community. Richard was fresh out of seminary; he and Glenda had been married less than a year. Major changes in their family life seemed to occur every few years from that point on. Their first two children, Andrew and Sarah, were born while they were still serving their first church. When Andy was born, Glenda became less involved with the ministry. Richard was left feeling somewhat frustrated and confused; he wanted to spend more time with his newborn son, but felt the constant pull of his church responsibilities. He managed, however, to set enough limits on ministry demands to allow him time for fatherhood. By the time Andy finished his terrible twos, the pastor and his wife felt fairly confident in their parenting skills.

Then Sarah was born. While Andy had generally been content and not overly fussy as a baby, Sarah was colicky and frail. Every evening for the first four months of her life, Sarah wailed relentlessly for two or three hours. Nothing seemed to help, and she would eventually cry herself to sleep. There were many sleepless nights for the whole family. Tension was often high between the tired parents, and even little annoyances seemed to take on enormous proportions. Andrew felt the stress of having a sibling, especially one who cried and demanded much attention. For several weeks he became more peevish and petulant. Richard and Glenda were exasperated with his renewed babyish behavior and often felt like running away from it all.

Needless to say, the couple had much less energy for the ministry during those months of colic. Parishioners noticed that there was often less verve in Richard's Sunday sermons. Most of them did not know why, since Richard was reticent to expose his family stresses in front of the congregation. Glenda's absence from church functions drew concern from many women in the church who correctly assumed that it must have something to do with the baby. Some would call to offer help along with a great deal of homespun advice. She felt, however, that they had already tried everything and all that could be done was to grin and bear it. Moreover, she too was reluctant to admit the level of her frustration and generally told her callers that everything was under control. Eventually Sarah's colic disappeared, and life became more manageable for everyone.

Soon thereafter the Edwards left to take their second church with a larger and more established congregation. Their third child, Rita, was born about a year later. Richard and Glenda found themselves continually balancing the demands of the ministry with the demands of rearing three children. And the latter responsibility, of course, kept changing according to the ages of the children.

By this time Andrew had entered school, and Sarah was toddling around the house. Fortunately, little Rita was an easy baby, much like her brother, Andrew. This was a blessing for the parents, who had new transitions to face with the two older children. Andrew's starting school stirred some anxiety in Richard as he remembered his own childhood. He had grown up in a small town where everyone knew that his father was a preacher. There were times when his classmates had been relentless in their teasing, and he had wished that his family would move to another city where no one would know he was a P.K. Richard worried that his son might have to face the same kind of teasing and wanted to protect him.

At the same time, Sarah, who had recently turned two, was helping her parents redefine how terrible the twos could be. Glenda and Richard thought they had seen it all with Andrew, but began to discover just how mild he had been compared with his younger sister. Yet, through a random blend of diplomacy, patient teaching, hair-tearing, and a bit of shouting, the Edwards family survived with its dignity intact.

Before they knew it, all three children were in school, and Glenda began to enjoy the luxury of a peaceful house during the day. As ministry would have it, however, the Edwardses were soon called to another church. It was a long-distance move to an entirely different climate, and the family took some time to get adjusted to their new surroundings. It was particularly difficult for Andrew, who was then eleven years old and had a stable group of friends at school.

Just when the Edwards family were beginning to settle into this third church home, Glenda discovered that she was pregnant. The other children had been planned, and the Edwardses had intended to stop at three. The couple were stunned and experienced mixed reactions. Glenda in particular had been looking forward to more freedom from the children, and now she found some of her dreams slipping away. In rearing three children, both she and Richard had learned something about reality and were willing to accept the help the new congregation offered. When Baby Mike was born, he had the loving care of not only his mother and father, but of three older siblings and several members of the congregation.

The Edwardses would move to two other churches as their children, one by one, went through their teenage years. There were some stormy moments as the kids began to try on new roles and identities in approaching adulthood. To Richard's silent delight, Andrew wanted to be a minister like his father and grandfather and enrolled first in Bible college and then at the denominational seminary. Sarah toyed with several ideas mixed with adolescent fantasy. At one point she wanted to be an actress and declared her intention to enroll in a performing arts academy. The next year she decided she would go to art school instead. In the end she surprised everyone: she eventually completed a master's degree in business administration and became a successful businesswoman, albeit with a flair for the dramatic.

Rita was the first of the children to marry—he was a young man she had dated for three years in college—and the first to make Richard and Glenda grandparents. This also made Mike an uncle while he was still in high school. Soon afterward, Rita's husband received a promotion at his job and with it a cross-country relocation. Her parents swallowed hard and blessed them while gently chastising them for taking away their new grandchild.

A year later, the family celebrated Mike's graduation from high school. Inwardly Richard and Glenda were both proud and grieved. Mike was the last child to leave home, and he would soon be attending college in another state. The Sunday after Mike left, Pastor Edwards preached a sermon about God the Father awaiting his children's homecoming. The house seemed too quiet, and the parents made the decision to move to a smaller home.

Changes in the children's lives required corresponding changes in their parents. After all, the children were not the only ones going through transitions. Richard and Glenda had to deal with redefining their roles not only as parents, but also as children of their own aged parents who were declining in health. But with the children grown and gone, Glenda finally felt she had the chance to pursue some personal dreams and decided to attend graduate school. At the same time that Glenda was expanding her horizons, Richard was looking inward. He began to question whether or not his years of investment in the ministry had really been worthwhile. For the most part he was content and felt that God had used him to do good things. On occasion, however, his frustration and doubts would get the better of him, especially when the ministry seemed to take a turn for the worse. At those times he toyed with the idea of leaving the pastorate and opening a neighborhood grocery store instead!

Now, after forty-two years of combined service in several congregations, Pastor Edwards was retiring. He stood on the platform with his family, silently ruminating on his mixed emotions while the associate pastor droned on endlessly. To some extent Edwards felt that he was being put out to pasture. The new generation of pastors being graduated from seminary seemed to be such specialists, trained in areas that didn't even exist when he was a seminary student. But he also knew that the congregation genuinely appreciated his skills, which he learned through years of pastoral experience rather than in the classroom.

Pastor Edwards was trying to cope with a sense of grief and loss, and he was wise enough to know it. He had invested more than half his life in the ministry. Although he and his family had dealt with some severely trying times over the years, in the main the ministry had given him a sense of fulfillment and prestige. What would it be like to step down from the pulpit? Somehow the honorary title of "Pastor Emeritus" seemed to offer little solace. He and Glenda were going to celebrate his retirement with a long-awaited trip to the Holy Land, and they had other plans as well. But what then? His retirement pension was adequate but not overwhelming. And what would he do with his time? Suddenly he was struck by a flash of insight: for the first time, he began truly to understand what his wife had experienced when the children married and left home.

*　　*　　*

This is only a thumbnail sketch of the life history of one clergy family. We have condensed several years into this fictional account, lingering only long enough to show the many ages and stages of their life together. Depending on where you are in your family's journey, you will recognize some of the joys and sorrows that go with each stage. These are some of the predictable stresses that a family typically experiences as its members grow and change.

Each stage of the family life cycle is marked off by a transition event. Most families experience similar transitions in similar order, and there are typical changes that should accompany each. Different writers, however, have divided up the family life cycle differently, depending on how many transitions they consider important.[3] When we collect the various accounts, the list of family transitions looks like this (in chronological order):

Premarital

Newly married, no children

Deciding to have children

Birth of the first child

Oldest child reaches toddlerhood

Oldest child enters school

Oldest child enters adolescence while parents enter mid-life

Children marry and/or leave home

Last child leaves home, leaving the couple alone again

Old age and retirement

Of course, not every family will go through all these stages in this particular order. Those who do not marry or have children and those who divorce or remarry will have a different number and sequence of stages. The usefulness of the life-cycle model, however, does not depend on its universality. The essential point is that every family will at some point encounter a change that requires reorganization. How a family reacts depends on its unique history, so no model can be fully universal. But to the extent that the stages are at least common, understanding them can help families have a better grasp of their lives.

We can see many of these transitions in the history of the Edwards family and how these interact with their being in the ministry. For two reasons, however, we cannot give you an exhaustive treatment of the life cycle of clergy families. First, the subject would easily require an entire book to itself. Second, very little writing or research has touched on this area. Much of what can be said must be either speculative or extrapolated piecemeal from research that was intended for another purpose. Thus we suggest that you refer to the books cited in the notes for a more complete account of the family life cycle. What we offer here is suggestive rather than comprehensive, intended to encourage you to think further on your family history.

How might the context of the ministry, as described in this book, affect the clergy family's life-cycle transitions? Here is just a sprinkling of observations.

The Newly Married Clergy Couple Before Children

The primary task of this stage is to become committed to the marriage, which requires that the couple realign their relationships to their parents and others. Sonya Rhodes calls this stage "Intimacy vs. Idealization":

> The major struggle in forming a relationship viable and durable enough to withstand the stresses of later stages concerns the efforts to achieve intimacy based on a realistic perception of the partner

as a whole person, as opposed to the idealization of one's partner as a romantic image, or disillusionment with one's partner as unresponsive.[4]

What happens to the newly married couple entering the ministry? As opposed to others who may have had the time to establish their marital relationship firmly, the new couple is faced with the task of establishing two intimate social relationships at the same time: to each other and to the congregation. It is easy to imagine how the time demands of ministry can pull the spouses away from each other, cutting into the time and energy they need to lay a solid foundation for their marriage. One young minister, who had been married just four months when he took his first church, told us, "Although the people in my small congregation have been very supportive, they still expect me to visit and spend time with them regularly. This leaves little time for my wife and me to do things together as a couple."

The minister's wife in particular may feel abandoned and frustrated. As we have said, she may feel that her husband is more married to the church than to her. One minister's wife, looking back over the early years of her marriage, wrote:

> Our most difficult years were when my husband first entered the ministry. As everyone told him what a good job he was doing, he began to spend more and more time in church activity. Although I was supportive of his ministry, I soon felt that he was neglecting our time together. If we hadn't gotten things worked out in those early years, I doubt that we would still be in ministry today.

There is yet another issue. The congregation's often idealized expectations of the clergy couple may not be conducive to the kind of realism that Rhodes discusses. A couple who have been married for some time before entering the ministry may have already established a realistic appreciation of each other's strengths and weaknesses. Couples still in the first flush of marriage, however, tend to romanticize each other. If a congregation expects them to be Mr. and Mrs. Perfect, how and when will the spouses learn to relate to each other as real human beings?

Congregations need to be sensitive to the needs of a newly married clergy couple. For their part, the couple must clearly recognize their need for time together and make their parishioners aware of this.

The Clergy Family With Young Children

The birth of children places still more time demands on the minister. One minister with two young children lamented to us that he had little time with his children, and when he did he was too tired. His family lived in a parsonage next to the church. His advice to aspiring ministers: "Get your own home and live at least a mile or two from the church building."

As we showed in chapter 8, clergy families with young children are often frustrated with schedule conflicts. One associate pastor and father of three school-age children complained that meetings scheduled at breakfast and in the evening for several nights a week took away from the precious few times he could be with his children. Another minister with three children told us that his kids complained he didn't have time to help with their homework. He regretted "not being able to relax and play and have free days and weekends together" with his family.

Again, there may be deeper issues involved. The minister who plays a symbolic role as father to the congregation may experience no conflict with this as long as he is childless. The arrival of a newborn, however, may induce the minister to withdraw some of his emotional investment from ministry, leaving his congregational family feeling neglected. This in turn may result in heightened demands for attention from the congregation. In a different scenario, the minister who is insecure about fatherhood may choose instead to invest himself more heavily in his congregational family, leaving the task of parenting to his wife. In either case it is important to note that the introduction of a child into the family can cause ripples in the relationship between the clergy family and the congregation.

The Clergy Family With Adolescents

Adolescence is a time when children attempt to establish a sense of identity that is not fully dependent on their family. They are trying to answer the question "Who am I?" This often entails the corresponding question "Who are my parents?" Whereas younger children generally accept their parents' values for their own, teenagers begin questioning these values as well as the motives and logic behind them.[5] This questioning, though a normal part of growing up, can be uncomfortable to the parents who suddenly find their cherished values subjected to close scrutiny.

Even if they don't like it, pastors tend to consider moving as part of their job description. Young children typically go along with the moves, helped by some needed reassurance. The pastor may be surprised, however, to find his teenaged children digging in their heels, strongly resisting a move to another church. This is because adolescents are beginning to derive important parts of their identity from outside the family, and thus leaving their peer groups is a more serious matter than before.

In whatever way a teenager's bid for independence manifests itself, clergy parents who cannot accept this step toward differentiation are apt to interpret their children's behavior as rejection or defiance. Parishioners who are sensitive to "rebellion" in their own households, moreover, may be even less tolerant of it in the P.K., who is expected to be a model child.

These transitional stresses are often complicated by the fact that one or both parents are encountering what is commonly called a mid-life crisis. The kernel of the mid-life crisis is a recognition that there is only half of life left, which prompts a soul-searching reevaluation of how the first half was spent. Those who have spent fifteen to twenty years investing themselves in a career, even the pastoral ministry, may begin wondering if it was all worthwhile.

This may be a time when pastors contemplate leaving the ministry. For them, the teenage P.K. may become the triangled excuse for leaving. Other ministers, who decide instead to invest their identities even more heavily into their vocation, may be more perturbed by the potentially disruptive behavior of their adolescent children. Clergy families in this stage of the life cycle need to recognize that there are two generations, not one, undergoing the stress of evaluating their identities.

The Clergy Family Launching Children

A new stage begins for clergy families when children leave home to marry, go to school, or take a job. The two questions facing families at this stage are whether the parents can let go

and whether the children want to leave. Some parents need to
have their children be dependent and thus find ways to sabotage
their independence. In other families, children have not gained
the confidence they need to find their way in the outside world,
and thus emotionally they cling to the parents for security.

This stage is very visible in clergy families. The level of the
parents' "success" is tested by decisions the children make.
Whom do they marry? (They had better be respectable Christians!) What college do they attend? (Let's hope it's a Bible
college, preferably the denominational Bible college!) What
vocations are they pursuing? (At least one of them *has* to be a
minister!)

Some Christians, clergy included, subscribe to a type of
"parental determinism," namely, the belief that parents have
the power to ensure that their children grow into full Christian
maturity. Certainly all parents play a major role in their
children's spiritual development. But can we also acknowledge
that a parent may do everything "right" and have children that
seem to make the "wrong" choices?

Clergy parents who have children with devout faith should be
thankful for God's grace. Those whose children turn away from
God, however, need the support and not the condemnation of
the community. And neither the parents nor the congregation
should deny God's ability to turn the hearts of the parents and
the children toward each other. Congregations need to help
clergy parents continue to love, comfort, and support their
children regardless of the life choices they make.

The Clergy Couple Alone Again

The stage that begins when all of the children have left home
is often referred to as "the empty nest." Usually this is seen as a
time of great loss for the mother of the brood, and it often is.
What is equally important, however, is that for the first time in
many years, the couple is left alone with each other. For some
couples it is a time of excitement as they look forward to sharing
the intimacy they once enjoyed and have cultivated over the
years. For others it is a time of despair as they come to realize
that they have invested all their emotional energies in their
children and have let themselves silently drift apart.

A congregation's expectations may unwittingly contribute to
the disintegration of the marital relationship in this stage. We

discussed in chapter 9 how intrusive congregations can whittle away at a clergy couple's sense of emotional closeness. Moreover, keeping up the appearances of being a model family can take its toll. Modeling a perfect marriage detracts from the realism needed to maintain a healthy intimacy. And the pressure of having perfect kids may pressure a clergy couple into triangling their anxieties into their children, thus increasing the sense of void when the children leave.

All couples need to foster marital closeness throughout their life together, not just when they first marry. Using children to keep a marriage together does not improve the relationship, but only delays the day of reckoning until the children are gone. Clergy parents who learn to balance their needs as a couple with the needs of their children will find that they still have something to be excited about, even when the nest is empty.

*   *   *

The theory of the family life cycle helps us to grasp the historical dimension of the clergy family's social ecology. Again, the ministry context can be understood as the weaving of three histories: those of the congregation, the families in the congregation, and the clergy family itself. The life-cycle model prompts us to look for the transitional stresses that are occurring at present in each of these on-going histories as well as for the transitions that were not successfully negotiated in the past.

In chapter 8 we discussed clergy family life in terms of the balance between stressors and resources. We wish to make a similar point here. Many of us, looking back on our childhood, have anger or resentment for what our parents either did or failed to do. Knowledge of the life cycle may help us to get a sense of the bigger picture. Instead of seeing ourselves as victims of our families, we can begin to see our parents as people who had their own life-cycle transitions to face. Like us, they had to find ways to cope with the stress of those transitions out of their limited emotional resources. And the resources available to them depended on whether or not the generation before them successfully negotiated *their* life-cycle transitions.

We would like to illustrate this by finishing the story of Mr. Mellon and his aging father. What was the pain that had kept these two men separate for so long? Mr. Mellon, an only child, had lost his mother suddenly in an auto accident when he was just a boy. He and his father were emotionally devastated, but did the best they could to cope. Soon his father began drinking, a little at first and then more and more. A few years later, when Mr. Mellon had turned ten, his father left and never came back, leaving the boy in the care of an uncle and aunt who lived nearby. Over the years the father wrote to him occasionally, but Mr. Mellon tore up the letters without reading them. He never forgave his father for abandoning him, especially so soon after his mother's death.

Now Mr. Mellon's father had contacted him again. Though he still burned with pain and anger, this time Mr. Mellon was willing to have his father come to beg his forgiveness. What his father told him, however, radically changed the course of their relationship.

For the first time, the father told his son how much his wife's death had devastated him. He had depended on her for all his emotional support, and when she died he felt lost and empty. What Mr. Mellon didn't know was that his grandfather had also been an alcoholic who in drunken stupors frequently beat his children. When Mr. Mellon's father began drinking, he felt that he had lost control and that he would become as abusive as his own father had been. Thus, in shame and defeat he waited until he felt his son was old enough to survive and then left before he could turn into his own worst nightmare.

Mr. Mellon was shocked. For so many years he had made his father out to be a horrible, abusive ogre. Now he began to see him as a frail human being who had done what he thought best in an impossible situation. His father had not had a good relationship with his own parents to draw on, and when his wife was suddenly whisked away by death, the emotional dam that had held back his childhood trauma collapsed. Now, near the end of his life, remorseful and empty, the father wanted a second chance with his son. Nothing, of course, could completely erase Mr. Mellon's own deep feelings of abandonment, betrayal, and loss. Understanding his father's history, however, helped him to put his own history in perspective and opened the door to reconciliation.

We, too, must learn to put our lives into historical perspective. If we take the time to look, we can see the transitional stresses that our families experienced at each stage of their life cycle.

And when we ask why our families may have failed at certain stages, we will discover the opposing demands that give us insight into our identity and our connection to generations past.[6] This longitudinal perspective gives us a more balanced, ecological sense of our family histories. Having achieved that, we will have more compassion for the histories of others.

Epilogue:
The Care and Feeding
of Clergy Families

Our purpose in this book has been to build an ecological perspective of the life of the minister's family. To that end we have approached the social ecology from several vantage points and introduced you to a great number of related ideas. Before we bring this to conclusion, let's briefly review what each chapter has contributed to the ecological perspective.

The goal of part 1 was to show the overall importance of understanding clergy family life in its social context, namely, in interaction with the congregation. We introduced the ecological mind-set in chapter 1 by using an example from the natural world and drawing parallels to the social world. Just as events and organisms are connected in the physical environment, so too are the lives of people who share a common social environment. These connections, however, may be difficult to see unless we actively look for them.

In chapter 2 we illustrated these ecological connections by using the theory of differentiation and triangles. Then we showed how these concepts can be applied to clergy families. Poorly differentiated groups, including some congregations, can be understood as a network of interlocking triangles. Because of this, events in two apparently remote corners of the social group may in fact be linked through a chain of triangles. Often, however, we are unaware of how we instinctively triangle others or how others triangle us, rendering the chain of interactions virtually invisible. If we train ourselves to look for key triangles in our social settings, even the most inexplicable or random events may suddenly begin to make sense.

Chapter 3 focused more specifically on the unique situation of the minister's family living in the context of a larger, congregational family. We highlighted two general themes: (1) the special role expectations placed on members of the clergy family, and (2) boundaries and the triple threat of idealization, impoverishment, and intrusion. In terms of boundaries, the problem of idealization is its creation of a double standard that isolates clergy family members from true peer relationships. This can be complicated by impoverishment, whereby the family is also prevented from establishing friendships outside the congregation. Finally, intrusion is the problem commonly known as "the fishbowl syndrome," in which clergy families experience the discomfort of living in glass houses. The lack of appropriate boundaries may leave them feeling depersonalized and taken for granted.

In chapter 4 we explored the implications of Edwin Friedman's concept that ministry involves the interaction of the clergy family with discrete families in the congregation as well as the congregation itself considered as a family. Each of these family groups has an idea of what constitutes "proper" family relationships. In social interaction these unquestioned assumptions can be seen as either a bias for one's own way of being a family or as a prejudice against someone else's. For that reason, we introduced Kantor and Lehr's model of closed-, open-, and random-type families. Our goal was to show how each type has both a positive and a negative side. Having a more balanced appreciation of our strengths and weaknesses and those of other families can help us move closer to the unity in diversity that should characterize the body of Christ.

In part 2 we returned to the theme of role expectations and examined the roles of each clergy family member in turn. Chapter 5 looked intently at the many roles of the parish pastor. In some cases, what others expect of him may conflict with what he expects of himself; in other cases, the expectations may be more compatible but still unrealistic. Our consistently ecological approach is to understand role conflicts in terms of (1) the different sources of expectations, and (2) the ways that the pastor's perception of his role fits with that of the congregation.

We examined the roles of the minister's wife in much the same way. Her expectations may either harmonize or conflict with the congregation's expectations. In chapter 6 we focused specifically on the themes of the intrusive role expectations and loneliness that many clergy wives experience. Their role conflicts, however, are different from their pastor-husbands' due to the evolving role of women in contemporary American society. The changes occurring at this level have created a kind of role ambiguity for clergy wives, who may find themselves struggling to reconcile traditional and modern values.

In chapter 7 we discussed the expectations that ministers' children receive from their parents, the congregation, and their peers. In some cases the children are expected to demonstrate perfect behavior; in others they are expected to embody the stereotype of the rebellious preacher's kid. Ecologically these expectations can be the vehicle by which the children are kept triangled between the clergy parents and the congregation.

Our discussion in part 3 moved beyond individual roles and focused on family and marriage relationships. Chapter 8 used the ecology of the balance between stressors and resources as a basis for understanding the typical problems that ministers' families report. Intrusive congregations increase the stress of clergy family life, while supportive, integrative congregations provide much-needed emotional resources.

Intrusion and integration also affect the quality of the clergy couple's marriage. In chapter 9 we discussed how idealization interferes with their ability to be honest with themselves and others about their marital relationship. This condition is complicated by the fact that intrusive congregations may contribute to a deteriorating sense of emotional closeness between the spouses. Clergy couples in supportive congregations, however, report greater satisfaction in marriage.

Just as the clergy family is nested within a congregation, the congregation is nested in turn within both a local community and a denominational structure. In chapter 10, therefore, we moved the discussion beyond the boundaries of the local church. We surveyed several social trends in modern religion that affect the life of the church and thus the clergy family. We showed how the makeup of both the larger community and the denomination may have a significant impact on clergy family life, in and through their relationship to the congregation.

Finally we added the dimension of time and history to the ecological model. In chapter 11 we argued that families and social groups carry the past into the present and our emotional inheritance from yesterday's generations is very much a part of our social ecology. We made this idea more explicit through the concept of the family-life cycle, where families must learn to balance demands for change against demands to stay the same. Knowing the typical transitional stresses that families face can help us have a handle on how stressful events of the past shape the demands of the present.

By now you may be saying to yourself, "Okay, okay—now tell me what we can *do* about all these things!" To this point we have deliberately refrained from making many pragmatic suggestions, for two reasons: (1) while practical advice can be helpful, it can also be useless or even dangerous. Families vary greatly. To bend an old phrase, "One family's meat is another family's poison." The more specific the advice, the greater the benefit or the damage; and (2) for advice to be beneficial we must be able to sort out what is or is not appropriate for our particular situation. It is much more important that we have a clear understanding of the problem than it is to have a handful of possible answers. Indeed, the family that truly understands the demands it must balance may discover some unique solutions. Whatever advice we do give is in no way meant to substitute for studious reflection on your own social ecology.

We have divided our closing chapter into three sections. The first can be read as an open letter to congregations, written by the clergy families who responded to our study. The second section complements the first by directly addressing the clergy family and its members. Finally we suggest some guidelines for ministers-to-be, particularly those who will soon be interviewing for church positions. In each section we will blend our comments with those of the families we surveyed.

So Where's the Owner's Manual?

Undoubtedly life would be a lot easier if every minister's family came equipped with an owner's manual entitled "How to Feed and Care for Your New Clergy Family." But of course, they don't, and thus each congregation must learn through personal experience.

There are, however, some general guidelines that can serve as a basic starting point. We asked clergy family members how their churches could help improve their lives. Five general themes emerged.

The Problem of Time

The most frequent response centered in the problem of time. As we saw in chapter 8, clergy family members feel they do not have the time they need away from church responsibilities, either as individuals or together as a family. The most common remedy suggested is to let the minister have more time off. Here is a sample of ministers' responses:

"Permit me to work just forty hours a week."

"Give me extra time off, such as one or two days per week, and an extended vacation."

"Give me a sabbatical every five years."

"Let me have every fifth weekend off to go somewhere away from the church."

A closely related matter is the need for a predictable schedule. Regardless of the work load and the actual amount of time off ministers have, they still need the predictability of a regular schedule. Two aspects were cited. First, pastors need consistent time to be with their spouses and children, and this should be considered in scheduling church events. Some congregations try to spread meetings over several weeknights in order to accommodate parishioners; if the pastor is required to be at all of them, he will have no free evenings left to spend with family. Second, once the schedule and work load have been worked out so that the pastor has adequate time for family life, the congregation should respect these boundaries. Don't call or schedule meetings on the pastor's day off.

The pastors' wives and children, of course, were in agreement regarding the need for predictable time together. Clergy wives suggested the following:

"Give us a free Sunday every two months or so."

"Provide more time and money for times away to recoup."

"Schedule a day off each week besides Saturday, and insist that the congregation honor his day off except for emergencies."

Minister's children had similar requests:

"Cut down on his work hours."

"Stop having meetings on Dad's day off."

Thus the first way for a congregation to support a clergy family is to make sure that parish responsibilities do not deprive the family members of time together. Once time boundaries have been established, respect them.

The Problem of Expectations

The second most common suggestion was for the congregation to develop more realistic expectations of the clergy family. Here are some suggestions from the wives:

"Realize that we have human needs just like you do."

"Accept us as real people, that we can err."

"Treat us as normal people; do not have higher expectations of us."

"Try not to be so judgmental."

"Realize that the pastor is a man and not a superman."

For many ministers, the desire for realistic expectations also entails a request that congregations take more responsibility for themselves:

"More consistent and responsible lay leadership would decrease demands on my time."

"Have lay leadership take responsible initiative in program areas."

Still another related alternative, mentioned by ministers, their wives, and their children alike, was a request that the congregation hire more staff to distribute the work load more realistically.

The Problem of Privacy

Another common theme centered on requests for more privacy. Many of the complaints had to do with telephone interruptions, while others cited actual intrusions into the family's living space. Some family members believe the solution is to keep a distance between the clergy family's home and the church building:

"Move the parsonage away from church property."

"Let me live in my own home; provide a housing allowance."

"Help us to buy a home away from the church."

"Move us across town."

Mere proximity to the church, however, is not the only issue. Certainly, being next door to the church increases the likelihood that parishioners will drop by unannounced or in other ways invade the home. But this does not in itself create the intrusive attitude in which clergy family feel they are being treated like a piece of church property. Thus, even if moving the pastor's family or providing a housing allowance should prove impossible, a congregation can learn to respect the clergy family's boundaries.

The Problem of Finances

A fourth theme was the clergy family's need for increased financial support. Almost all the responses in this category were requests for an increase in salary. One minister, however, had an additional creative suggestion: "Pay travel expenses so my wife could travel with me more frequently."

Often the requests were tied to other specific needs that have already been mentioned, such as money for family vacations or for a home away from the church.

In general, congregations need to recognize that the clergy family has the same human needs as other families. The congregation that truly cares for its clergy family will be creative in looking for tangible ways to show its support. We suggest, for example, tailoring the care of the clergy family to the stresses of their stage in the life cycle. Providing a "date night" may be more important to recently married clergy than for those who have been married several years. Reevaluating implicit and explicit expectations of P.K.s may help take some stress off the minister's family with teenage children. And of course, clergy families with newborns or young children are always in need of a capable, free baby-sitter. For families who are geographically removed from the children's grandparents, the couple may greatly appreciate older parishioners who can become substitute grandparent figures for their children.

Taking Care of Your Own Family Life

As we have said before, the relationship between the clergy family and the congregation is a two-way street. The congregation's responsibility to care for the minister's family is matched by the family's responsibility to care for itself.

First, clergy couples should ask themselves in what ways they may sabotage their own family life. A minister who is married to the church is not simply a victim of congregational demands. Similarly, whether a congregation has unrealistic expectations of a minister or his wife is only half the story. Do they also have unrealistic expectation of themselves? Or are they colluding with the congregation's expectations in some other way? Any pastor's family can be the victim of an unfortunate match with a congregation or bad timing. But the clergy family who constantly lament being victimized by one congregation after another should seriously ask themselves how they invite and even unconsciously encourage such treatment.

Second, ministers' families must learn to ask for what they need rather than waiting for the congregation to be struck by divine revelation. To some extent, family members may have a difficult time asking anybody for anything, quite apart from their roles as leaders of the congregation. But it may also be that their refusal to ask is an implicit acceptance of the idealized expectation that they have fewer needs than other families. To cultivate the ability to know when you need help and to ask for it is to cultivate differentiation.

These are general comments directed to the clergy family as a whole. In our study we also asked members of the pastor's family what advice they had for their peers. Here is what they told us.

Advice From Ministers

What advice do ministers have for other ministers? Many of the pastors responding to our survey emphasized their responsibility to be firmly committed to family time:

"Decide immediately that family time is the most important appointment each week."

"Schedule time for family activities, and hold that time as important as Sunday worship."

"Find a way to prevent work, ministry, and church from robbing your wife and children of special times—special times as defined by family."

"You must learn to say NO!"

Often, of course, this is easier said than done. The point is that the minister shares responsibility with the congregation for protecting family time. Some pastors made more specific suggestions on how to do this:

"Take half a day off each week no matter what."

"Work only forty hours a week and enjoy being with family and spending quality time with them."

"Be sure to insist on some time off every week, one month vacation, and two weeks of study time away from the church."

"Take one or two days off, plus two to three evenings a week."

"Take off at least one day per week and do not answer the phone. Spend two nights at home uninterrupted."

"Set aside a date night every week, with God being the only one having veto power."

Overall, these ministers spoke forcefully about the importance of making the family a top priority. Arrangement of their time varies from situation to situation, but the key is that once an appropriate plan is made, the minister should stick to it.

Advice From Ministers' Wives

Clergy wives also stressed the need to keep church responsibilities from encroaching on family time. Here is a sample of the more protective advice they gave to other ministers' wives:

"Demand one day off per week and make sure he takes it; even God rested one day."

"Choose the day off wisely and keep it. It's yours!"

"Insist upon dates set aside in the calendar for husband/wife and family activities."

Another common theme is that clergy wives should be intentional about supporting their husbands:

"Try and support him in every area. Pray for and encourage him continually."

"Love and support your husband above all, especially in the down times."

"Understand his calling, try to be helpful to him, and give him love and support."

"Be supportive of his ministry, and as much as possible make home life relaxed."

We must note that these suggestions seem to come from the perception of the clergy wife as William Douglas's "background supporter." As we saw in chapter 6, the majority of clergy wives in two studies described themselves this way. In contrast, other clergy wives encouraged their peers to pursue the more individualistic goal of being themselves:

"Be yourself and encourage the rest of your family to do the same."

"Develop personally. Don't let others' expectations lock you into what you feel you need to do and be for them. Be free to be yourself."

"Don't even try to be the perfect pastor's wife; just be yourself and do what is real for you. If some don't like it, that's their problem not yours."

The ambiguity of the clergy wife's role, as we discussed, lies in its mix of these traditional and contemporary expectations. The two strands are brought together in the lengthier advice of one clergy wife:

"Don't marry a minister unless you know who you are as an individual and are willing and eager to support your husband's career in all its many facets. Get your personal rebellion over with before you marry a minister. It's real hard to do it afterwards. The price is very high."

The unspoken conflict here can be phrased in a question: What happens if the minister's wife discovers that being herself pulls her away from the ministry rather than toward it?

We prefer not to make a value judgment as to whether one of Douglas's types is best or most functional. As we have tried to argue, what is "best" is not an a priori judgment, but a matter of fit between the individual minister's wife and her social context. Our counsel, again, is for honest self-reflection; it is better to recognize and wrestle with one's ambivalence than to try to bury it.

Advice From Ministers' Children

In a manner similar to clergy wives, the ministers' children advised their peers to support their parents. Here are some of their comments:

"Keep communication open with your parents."

"Support the ministry and know that it's God's will; go ahead and treat your dad like an ordinary person and love him."

"Pray for daddy and let him know you support him. At sometime or other, I think, he will be confronted with the fact that there are some un-Christian people in his Christian community. Inevitably, there are some people who will expect too much out of one man and will cause daddy a certain amount of stress. Keep showing him love."

Ministers' children also emphasize the importance of family time. If the congregation and the clergy couple share responsibility for protecting this valuable commodity, the children also recognize that they must play their part. Their advice seems to mix maturity with a sense of regret, particularly for the lack of time they can spend with their fathers:

"Try to be home when your dad is and encourage your parents to plan activities and things with you; suggest ideas and don't be afraid to remind your parents of family plans."

"Spend as much time with your parents as possible while you're young."

"Make sure you spend time with your father and do something together once in a while."

"Take time out specifically for activities together and don't let church functions be the only thing you do together."

"Make sure your father limits the number of evenings he goes out each week."

"If you feel neglected, tell your father; don't keep it inside."

Preparing for the Ministry

Finally, what of those who are preparing to enter the ministry? We hope, of course, that this book has given you a realistic look at some of the kinds of stress you may encounter in your family life. The suggestions above apply to you as well.

At the risk of repeating ourselves to the point of tedium, we must say again that we do not intend to paint a gloomy picture of the ministry. Many, if not most, clergy families find their lives rewarding. By the same token, we do not wish to create the opposite error and say that clergy family life is wonderful. The issue is not simply what a minister's family life looks like or whether it is good or bad; the issue is the kinds and amount of stress your family will experience in the ministry. The answer depends on the unique combination of your history and the history of the congregation you serve. To take an ecological perspective requires that you understand your particular stressors in that context.

We have both general and specific suggestions for those preparing to enter the ministry. First, take a hard look at your own role expectations. How do you understand the role of the minister? Of the minister's spouse? What roles and functions do you find rewarding? Which do you find awkward or even repellent? What personal emotional needs will being a minister fulfill for you? These are hard questions with many of the answers locked away in the deeper recesses of your mind and emotions. You will not be able to answer them all and may not be able to answer any of them fully. It is helpful, though, to keep them in mind as you prepare for and enter the ministry. Periodic and thoughtful reflection may help you to catch problems in their early stages, but assuming that "everything will work out" may only ensure that problems will grow past the point of an easy solution.

A related question is to ask yourself how being in the ministry will affect you at your stage of the life cycle. Are you married? If not, do you hope to marry before or after entering the ministry? Do you have children? What are their ages? The demands of ministry will pose different issues for your family at different stages. Suppose at mid-life you discover that you may not be so gifted for the ministry as you had once hoped. Would you be able to leave the ministry? If not, why not? Answering these questions may help you to identify some of the pressures you have inherited from past generations, giving you one more critical piece of the ecological puzzle.

Added to these issues of emotional preparedness are the more pragmatic considerations. When you interview for a possible position at a church, you should do more than establish theological compatibility and your fitness for the job. Anticipate the needs of your family and ask pertinent questions. Based on the cost of living in your community, will the salary be adequate for a family the size of yours? If not, what else can be negotiated? What will the church expect of the minister's spouse? Will the spouse be paid for his or her contribution?

When does the minister get time off? Study leave? What kind of regular time can be allowed for family life and vacations? Again, experienced clergy families have strong recommendations in regard to time demands:

> "Have strong family priorities and get these written into the contract."

> "Refuse to go to a church which does not insist that their minister spend no more than fifty hours a week in church-related activities."

> "Carefully guard the number of nights worked during the first two years; limit it to three nights and stick to it legalistically because it will set the pattern for years to come."

You may be reticent to ask such direct questions. But how eager should you be to go to a congregation that would be offended by your asking? It is better to bear the discomfort of asserting yourself before the decision is made than to regret the decision later.

Two final questions that are crucial to understanding the emotional climate you will be stepping into are why and how the previous pastor left.[1] Even experienced clergy may neglect to find this out. Was the separation traumatic for the church? Did the pastor leave because of a conflict? If so, with whom? Remember that there is often a honeymoon period when you first arrive at a church; don't fool yourself into thinking that the person who had a conflict with the previous pastor won't eventually have any problems with you.

You can begin to get a feel for these matters even from the first contact. Who approaches you personally? This may give you a sense of who the key people in the congregation are. What information do they volunteer, that is, without being asked? Some parishioners and church staff may be eager for you to see them in a particular way and begin to paint that picture for you from the very start. What information are they reluctant to give? This may point you to areas of concern or conflict. Is the church pressing for a quick decision without apparent reason? This can help you get a sense of the level of anxiety in the congregation.

We are not suggesting that you must find the perfect congregation before you accept a call or take up an assignment. It is a matter of making a fully informed and realistic decision, one which takes serious account of your family's life. Take every opportunity to learn more about the ecology of the church you are considering or the one that you are already serving. The better your understanding of the social environment, the better the fit you and your family can achieve there.

*   *   *

The social and emotional world of the clergy family is complex and often confusing. Ministers and their family members are as human as anyone else in the congregation. And when a group of people share as much of their lives and work with each other as pastors' families and parishes do, some conflict of emotional needs is bound to arise. In some churches both the minister and the congregation are mindful of their own and each other's needs. In other congregations, however, the clergy family are put in the position of having to meet the needs of others, often at the expense of having anyone to minister to them. The relationship will not necessarily be adversarial; the clergy family may simply feel torn between conflicting responsibilities. One minister's wife told us, "Often my own feelings are confusing. I know my husband's job is awesome. I know others need him. I want him to be there for these people. I want the kingdom to grow and our church to do well. But I need him, our children need him, and we need time together."

Both the congregation and the clergy family need the pastor. But the pastor also needs to learn how to be with his family, and the parishioners with theirs. Even in the best of situations, this is still a lesson that many of us need to learn and relearn. One pastor wrote to us, "I think that the characteristics of the congregation play a large role in the minister's family life and its relationship to the church. I pastor a young and growing congregation which is sensitive to the needs of my family. I am my worst enemy." This is an ecologically insightful remark. The patterns of relationship in a local church may either enhance or diminish the quality of the clergy family's life. But clergy also have their personal issues that keep them from connecting with their families as they should.

The solution is not for the minister's family to become demanding and parade their needs before the congregation. Rather, every family in the church must begin to develop an ecological sense of the unity of the body of Christ:

The eye cannot say to the hand, "I don't need you!" And the head cannot say to the feet, "I don't need you!" On the contrary, those parts of the body that seem to be weaker are indispensable, and the parts that we think are less honorable we treat with special honor. . . . But God has combined the members of the body and has given greater honor to the parts that lacked it, so that there should be no division in the body, but that its parts should have equal concern for each other. If one part suffers, every part suffers with it; if one part is honored, every part rejoices with it.[2]

These words of the apostle Paul should strike home to pastor-centered congregations. The church as the body of Christ and the family of God is not a metaphor, but a fact of how God has placed us in relationship to each other. Every part of the body is to have equal concern for the other. If any family in the body suffers, including the minister's family, then the whole body suffers. And clergy families must not believe for a moment that they do not truly need the support of the congregation, for this is just as much a denial of our oneness in Christ.

Taking an ecological approach seriously means recognizing the relationships that already exist, even the ones we cannot see. It means understanding our connectedness to one another, even if we have reasons for denying it. Not recognizing how we are linked to each other is a liability; appreciating those links is a strength. Clergy families and congregations must learn that every family in the church is important and that each must care for the other.

Looking at the apostle's words, we realize that we had the owner's manual all along.

Notes

Preface

1. J. C. Wynn, "Pastors Have Family Problems Too,' *Pastoral Psychology* 11 (September 1960): 10.

1. Setting the Stage

1. Charles Stewart, *The Minister As Marriage Counselor* (New York: Abingdon, 1961) and *The Minister As Family Counselor* (Nashville: Abingdon, 1979); William Hulme, *The Pastoral Care of Families* (Nashville: Abingdon, 1962); J. C. Wynn, *Pastoral Ministry to Families* (Philadelphia: Westminster, 1957) and *Family Therapy in Pastoral Ministry* (San Francisco: Harper & Row, 1982).

2. Ben Patterson, "Do You Rate Your Family Too High?" *Leadership* 2 (Fall 1981): 43–45.

3. Roger C. Palms, "Four Keys to Better Family Life," *Leadership* 2 (Fall 1981): 40.

4. Ibid., 42.

5. For a detailed, illustrated history of Mono Lake, see David Gaines, *Mono Lake Guidebook* (Lee Vining, Calif.: Kutsavi Books, 1981).

6. Martin Gardner, *aha! Gotcha: Paradoxes to Puzzle and Delight* (New York: W. H. Freeman, 1982), 119.

7. Ibid.

8. The terms "horizontal" and "vertical" are used similarly by Paul Watzlawick, Janet Beavin, and Don Jackson in *Pragmatics of Human Communication* (New York: W. W. Norton, 1967), 123.

2: Triangles in the Pastoral Ministry

1. Murray Bowen, *Family Therapy in Clinical Practice* (New York: Jason Aronson, 1978).

2. Jordan Paul and Margaret Paul, *Do I Have to Give Up Me to Be Loved by You?* (Minneapolis: CompCare Publishers, 1983).

3. Bowen, *Family Therapy in Clinical Practice*, 362.

4. Ibid., 365.

5. Ibid.

6. Ibid., 366.

7. For example, see the illuminating case studies of the families of schizophrenic children in R. D. Laing and A. Esterson, *Sanity, Madness, and the Family* (New York: Penguin, 1964).

8. On the notion of the adolescent identity crisis and its central role in human develpment, see Erik Erikson, *Childhood and Society*, 2d ed. (New York: W. W. Norton, 1963) and *Identity: Youth and Crisis* (New York: W. W. Norton, 1968).

9. David and Helen Seamands, "The Story of Raising a Pastoral Family," *Leadership* 2 (Fall 1981): 18.

10. Bowen, *Family Therapy in Clinical Practice*, 538–39.

11. Ibid., 485.

12. Ibid., 478.

13. Thomas Fogarty, "Triangles," in *The Family: The Best of the Family 1973–1978*, ed. E. G. Pendagast (New Rochelle, N.Y.: Center for Family Learning), 42.

14. Eric Berne, *Games People Play* (New York: Grove, 1964).

15. See Michael P. Nichols, *The Self in the System* (New York: Brunner/Mazel, 1987), 91–96.

16. Nancy Platt and David Moss, "Self-Perceptive Dispositions of Episcopal Clergy Wives," *Journal of Religion and Health* 15 (1976): 195.

17. Bowen, *Family Therapy in Clinical Practice*, 373.

18. These principles are adapted from *balance theory*. See the summary of balance theory in Lynn Hoffman, *Foundations of Family Therapy* (New York: Basic Books, 1981), 126–31. See also C. Cartwright and F. Harary, "Structural Balance: A Generalization of Heider's Theory," *Psychological Review* 63 (1956): 277–93.

19. The same idea applied to families is known to therapists as "pseudo-mutuality." See Lyman C. Wynne, Irving M. Ryckoff, Juliana Day, and Stanley I. Hirsch, "Pseudo-Mutuality in the Family Relations of Schizophrenics," *Psychiatry* 21 (1958): 205-220.

20. The same argument could be extended beyond the boundaries of the local congregation to shed light on religious, racial, and political prejudice.

3. A Family Within a Family

1. 2 Corinthians 6:18.

2. Galatians 4:6.

3. Ephesians 2:19–20.

4. Edwin Friedman, *Generation to Generation: Family Process in Church and Synagogue* (New York: Guilford, 1985), 197.

5. Ibid., 198. Emphasis in original.

6. Ibid., 198.

7. William Douglas, "Minister and Wife: Growth in Relationship," *Pastoral Psychology* 12 (December 1961): 38.

8. Friedman, *Generation to Generation*, 198.

9. These family descriptions are suggested by the typology developed by David Kantor and William Lehr, *Inside the Family* (San Francisco: Jossey-Bass, 1975), 116–42. The typology will be described further in chapter 4 of our book.

10. Kantor and Lehr, *Inside the Family*, 26–28.

11. Salvador Minuchin, *Families and Family Therapy* (Cambridge, Mass.: Harvard University Press, 1974), 53ff.

12. These are functionally similar though not identical to Bowen's notions of emotional cutoff and emotional fusion, which are discussed in chapter 2.

13. Cameron Lee tells the story.

14. Margaretta K. Bowers, *Conflicts of the Clergy* (New York: Thomas Nelson, 1963), 12.

15. Ruth Rehmann, from *Der Mann auf der Kanzel*, quoted by Alice Miller, *For Your Own Good*, 2d ed., trans. by Hildegarde and Hunter Hannum (New York: Farrar, Straus, Giroux, 1984), 32–33.

16. John G. Koehler, "The Minister as a Family Man," *Pastoral Psychology* 11 (September 1960): 11–15.

17. Rob Suggs, in *Leadership*, 1984.

18 This metaphor has also been used by J. C. Wynn, "Consider the Children," *Pastoral Psychology* 11 (September 1960): 23–26.

19. Wallace Denton, "Role Attitudes of the Minister's Wife," *Pastoral Psychology* 12 (December 1961): 17.

20. Pauline G. Boss, "Family Boundary Ambiguity: A New Variable in Family Stress Theory," *Family Process* 23 (1984): 535–46, and "Normative Family Stress: Family Boundary Changes Across the Life-Span," *Family Relations* 29 (1980): 445–50.

21. Keith Madsen, *Fallen Images: Experiencing Divorce in the Ministry* (Valley Forge, Pa.: Judson, 1985), 38.

22. Robert P. Rankin, "The Ministerial Calling and the Minister's Wife," *Pastoral Psychology* 11 (September 1960): 17.

23. Gerald J. Jud, Edgar W. Mills, Jr., and Genevieve Walters Burch, *Ex-Pastors: Why Men Leave the Parish Ministry* (Philadelphia: Pilgrim, 1970), 4. Emphasis in original.

4. Family Types or Stereotypes?

1. Edwin Friedman, *Generation to Generation: Family Process in Church and Synagogue* (New York: Guilford, 1985), 36.

2. 1 Corinthians 12:12, 18–20.

3. Arthur B. Shostak, "Singlehood," in *Handbook of Marriage and the Family,* ed. Marvin B. Sussman and Suzanne K. Steinmetz (New York: Plenum, 1987), 355–67.

4. Sharon K. Houseknecht, "Voluntary Childlessness," in Sussman and Steinmetz, *Handbook of Marriage and the Family,* 369–95.

5. Eleanor D. Macklin, "Nontraditional Family Forms," in Sussman and Steinmetz, *Handbook of Marriage and the Family,* 317–53.

6. Patricia A. Gongla and Edward H. Thompson, Jr., "Single-Parent Families," in Sussman and Steinmetz, *Handbook of Marriage and the Family,* 397–418.

7. David Kantor and William Lehr, *Inside the Family* (San Francisco: Jossey-Bass, 1975), 116–42. See chapter 3, note 6. The research was done through the Institute for the Study of Family and Youth in Cambridge, Massachusetts, hence the name "Cambridge" typology.

8. Jay Haley, "Family Experiments: A New Type of Experimentation," *Family Process* 1 (1962): 266.

9. Kantor and Lehr, *Inside the Family,* 162.

10. Ibid., 116–17.

11. Ibid., 146.

12. Ibid., 162.

13. See Paul Watzlawick, John Weakland, and Richard Fisch, *Change: Principles of Problem Formation and Problem Resolution* (New York: W. W. Norton, 1974), 31ff.

14. Kantor and Lehr, *Inside the Family,* 151ff.

15. Larry Constantine, for example, has extended Kantor and Lehr's model to include the "synchronous" family whose core purpose is "harmony through identification." See his book *Family Paradigms: The Practice of Theory in Family Therapy* (New York: Guilford, 1986), 18ff.

16. 1 Corinthians 12:21.

5. The Roles Ministers Play

1. The terms to be defined are derived from "role theory," a subdiscipline of the sociological theory known as "symbolic interactionism."

2. Wesley Burr et al., "Symbolic Interaction and the Family," in *Contemporary Theories About the Family,* vol. 2, ed. Wesley Burr, Reuben Hill, F. Ivan Nye, and Ira L. Reiss (New York: Free Press, 1979), 54.

3. Donald Smith, *Clergy in the Cross Fire* (Philadelphia: Westminster, 1973), 24.

4. Burr et al., "Symbolic Interaction," 57.

5. Edgar Mills, "Types of Role Conflict Among Clergymen," *Ministry Studies* 2 (1968): 13–15.

6. This says nothing, however, about the intensity of the role conflict. Some conflicts may be minor and easily dealt with. The focus is on the complexity of the minister's role set.

7. This is described as "role ambiguity" by James D. Anderson, "Pastoral Support of Clergy Role Development Within Local Congregations," *Pastoral Psychology* 22 (March 1971): 11.

8. In particular Gregory Bateson and his colleagues developed the notion of the double-bind to explain the development and maintenance of schizophrenia. The classic papers on the double-bind theory have been reprinted in Gregory Bateson, *Steps to an Ecology of Mind* (New York: Ballantine, 1972).

9. "Verbal" communication refers mainly to the *content* of what is said while "nonverbal" communication refers to *how* it is said. Nonverbal communication also refers to all other forms of communication that do not involve speech, such as facial expressions and body gestures.

10. Gregory Bateson et al., "Toward a Theory of Schizophrenia," in Bateson, *Steps to an Ecology of Mind*, 217.

11. Charles Glock and Philip Roos, "Parishioners' Views of How Ministers Spend Their Time," *Review of Religious Research* 2 (1961): 170–75. We address the research relating to clergy roles and the time spent in each in the discussion of combined internal/external role conflicts.

12. For other research on congregational expectations and perceptions, see the following: Richard Maddock, Charles Kinney, and Morris Middleton, "Personality vs. Role-Activity Variables in the Choice of a Pastor," *Journal for the Scientific Study of Religion* 12 (1973): 449–52; Everett Perry and Dean Hoge, "Faith Priorities of Pastor and Laity as a Factor in the Growth or Decline of Presbyterian Congregations," *Review of Religious Research* 22 (March 1981): 221–32.

13. Edward S. Golden, "Psychological Problems of the Clergy," in *Psychological Testing for Ministerial Selection*, ed. William C. Bier (New York: Fordham, 1970), 212. Note that the term "double bind" is not used in the same technical sense as it was above.

14. William B. Presnell, "The Minister's Own Marriage," *Pastoral Psychology* 25 (1977): 278.

15. Quoted by Koehler, "The Minister as Family Man," 13.

16. Golden, "Psychological Problems of the Clergy," 217.

17. Ibid.

18. Robert L. Carrigan, "Psychotherapy and the Theological Seminary," *Journal of Religion and Health* 6 (1967): 94–95.

19. For further discussion and examples, see G. C. Anderson, "Emotional Health of the Clergy," in *The Minister's Own Mental Health*, ed. Wayne Oates (Great Neck, N.Y.: Channel Press, 1961), 35;

and Dean Johnson, "Self-Understanding in Pastoral Counseling," *Pastoral Psychology* 6 (September 1955): 27–34.

20. Gotthard Booth, "The Psychological Examination of Candidates for the Ministry," in *The Ministry and Mental Health*, ed. Hans Hofmann (New York: Association Press, 1960), 101.

21. J. C. Wynn, *Family Therapy in Pastoral Ministry*, 107.

22. Golden, "Psychological Problems of Clergy," 219.

23. Carl Christensen, "The Occurrence of Mental Illness in the Ministry: Family Origins," *Journal of Pastoral Care* 14 (1960): 60. This is similar to the concept of *pseudomutuality* in Lyman Wynne et al., "Pseudomutuality in the Family Relations of Schizophrenics," *Psychiatry* 21 (1958): 205–22.

24. Carl Christensen, "The Occurrence of Mental Illness in the Ministry: Psychoneurotic Disorders" and "The Occurrence of Mental Illness in the Ministry: Personality Disorders," *Journal of Pastoral Care* 17 (1963): 2–3, 134.

25. See Edward Thornton, "Emotional Disorders of Persons in Church-Related Vocations," in *The Minister's Own Mental Health*, ed. Wayne Oates (Great Neck, N.Y.: Channel Press, 1961), 179–87; and Herbert Anderson and C. George Fitzgerald, "Use of Family Systems in Preparation for Ministry," *Pastoral Psychology* 27 (1978): 49–61. For a more detailed discussion of the intrapsychic dynamics of the "good" child, we highly recommend Alice Miller, *The Drama of the Gifted Child*, trans. Ruth Ward (New York: Basic Books, 1981).

26. Margaretta K. Bowers, *Conflicts of the Clergy* (New York: Thomas Nelson, 1963), 98.

27. Ibid., 101.

28. Kirk A. Kennedy, Bonita N. Eckhardt, and W. Mack Goldsmith, "Church Members' Expectations of Clergy Personality," *Journal of Psychology and Christianity* 3 (Fall 1984): 11. Emphasis added.

29. Samuel Blizzard, "The Minister's Dilemma," *Christian Century*, (25 April 1956): 508–10. Similar results are reported by Gerald J. Jud, Edgar W. Mills, Jr., and Genevieve Walters Burch, *Ex-Pastors: Why Men Leave the Parish Ministry* (Philadelphia: Pilgrim, 1970), 72–73.

30. Charles Coates and Robert Kistler, "Role Dilemmas of the Protestant Clergyman in a Metropolitan Community," *Review of Religious Research* 6 (1965): 147–52.

31. For those interested in further reading, we suggest the following titles: Jurg Willi, *Couples in Collusion* (New York: Jason Aronson, 1982); David Klimek, *Beneath Mate Selection and Marriage* (New York: Van Nostrand Reinhold, 1979); Clifford Sager, *Marriage Contracts and Couple Therapy* (New York: Brunner/Mazel, 1976); William Lederer and Don Jackson, *The Mirages of Marriage* (New York: W. W.

Norton, 1968). Only Willi's book focuses explicitly on "collusion"; the other works, however, offer similar or related insights.

32. Kirk A. Kennedy, Bonita N. Eckhardt, and W. Mack Goldsmith, "Church Members' Expectations of Clergy Personality," *Journal of Psychology and Christianity* 3 (Fall 1984): 15–17.

6. Married to the Minister

1. Again, as we noted in the preface, we will be using the term "minister's wife" instead of the more general "minister's spouse," in order to remain consistent with the published literature and our own research. We assume that some of the same dynamics would apply to the male spouses of female clergy, but also strongly suspect that this much less common situation would pose some striking differences.

2. Elizabeth Dodds, "The Minister's Homemaker," *Pastoral Psychology* 11 (September 1960): 30.

3. Wallace Denton, "Role Attitudes of the Minister's Wife," *Pastoral Psychology* 12 (December 1961): 23.

4. See figure 8.1 in chapter 8.

5. Duane Alleman, "The Psychosocial Adjustment of Pastors' Wives" (Ph.D. diss., Graduate School of Psychology, Fuller Theological Seminary, 1987), 132.

6. Ibid., 134.

7. Marietta Hobkirk, "Some Reflections on Bringing Up the Minister's Family," *Pastoral Psychology* 12 (December 1961): 29.0

8. Denton, "Role Attitudes," 19.

9. See Pat Valeriano, "A Survey of Ministers' Wives," *Leadership* 2 (Fall 1981): 67.

10. Ibid. .

11. Ibid., 69.

12. Alleman, "Psychosocial Adjustment," 93.

13. Ibid., 87ff.

14. Theodore Hsieh and Edith Rugg, "Coping Patterns of Ministers' Wives," *Journal of Psychology and Christianity* 2 (Fall 1983): 79–80.

15. Ibid., 80.

16. The term "two-person career" was coined by Hanna Papanek, who defines it thus: "a three-way relationship between the employer and two partners in a marriage. . . . The wife is drawn into the orbit of the employing institution because of her marital bonds." See Papanek, "Men, Women, and Work: Reflections on the Two-Person Career," *American Journal of Sociology* 78 (1973): 852–72.

17. D. P. Thomson, ed., "The Minister's Wife—Her Life, Work, and Problems" (Report of a conference held at St. Ninian's Training Centre, Crieff, Perthshire, Scotland, 1964), 42–43.

18. William Douglas, *Ministers' Wives* (New York: Harper, 1965). See also two earlier articles by Douglas, "Ministers' Wives: A Tentative Typology," *Pastoral Psychology* 12 (December 1961): 10–16, and "Minister and Wife: Growth in Relationship," *Pastoral Psychology* 12 (December 1961): 35–39.

19. Mary Taylor, "Two-Person Career or Two-Career Marriage?" *Christian Ministry* 8 (January 1977): 19.

20. Alleman, "Psychosocial Adjustment," 103.

21. Douglas, *Ministers' Wives*, 231.

22. Robert P. Rankin, "The Ministerial Calling and the Minister's Wife," *Pastoral Psychology* 11 (September 1960): 18–20.

23. Quoted by Elizabeth Dodds, "The Minister's Homemaker," *Pastoral Psychology* 11 (September 1960): 28.

24. Taylor, "Two-Person Career," 19.

25. Alleman, "Psychosocial Adjustment,"79.

26. Shirley Hartley, "Marital Satisfaction Among Clergy Wives," *Review of Religious Research* 19 (1978): 188.

27. Alleman, "Psychosocial Adjustment," 86.

28. Richard Blackmon, "The Hazards of the Ministry" (Ph.D. diss., Graduate School of Psychology, Fuller Theological Seminary, 1984).

29. Barbara Prasse, "The Changing Roles of the Minister's Wife," *Christian Ministry* 2 (July 1971): 12.

30. Thomson, ed., "The Minister's Wife," 12.

31. Alleman, "Psychosocial Adjustment," 83.

32. Ibid., 76.

7. Perfect Kids: The Pressures of the P.K.

1. This quotation is taken from an anonymous response to our survey. All subsequent quotations that are not footnoted also come from this survey.

2. The quotation is taken from a study of P.K.s done by Paul Haakenson, a P.K. and student at St. Olaf College. See Paul Haakenson, "P.K. Stories" (Unpublished manuscript, St. Olaf College), 8. The authors are grateful for Mr. Haakenson's allowing them to use his original material in this book.

3. Alice Miller, *For Your Own Good*, 2d ed., trans. by Hildegarde and Hunter Hannum (New York: Farrar, Straus, Giroux, 1984), 265.

4. Pat Valeriano, "A Survey of Ministers' Wives," *Leadership* 2 (Fall 1981): 66.

5. J. C. Wynn, "Consider the Children," *Pastoral Psychology* 11 (September 1960): 23.

6. Haakenson, "P.K. Stories," 4.

7. Wynn, "Consider the Children," 23.

8. Roger L. Dudley, "Alienation From Religion in Adolescents From Fundamentalist Religious Homes," *Journal for the Scientific Study of Religion* 17 (1978): 389–98.

9. Martin A. Johnson, "Family Life and Religious Commitment," *Review of Religious Research* 4 (1973): 144–50.

10 Galatians 4:6.

11. For a more detailed discussion of the role of grace in family relationships and emotional development, see Cameron Lee, "The Good Enough Family," *Journal of Psychology and Theology* 13 (1985): 182–89; and W. W. Meissner, *Life and Faith* (Washington: Georgetown University Press, 1987).

12. Quoted in Wynn, "Consider the Children," 26.

13. Haakenson, "P.K. Stories," 8.

14. Mary LaGrand Bouma, *Divorce in the Parsonage* (Minneapolis: Bethany Fellowship, 1979), 69.

15. Haakenson, "P.K. Stories," 8.

16. Valeriano, "A Survey of Ministers' Wives," 69.

17. Haakenson, for example, notes what he calls the "rebel/saint" dichotomy used to describe P.K.s. See Paul Haakenson, "P.K. Stories" and "Growing Up in a Glass House: A Comprehensive Study of Pastors' Children" (Unpublished manuscript). The rebel/saint distinction is used by Mary LaGrand Bouma, "Pastors' Kids, Ministering Children," *Leadership* 2 (Fall 1981): 30–38.

18. Daniel Blain, "Fostering the Mental Health of Ministers," *Pastoral Psychology* 9 (May 1958): 9–18. It is noteworthy that Blain speaks of the minister's son rather than of the minister's child. At present we know of no research that distinguishes the experiences of ministers' sons from ministers' daughters. In this chapter we do not make any such gender distinctions.

19. David L. Rosenhan, "On Being Sane in Insane Places," *Science* (1973): 250–58.

20. Erik Erikson, *Identity: Youth and Crisis* (New York: W. W. Norton, 1968), 172ff.

21. Wynn, "Consider the Children," 23.

22 See the discussion of intrusion and integration in chapter 8.

23. Haakenson, "P.K. Stories," 3. The analysis that follows is not an attempt to read between the lines of Haakenson's excerpt. Our intent is to use the vignette as a general example of how triangles may occur and where to look for them.

24. Howard Clinebell, "Counselor to Ministers' Families," *Christian Ministry* 2 (July 1971): 40. See also Bouma, "Pastor's Kids, Ministering Children," 32.

25. Haakenson, "P.K. Stories," 3.

26. Ibid.

27. J. C. Wynn, *Pastoral Ministry to Families* (Philadelphia: Westminster, 1957), 188.

28. Louis McBurney, in Dean Merrill, *Clergy Couples in Crisis: The Impact of Stress on Clergy Marriages* (Waco, Tex.: Word, 1985), 116.

8. Stress and the Minister's Family

1. Some readers may ask, "Isn't the pastor *supposed* to keep from getting triangled between the congregation and the children?" Yes, if that were in fact happening. In this case, however, the minister's action should not be interpreted as a differentiated attempt to stay out of a triangle. The matter has to be decided from two points of view. First, was the criticism of the children realistic or exaggerated? To the extent that the criticism is realistic, the pastor can affirm it. This begs the question, however, of why such a realistic criticism had to come from the congregation instead of from the parents. Second, where is the real conflict? If the real issue is between the congregation and the pastor, then the pastor's hands-off solution can be seen as colluding with the congregation to triangle the children.

2. A thorough description of the study plus reports of the statistical findings can be found in the senior author's doctoral dissertation: Cameron Lee, *The Social and Psychological Dynamics of the Minister's Family* (Ann Arbor, Mich.: University Microfilms International, 1987).

3. The ministers selected for this survey study were drawn from the doctor of ministry program at Fuller Theological Seminary. A total of 127 ministers, 117 ministers' wives, and 47 children responded. The ministers ranged in age from twenty-six to seventy-four years, with an average age of forty. The wives ranged from twenty-four to sixty-three years of age, with an average of thirty-nine. The children were from nine to twenty-nine years old, averaging sixteen years old. The group represented more than thirty denominations and various levels of experience.

4. We must be careful not to overgeneralize here. We have done the survey with other groups, and though the same themes tend to emerge, the order of the frequency of occurrence can change.

5. Nick Stinnett and John DeFrain, *Secrets of Strong Families* (Boston: Little, Brown, 1985).

6. David and Vera Mace, *What's Happening to Clergy Marriages?* (Nashville: Abingdon, 1980), 84.

7. Note that the surveys used the word "spouse." All the spouses who responded, however, were women.

8. Each person was asked to rate each of the eleven items on a Likert-type scale, ranging from a score of 1 ("no problem at all") to 4 ("a great problem"). Responses from ministers were treated as a group, as

were responses from ministers' wives and children respectively. The mean score for each group on each item was computed, then arranged into rank order to generate the figures in table 8.1.

9. All the surveys were coded to allow us to identify responses coming from the same family. For this part of the study, we used only those surveys that could be matched in family sets, that is, one survey each from a minister, his wife, and one child. This gave us forty-one families.

10. The items for intrusion and integration were reworded versions of items from the "Family Adaptability and Cohesion Evaluation Scales (FACES)," a self-report test designed by David Olson, Richard Bell, and Joyce Portner for family research (Unpublished, University of Minnesota, 1978).

11. The minister's items were as follows:

- "Being in ministry has made . . ."
- ". . . my spouse's role as partner to me . . ."
- ". . . my role as a parent to my children . . ."
- ". . . my role as a partner to my spouse . . ."
- ". . . our children's lives . . ."
- ". . . our life as a family . . ."

The items for the minister's spouse were similar:

- ". . . my role as a partner to my spouse . . ."
- ". . . my spouse's role as a parent to our children . . ."
- ". . . my spouse's role as partner to me . . ."
- ". . . our children's lives . . ."
- ". . . my role as a parent to our children . . ."

12. See Lee, *The Social and Psychological Dynamics of the Minister's Family*, 242ff.

9. Are We Married to the Congregation, or to Each Other?

1. David Mace and Vera Mace, *What's Happening to Clergy Marriages?* (Nashville: Abingdon, 1980).

2. See Keith Madsen, *Fallen Images: Experiencing Divorce in the Ministry* (Valley Forge, Pa.: Judson, 1985).

3. William Douglas, "Minister and Wife: Growth in Relationship," *Pastoral Psychology* 12 (December 1961): 37.

4. The item is adapted from Spanier's Dyadic Adjustment Scale. See G. Spanier and C. Cole, "Toward Clarification and Investigation of Marital Adjustment," *International Journal of Sociology of the Family* 6 (1974): 121–46.

5. Our special thanks to Dr. Bill Hogue, Executive Director, and the Reverend Michael Carlisle of the Southern Baptist General Convention

of California for their support and assistance. Our thanks also to the numerous people of the Seventh-day Adventist Church who helped in the distribution and collection of the questionnaires.

6. For example, see Norval D. Glenn and Charles N. Weaver, "A Multivariate, Multisurvey Study of Marital Happiness," *Journal of Marriage and the Family* 40 (1978): 269–82; and Vernon H. Edmonds, "Marital Conventionalization: Definition and Measurement," *Journal of Marriage and the Family* 29 (1967): 681–88.

7. Walter R. Schumm, "Religiosity and Marital Satisfaction: Can Marital Conventionalization Explain Away the Relationship?" *Journal of Psychology and Christianity* 1 (Summer 1982): 16–21; Richard A. Hunt and Morton B. King, "Religiosity and Marriage," *Journal for the Scientific Study of Religion*, 17 (1978): 399–406.

8. Ministers were asked to rate their satisfaction with their own behavior, both as "companion to my spouse" and as "lover to my spouse." Spouses (wives) were asked to rate the minister "as companion to me" and "as lover to me." All ratings used a four-point Likert scale where scores of 1 through 4 corresponded to "very unsatisfied," "unsatisfied," "satisfied," and "very satisfied" respectively. Ministers gave themselves a mean rating of 3.16 as companions and 3.1 as lovers; wives rated them 3.36 as companions and 3.41 as lovers.

9. Mace and Mace, *Clergy Marriages*, 36ff.

10. Nick Stinnett and John DeFrain, *Secrets of Strong Families* (Boston: Little, Brown, 1985), 100ff.

11. William Lederer and Don Jackson, *The Mirages of Marriage* (New York: W. W. Norton, 1968), 373.

12. Ibid., 156.

13. Gerald J. Jud, Edgar W. Mills, Jr., and Genevieve Walters Burch, *Ex-Pastors: Why Men Leave the Parish Ministry* (Philadelphia: Pilgrim, 1970), 87.

14. We found this to be true in all three samples of clergy couples: doctor of ministry, Southern Baptist, and Seventh-day Adventist.

15. Both the variable and its measurement are borrowed from the research of David Olson and his associates at the University of Minnesota. See especially David Olson, Douglas Sprenkle, and Candyce Russell, "Circumplex Model of Marital and Family Systems: I. Cohesion and Adaptability Dimensions, Family Types, and Clinical Applications," *Family Process* 18 (1979): 29–45; and David Olson, Richard Bell, and Joyce Portner, "FACES II [Family Adaptability and Cohesion Evaluation Scales]" (Unpublished manuscript, University of Minnesota, 1982).

16. In Olson's original model, either very high or very low levels of cohesion were held to be problematic. In later research, however, Olson and his colleagues discovered that in "normal" (i.e., nonclinic)

groups, higher levels of cohesion may be desirable. See David Olson, Hamilton McCubbin et. al., *Families: What Makes Them Work* (Beverly Hills: Sage Publications, 1983).

17. Ministers in the doctor of ministry group were presented with ten facets of ministry and asked to rate their level of satisfaction with each on a five-point scale from a low of "very unsatisfying" to a high of "extremely satisfying." The ten items were as follows:

- Members' willingness to study and be trained
- Your own freedom to preach, teach, and act as you see fit
- The amount of time you have for family and private life
- The congregation's appreciation of your work or involvement
- The possibility that you can make a significant contribution to the vitality and mission of that organization
- Your salary and living arrangements
- Members' willingness to carry out their Christian witness in the world
- The opportunity to exert creative leadership and try out new ideas
- The degree to which laity share the leadership tasks of the church
- The degree to which the work utilizes your strengths rather than your weaknesses as a minister

10. Beyond the Local Church

1. John Coleman, "Situation for Modern Faith," *Theological Studies* 39 (1978): 601–32.

2. The period of the papacy of Gregory VII (Hildebrand) was crucial in the history of church-state relations. In the end, Henry was the victor and the pope died in exile. See Kenneth Scott Latourette, *A History of Christianity*, vol. 1 (New York: Harper & Row, 1975), 470–73.

3. See especially Langdon Gilkey, *Religion and the Scientific Future* (New York: Harper, 1970).

4. Peter Berger, "From the Crisis of Religion to the Crisis of Secularity," in *Religion in America: Spiritual Life in a Secular Age*, ed. Mary Douglas and Steven Tipton (Boston: Beacon, 1983), 21.

5. Harry Emerson Fosdick, *On Being a Real Person* (New York: Harper, 1943): quoted in Paul Vitz, *Psychology as Religion: The Cult of Self-Worship* (Grand Rapids: Eerdmans, 1977), 70–71.

6. Richard Sennett, *Authority* (New York: Random House, 1970).

7. For fans of Garrison Keillor, both Lake Wobegon's Lutheran Church and Our Lady of Perpetual Responsibility Catholic Church are examples of community churches.

8. Robert E. Mitchell, "When Ministers and Parishioners Have Different Social Class Positions," *Review of Religious Research* 7 (1965): 28–41.

9. Hart M. Nelsen and Robert F. Everett, "Impact of Church Size on Clergy Role and Career," *Review of Religious Research* 18 (1976): 62–73.

10. See chapter 9. Also see Cameron Lee, *The Social and Psychological Dynamics of the Minister's Family* (Ann Arbor, Mich.: University Microfilms International, 1987), chaps. 10–13.

11. Donald McGavran, *Understanding Church Growth* (Grand Rapids: Eerdmans, 1970).

12. For example, see David Mace and Vera Mace, *What's Happening to Clergy Marriages?* (Nashville: Abingdon, 1980), 78.

13. Duane Alleman, "The Psychosocial Adjustment of Pastors' Wives" (Ph.D. diss., Graduate School of Psychology, Fuller Theological Seminary, 1987), 80. Alleman's dissertation study was cited in chapter 6.

14. Richard Blackmon, "The Hazards of the Ministry" (Ph.D. diss., Graduate School of Psychology, Fuller Theological Seminary, 1984), cited also in chapter 6.

15. For a study of how American individualism has affected both family and religious life, see Robert Bellah et. al., *Habits of the Heart: Individualism and Commitment in American Life* (New York: Harper Perennial, 1985). An exhaustive study of the differences between denominational groups can be found in David Schuller, Merton Strommen, and Milo Brekke, eds., *Ministry in America* (San Francisco: Harper & Row, 1980). For the effects of modern culture on our sense of community, see S. D. Gaede, *Belonging* (Grand Rapids: Zondervan, 1985).

Religious pluralism and the privatization of religion are treated in an unusual Screwtape-letter style by Os Guinness in *The Gravedigger File: Papers on the Subversion of the Modern Church* (Downers Grove, Ill.: InterVarsity Press, 1983). Privatization in family life and the phenomenon of cultural religion are discussed by J. A. Walter, *Sacred Cows: Exploring Contemporary Idolatry* (Grand Rapids: Zondervan, 1979). The last three authors all acknowledge a debt to the work of Peter Berger.

11. Moving Through Time: The Minister's Family Across the Life Cycle

1. See Elizabeth Carter and Monica McGoldrick, eds., *The Family Life Cycle: A Framework for Family Therapy* (New York: Gardner, 1980); Sonya Rhodes and Josleen Wilson, *Surviving Family Life* (New

York: Putnam, 1981); and Mel Roman and Patricia Raley, *The Indelible Family* (New York: Rawson, Wade, 1980).

2. This is an adaptation of Carter and McGoldrick's notion of horizontal and vertical stressors. See their book *Family Life Cycle*, chapter 1.

3. See the sources listed in note 1 plus Evelyn Millis Duvall, *Family Development* (Philadelphia: Lippincott, 1978).

4. Sonya Rhodes, "Developmental Approach to the Life Cycle," *Social Casework* 58 (1977): 303.

5. The stereotype of the rebellious teenager is an extreme of the normal adolescent questioning. Some researchers challenge this stereotype and claim that the majority of teenagers do not rebel openly against their parents.

6. A particularly useful tool in this regard is the family genogram, an in-depth family tree that goes beyond names and dates and searches out patterns of relationship repeated over the generations. It can be used either as an adjunct to counseling or for self-reflection. See Monica McGoldrick and Randy Gerson, *Family Genograms* (New York: W. W. Norton, 1986).

Epilogue: The Care and Feeding of Clergy Families

1. See Edwin Friedman's discussion of this in *Generation to Generation: Family Process in Church and Synagogue* (New York: Guilford, 1985), cited first in chapter 3.

2. 1 Corinthians 12: 21–23a, 25–26.

Index

CPSIA information can be obtained at www.ICGtesting.com
Printed in the USA
LVOW080357070912

297769LV00003BA/35/A